Tower of Transformational Leadership

Published by
Kenway Publications
an imprint of
East African Educational Publishers Ltd.
Elgeyo Marakwet Close, off Elgeyo Marakwet Road, Kilimani, Nairobi
P.O. Box 45314, Nairobi - 00100, KENYA
Tel: +254 20 2324760
Mobile: +254 722 205661 / 722 207216 / 733 677716 / 734 652012
Email: eaep@eastafricanpublishers.com
Website: www.eastafricanpublishers.com

East African Educational Publishers also has offices or is represented in the following countries: Uganda, Tanzania, Rwanda, Malawi, Zambia, Botswana and South Sudan.

© George Magoha, 2017

All rights reserved

First published 2017

ISBN 978-9966-56-207-4

Printed in Kenya by
Ramco Printing Works Ltd,
Ramco Unit 2, Ramco Industrial Group Complex, Mombasa Road,
P.O. Box 27750 – 00506, Nairobi, Kenya

George Magoha

Tower of Transformational Leadership

Kenway Publications

KENWAY BIOGRAPHICAL WORKS

1. SUSAN WOOD: *A Fly in Amber*
2. MICHAEL BLUNDELL: *A Love Affair with the Sun*
3. JOMO KENYATTA: *Facing Mount Kenya*
4. PROF JOSEPH MAINA MUNGAI: *From Simple to Complex: The Journey of a Herdsboy*
5. GG KARIUKI: *Illusion of Power*
6. WAITHAKA WAIHENYA: *The Mediator: General Sumbeiywo and the Sudan Peace Process*
7. MADATALLY MANJI: *Madatally Manji: Memoirs of a Biscuit Baron*
8. ALLAN DONOVAN: *My Journey Through African Heritage*
9. YUSUF K DAWOOD: *Nothing but the Truth*
10. DOUGLAS COLLINS: *Tales from Africa*
11. ANNABEL MAULE: *Theatre Near the Equator*
12. ELIJAH MALOK: *The Southern Sudan: Struggle for Liberty*
13. VALERIE CUTHBERT: *Wings of the Wind*
14. DAVID GOLDSWORTHY: *Tom Mboya: The Man Kenya Wanted to Forget*
15. OGINGA ODINGA: *Not Yet Uhuru*
16. TOM MBOYA: *Freedom and After*
17. NGŨGĨ WA THIONG'O: *Dreams in a Time of War*
18. NJENGA KARUME with MUTU WA GETHOI: *Beyond Expectations: From Charcoal to Gold*
19. WANJIRU WAITHAKA and EVANS MAJENI: *A Profile of Kenyan Entreprenuers*
20. KEVIN LILLIS: *Running for Black Gold: Fifty Years of African Athletics*
21. PETER KAGWANJA with HUMPHREY RINGERA: *Kiraitu Murungi: An Odyssey in Kenyan Politics*
22. NGŨGĨ WA THIONG'O: *In the House of the Interpreter*
23. ROBERT F STEPHENS: *Kenyan Student Airlifts to America, 1959-1961: An Educational Odyssey*
24. JEREMIAH GITAU KIEREINI: *A Daunting Journey*
25. JOE KHAMISI: *Dash before Dusk: A Slave Descendant's Journey in Freedom*
26. GEORGE MAGOHA: *Tower of Transformational Leadership*

Contents

Acknowledgements vi

Dedication vii

Acronyms and Abbreviations viii

Foreword by Dr. Manu Chandaria xiv

Foreword by Professor P.L.O. Lumumba xvii

Chapter 1: Formative Years 1

Chapter 2: Return to Kenya 55

Chapter 3: Influences in My Life 81

Chapter 4: Transformative Leadership 96

Chapter 5: Servant Leadership 114

Chapter 6: My Ten-Year Agenda as Vice-Chancellor 124

Chapter 7: Lessons Learnt 226

Chapter 8: With the Benefit of Hindsight 245

Chapter 9: My Professional Work as a Medical Regulator 252

Chapter 10: Reflections 294

Chapter 11: KNEC: Return to Credibility 307

Index 348

ACKNOWLEDGEMENTS

I wish to thank the Almighty God for the gift of life, excellent education and continuous good health that has enabled me to write this memoirs. I am greatly indebted to Dr. Geoffrey Griffin, the Founder and Director of Starehe Boys Centre whose strict discipline enabled me to discover and harness my academic potential; and Professor Joseph Maina Mungai for encouraging and convincing me to study medicine.

I wish to acknowledge and thank my elder brother John Obare, and his wife Agatha Obare for hosting me during part of my primary and secondary school years in Nairobi.

I must not forget to thank Dr. James Angawa who was responsible for professionally and competently managing my medical condition resulting in my continued good health and uninterrupted school attendance.

Njeri Muhoro was not only part of my excellent public relations team during my tenure as Vice-Chancellor of the University of Nairobi, but she also encouraged me to commence the work on my memoirs immediately after the expiry of my ten-year tenure as Vice-Chancellor. She was most instrumental in the conceptualization, compilation and critical appraisal of the first draft of the manuscript. In all these, she was ably assisted by my personal assistant as Vice Chancellor, Simeon Odera. To them I say thank you for all the effort.

I also acknowledge; Dr. Ibrahim Otieno, director ICT University of Nairobi, Daniel Yumbya (CEO), Duncan Mwai (ICT manager), Aziza Athman, Rose Wafukho and Sarah Were, of Medical Practitioners and Dentists Board of Kenya for their invaluable input on various dynamic logistics including collation of pictorials.

DEDICATION

To

My parents, Bernard Boniface Magoha and Joan Sarah Aloo;

My dear wife, Dr. Odudu Barbara Magoha;

And my son, Dr. Michael Augustus Achianja Magoha.

ACRONYMS AND ABBREVIATIONS

A&F	-	Administration and Finance
AA	-	Academic Affairs
AAU	-	Association of African Universities
ACCA	-	Association of Chartered Certified Accountants
ACU	-	Association of Commonwealth Universities
ADC	-	Agricultural Development Corporation
AHPRA	-	Australian Health Practitioners Regulation Agency
AIE	-	Authority to Incur Expenditure
AMCOA	-	Association of Medical Councils of Africa
AMSUN	-	Association of Medical Students of the University of Nairobi
ANSTI	-	African Network for Scientific and Technological Institutions
ASARECA	-	Association for Strengthening Agricultural Research in Eastern and Central Africa
C4D	-	Computing for Development Laboratory
CAD	-	Canadian Dollars
CAE	-	College of Agriculture and Engineering
CBA	-	Collective Bargaining Agreements
CBD	-	Central Business District
CCTV	-	Closed Circuit Television
CCU	-	Central Catering Unit
CDC	-	Centre for Disease Control
CEBIB	-	Centre for Biotechnology and Bioinformatics
CEES	-	College of Education and External Studies
CFI	-	Canadian Foundation for Innovation
CHS	-	College of Health Science
CIC	-	Commission for the Implementation of the Constitution

CIPL	-	Centre for International Programs and Links
COREVIP	-	Conference of Rectors, Vice Chancellors, and Presidents of African Universities
COVIDSET	-	Conference of Vice Chancellors, Provosts, Deans of Science, Engineering and Technology
CREST	-	Centre for Research Evaluation, Science and Technology
CRM	-	Customer Relationship Management system
CUE	-	Commission for University Education
DCI	-	Directorate of Criminal Investigation
DFID	-	Department for International Development
DRUSSA	-	Development of Research Uptake in Sub-Saharan Africa
DVC	-	Deputy Vice-Chancellor
EAC	-	East African Community
EACC	-	Ethics and Anti-Corruption Commission
EBS	-	Elder of the Burning Spear
EDAC	-	Erectile Dysfunction Advisory Council
EIFL	-	Electronic Information for Libraries
FGM	-	Female Genital Mutilation
FIMS	-	Financial Information Management System
FKE	-	Federation of Kenya Employers
FRCS	-	Fellow Royal College of Surgeons
GSU	-	General Service Unit
HABRI	-	Housing and Building Research Institute
HAMIS	-	Hostel Administration Management Information System
HIV	-	Human Immunodeficiency Virus
HRMIS	-	Human Resource Management Information System
IAMRA	-	International Association of Medical Regulatory Authorities
IAVI	-	International AIDS Vaccine Initiative

ICDC	-	Industrial Commercial Development Corporation
ICIPE	-	International Centre for Insect Physiology and Ecology
ICT	-	Information Communications and Technology
ICTC	-	Information and Communication Technology Centre
IDRC	-	International Development Research Centre
IFC	-	International Finance Corporation
ILO	-	International Labour Organization
ILRI	-	International Livestock Research Institute
INASP	-	International Network for the Availability of Scientific Publications
INFLA	-	International Federation of Library Associations and Institutions
INTERAF	-	Inter-African Universities Program 1967
ISO	-	International Organization for Standardization
JKML	-	Jomo Kenyatta Memorial Library
JKUAT	-	Jomo Kenyatta University of Agriculture and Technology
KAVI	-	Kenya AIDS Vaccine Initiative
KCPE	-	Kenya Certificate of Primary Education
KCSE	-	Kenya Certificate of Secondary Education
KEBS	-	Kenya Bureau of Standards
KENET	-	Kenya Education Network
KIE	-	Kenya Industrial Estates
KLISC	-	Kenya Library and Information Services Consortium
KMPDB	-	Kenya Medical Practitioners and Dentists Board
KNEC	-	Kenya National Examinations Council
KNH	-	Kenyatta National Hospital
KNTC	-	Kenya National Trading Corporation

KRA	-	Kenya Revenue Authority
Kshs	-	Kenya Shillings
KUCCPS	-	Kenya Universities and College Central Placement Service
KUDHEIHA	-	Kenya Union of Domestic, Hostels, Educational Institutions, Hospitals and Allied workers
KULC	-	Kenya University Librarians Committee
KUSU	-	Kenya Universities Staff Union
KWS	-	Kenya Wildlife Service
LAN	-	Local Area Network
LL.D	-	Doctor of Laws
MBS	-	Moran of the Order of the Burning Spear
MD	-	Managing Director
MEPI	-	Medical Education Partnership Programme Initiative
MKU	-	Mount Kenya University
MMed	-	Master of Medicine
NASA	-	National Aeronautics and Space Administration
NASCOP	-	National AIDS and STIs Control Programme
NEPAD	-	New Partnership for African Development
NHS	-	British National Health Service
NIH	-	National Institutes of Health
NIS	-	National Intelligence Service
NREN	-	National Research and Education Network
NUARSA	-	Nairobi University Arts Students Association
NYS	-	National Youth Service
OHCHR	-	Office of the High Commission for Human Rights
OMR	-	Optic Mark Reader
OPAC	-	Online Public Access Catalog
OSD	-	Organizations Systems Design

PACE	-	Partnership for Advanced Clinical Education
PAUSA	-	Pan African Urological Surgeons Association
PAYE	-	Pay As You Earn
PC	-	Perform Ace Contracting
PCC	-	Professional Conduct Committee
PEPFAR	-	President's Emergency Plan Fund for AIDS Relief
PIC	-	Preliminary Inquiry Committee
PRIME-K	-	Partnership for Innovative Medical Education for Kenya
PS	-	Permanent Secretary
PS	-	Principal Secretary
PSIP	-	Public Service Integrity Programme
PwC	-	PricewaterhouseCoopers
QMS	-	Quality Management System
RBA	-	Retirement Benefits Authority
RBM	-	Results Based Management
RDBMS	-	Relational Database Management System
RPE	-	Research, Production and Extension
RRI	-	Rapid Results Initiative
SA	-	Student Affairs
SALAR	-	Students Association for Legal Aid and Research
SEMI's	-	Seed Enterprise Management Institute
SEP 2009	-	Stanford Executive Program 2009
SMIS	-	Students Management Information System
SONU	-	Students Organization of Nairobi University
SUNY	-	State University of New York
SWA	-	Students Welfare Authority
TRECC Africa	-	Training for Resource Efficiency and Climate Change Adaptation in Africa

ACRONYMS AND ABBREVIATIONS

TSC	-	Teachers Service Commission
UASU	-	University Academic Staff Union
UMB	-	University Management Board
UNES	-	University of Nairobi Enterprises and Services
UNESCO	-	United Nations Educational Scientific and Cultural Organization
UNISEED	-	University of Nairobi's Seed Company
UNITID	-	University of Nairobi's Institute of Tropical and Infectious Diseases
UNDP	-	United Nations Development Programme
UNTESU	-	Universities Non-Teaching Staff Union
UNU	-	United Nations University
UONAA	-	University of Nairobi Alumni Association
USAID	-	United States Agency for International Development
VC	-	Vice-Chancellor
VHF	-	Very High Frequency
VoIP	-	Voice over Internet Protocol
WHO	-	World Health Organization
WMI	-	Wangari Maathai Institute
WOSWA	-	Women Students Welfare Association

FOREWORD BY DR. MANU CHANDARIA

I take great pleasure and honour in writing a Foreword for the memoirs of one of the most brilliant sons of our great country – Professor George Magoha. Professor Magoha stands out as the first competitively recruited Vice-Chancellor of the University of Nairobi, since its inception. Despite his very humble background and many youthful challenges, his measurable impact while at the helm of the University of Nairobi will definitely be remembered for many generations to come. I was privileged to serve with him as a member of the University of Nairobi Council for a total of 12 years, during which period he served the University in various capacities: one year as Principal of the College of Health Sciences; two and half years as Deputy Vice-Chancellor in charge of Administration and Finance; and the rest as Vice-Chancellor and Chief Executive Officer.

His no-nonsense, hands-on and transformative approach to management swiftly and effectively brought discipline to the entire University. This memoirs clearly reveals how Professor Magoha, a urological and transplant surgeon, led the University of Nairobi as the Vice-Chancellor and Chief Executive Officer by example, formed transformative and cohesive management teams, and got on with the job of managing the University. He was undoubtedly an excellent role model for staff and students. He shunned tribalism and petty politics and fully embraced productivity and meritocracy as indicators of success. But perhaps some of the most important qualities I admired him for were his passion for his work, and that he approached his responsibilities with humility and boundless energy. In this way he inspired his teammates, staff and students. He ensured that he completed his tasks on time as an example to others, and didn't spare anyone who did not.

The memoirs clearly describes how he instilled very strict financial discipline at the University, an action that resulted in its turnround – from a state of massive deficit to a healthy financial position ten years later. This also resulted in availability of the much-needed funds, which I can confidently say, he utilized very wisely with utmost integrity and distinction.

In this memoirs, Professor Magoha describes how he improved the academic infrastructure by completing many stalled projects and modernizing the examination process through the construction of an excellent four-storey Central Examination Centre at Chiromo Campus, and modernizing ICT infrastructure and campus connectivity including the purchase of over 9,000 computers and the establishment of many Internet hotspots across the University. Professor Magoha's game-changer however was the concept, planning and construction of the ultramodern 22 storey University of Nairobi Towers which even incorporates a helipad. I confirm as he writes in the memoirs that the University of Nairobi Towers was constructed at a cost of about Kshs 2.8 billion, without borrowing any money from the bank, and without requesting for funds from the exchequer. The bulk of the money for the construction was as a result of very prudent financial management, including wise investment of surpluses. The rest of the money came from two donors, both passionately approached by Professor Magoha. I am very proud to have contributed Kshs 50 million through the Chandaria Foundation towards the construction of the Chandaria Arts Theatre and Auditorium, which is located within the Towers.

The richness of this memoirs as a factual historical document is well illustrated by the excellent improvement in academic infrastructure, which naturally led to the quick internationalization of the university. This, coupled with good corporate governance, performance contracting processes and the formulation of various policy frameworks, catapulted the University into 'World-Class Excellence'. Indeed, to date only the University of Nairobi has achieved the grade of 'EXCELLENCE': ISO 9001:2008 Certification, thanks to the stewardship of Professor Magoha.

Under Professor Magoha's able leadership, the University of Nairobi graduated a staggering 95,000 graduates during his ten-year-tenure as Vice-Chancellor, much more than the 70,000 graduated in the previous forty-two years of the University's existence. This was because of much-improved students and staff discipline that resulted in the non-significant disruption of academic programmes over the ten years. It is also significant to note from the memoirs that, the University was producing over one hundred PhDs annually, contributing to the expansion of the much-needed intellectual human resource capacity nationwide.

In addition to diligently serving the University with distinction, at professional level Professor Magoha remained a sterling academic who has trained numerous surgeons and urologists for this country and the African continent. His surgical and urological publication profile is also excellent and very commendable especially on prostate cancer. Furthermore, he has simultaneously played a significant role in Medical and Dental Regulation in Kenya, East African Partner States and the African continent as Chairman of Medical Practitioners and Dentists Board of Kenya, President of the Association of Medical Councils of Africa (AMCOA), and, recently, Chairman of the Kenya National Examinations Council (KNEC).

There is no doubt in my mind that Professor Magoha will be remembered very positively for his great transformative leadership at the University. He is undoubtedly one of the greatest academic leaders the University of Nairobi has ever had. I would add further that having known many Vice-Chancellors over a period of the last forty years, he stands tall among them all.

Dr. Manu Chandaria
(OBE, CBS, EBS)

FOREWORD BY PROFESSOR P.L.O. LUMUMBA

The task of managing a university in Africa is a formidable one, yet when the history of the University of Nairobi under the tenure of Professor George Albert Omore Magoha is written, his friends and foes alike will admit that he served with distinction.

Those who have come to know Professor Magoha through his public persona as the Vice-Chancellor know very little of this great Kenyan, who has bestrode the landscape of his profession like the fabled colossus.

While this book is aptly titled *Tower of Transformational Leadership*, Professor Magoha sets the stage for his area of focus by giving us glimpses of his personal history to the extent that it is germane in helping us understand him.

He delves into the subject of transformative leadership by taking the reader back to the advertisement that was placed in the *Economist Magazine* inviting applications for the position of Vice-Chancellor of the University of Nairobi. He states:

> Transformative change however is not an easy concept to grasp. Looking back, I encountered some challenges to get the University community to embrace the concept and to practice it in their everyday activities. The individual to be VC, and CEO of the University, was defined as one who should be able to manage participatory planning processes and to set long and short term strategic visions and goals; to promote efficiency and good order including the welfare, conduct, and discipline of staff and students. The person appointed was to be an innovative, visionary leader capable of building a dynamic and motivated management team. Of particular importance in the equation was the ability to formulate and execute a change management programme to ensure the sustainability and transformation of the University, on the path to world class excellence.

The concept of transformational leadership was not one that was unique to Kenya but the author states what it entailed as he wrapped his mind on it. He says:

> Transformative leadership is a management style where the leader is charged with identifying needed change, and creating a clear vision to guide the change not only through inspiration, but also execution of the change in tandem with the organizational needs. Transformative leaders also motivate and raise the morale of the team members by using several methods, that connect the leader, team members and workers to take greater sense of self identity and self in the organization and the collective identity of the organization. The transformative leader should be a role model for the workers, in order to inspire them and raise their interest in the organization and be able to challenge them to take greater ownership of their work.

The central plank of Professor Magoha's exposé on transformational leadership is that a firm family foundation and educational background is a fundamental prerequisite in one's preparation for the challenging task of managing an institution particularly at a time when its survival depends on transformation whose impact shakes the old order to its very core.

In his incisive analysis of what constitutes transformational leadership, Professor Magoha has not allowed himself to be confined to the proverbial 'box'. He has examined leadership in its different facets and nuances and ably demonstrated that a transformational leader must be a visionary servant capable of working with people from diverse backgrounds.

While Professor Magoha will be remembered for his sterling ten years stint at the University of Nairobi, it must not be forgotten that he contemporaneously served as the Chairman of the Kenya Medical Practitioners and Dentists Board and helped regulate the medical profession in different parts of Africa with equal zeal and efficiency.

After reading this book, those who have had the privilege of working with him will understand why in his quest for excellence, he brooks no nonsense yet he remains a collegiate consensus builder in his leadership style.

Professor Magoha's result-oriented leadership has yielded many fruits for the University of Nairobi, which remains a premier institution even after the end of his tour of duty; giving meaning to the statement that one is not deemed successful until his successor succeeds.

It is noteworthy that his transformational leadership has once again been embraced through his appointment to rescue the Kenya National Examinations Council which had been mired in corruption and mediocrity.

I applaud Professor Magoha's gem of a book because it is the testimony of one who has been tried, tested and found worthy.

Professor P.L.O. Lumumba,
LL.D, D.Litt (hc), CPS (K), MKIM
DIRECTOR/CHIEF EXECUTIVE OFFICER
KENYA SCHOOL OF LAW

*In an academic gown, as the Vice-Chancellor,
University of Nairobi, 2005*

CHAPTER ONE

Formative Years

Hard work has never killed anyone; neither have honesty, integrity and fair treatment.

Early Memories

Among some of my earliest memories are my mother Sarah's love for me. Early in life she taught me how to perform all household chores including fetching water from the stream, fetching firewood, cooking, tilling the farm, grazing and milking cows. She believed that hard work has never killed anyone and neither have honesty, integrity and fair treatment of others.

I recognize now that, in this way she taught me the true values of love, honesty, integrity, fairness, faithfulness, hard work and above all, the fear of God. She was a strict but fair disciplinarian and I believe that it is such instruction early in my formative years, that had a lasting impression or influence and which I have always tried to encourage others to emulate.

Another of my early memories is my paternal grandmother, a healer, who never hesitated to point out to me shrubs and trees with medicinal value. In a sense perhaps, the art of healing was inculcated in my conscience early and may be that's why I became a medical doctor.

My Ancestral Roots

I belong to the K'Anyango clan from Marenyo sub-location of East Gem location, Gem Sub-county of Siaya County. This clan is well known for education and the discipline imparted to their children. This is exemplified by the fact that one of the first native Kenyan judges of the Court of Appeal, when it was the highest court in Kenya, Justice Raymond Otieno Masime came from this clan. The clan also boasts of having many other professionals including lawyers, economists, scientists, administrators, teachers, architects, medical specialists and university professors.

My father, Bernard Boniface Magoha, was the second born in a family of eight siblings, four males and four females. My mother, Joan Sarah Aloo, was the second born in a family of four: Charles Arnold Agunga who passed on while on training in Namliango, Makerere Uganda before I was born, Pauline Anyango who passed on in 1958 and my only surviving aunt, Elizabeth Omore. My maternal grandfather, Romulus Omore, was a catechist at Aluor Catholic Mission while my maternal grandmother, Veronica Akongo, of the Waohra clan in Sakwa, Siaya County was a cook at St. Mary's School, Yala. I am named after my maternal grandfather. My paternal grandfather, Lucas Ogola was a farmer while my paternal grandmother, Maria Akumu was a housewife and also a healer: she had extensive knowledge of various leaves and herbs with healing potential.

Family Tree

I was born on 02 July, 1952 at the then Kisumu Provincial Hospital, to Bernard Boniface Magoha and Joan Sarah Aloo. My parents met at a church service at Mill Hill Catholic Mission in Yala, and married in a white Catholic Church wedding at St. Peter Clavers Catholic Church, Yala in the present Siaya County. Perhaps, on reflection, it is why my father remained monogamous.

My parents were blessed with ten children, three girls and seven boys. The first child, William Edward Ogola was born in 1937, followed by the second child, John Francis Obare, in 1939. The third child Mary Consolata Magoha was born in 1941 but passed on soon after birth. The fourth child, Mary Magdalene Owuor, was born in 1943, and Charles Arnold Agunga Magoha, the fifth child, was born in 1946. The sixth child, Michael Achianja Magoha, was born in 1949 but passed on in 1971 when he was just about to complete his high school education. I am the seventh born, and was born in 1952. The eighth child, Richard Alex Nyabera Magoha was born in 1954, while the ninth born, Joseph Vincent Oyile Magoha was born in 1956. The lastborn, Pauline Magoha Dola, was born in 1960.

Early Life

Although both of my grandfathers died before I was born, I was privileged to have my grandmothers for the first 20 years of my life. Sharing stories with them strengthened my understanding of our culture. My maternal grandmother for instance, strengthened and anchored my strong belief in the Christian doctrine, while my paternal grandmother would take me to the bush and meticulously show me certain leaves that could be used as herbal medicine to cure various ailments.

My parents were stounch Catholics and disciplinarians. My father never stayed home much. As a primary school headmaster he lived in various primary schools run by the Mill Hill Catholic Mission in central Nyanza, the present day Kisumu and Siaya counties. Some of the schools in which my father was headmaster are Manyuanda and Reru in the present day Kisumu County, and Jina, Kagilo and Muhanda in the present day Siaya County.

We lived a very simple village life but were reasonably well fed on a diet of ugali, traditional vegetables, fish and occasionally meat and *nyoyo* (boiled maize and beans). The servings however were never generous as we were many siblings. I learned my first lesson of equality in life early: my mother would put in each of our hands a small piece of fish or meat but the ugali and soup plates remained common to all. This was to ensure that the weaker and slower siblings also had a balanced diet. Breakfast was always porridge although occasionally, when my parents could afford it, there would be a cup of tea. Meat and tea were only possible because of my father's dedication to his family. At night we all slept together on a mat on the floor, sharing one big blanket except for the youngest born, who had a bed because she was a baby. Bedbugs and jiggers were, at this time in our lives a challenge.

However, we were lucky that my mother had a certain white cream which was very effective in controlling them. I am not sure what this white cream was, but I know that it worked well and that my father could afford it.

My mother was not only a housewife but also a dryfish trader. During school holidays, I proudly carried the dryfish for her to and from Yala market twice a week, on Tuesdays and Fridays. It mattered least to me that I was the man among women in the market, because I loved my mother dearly. I spent most of my formative years under her strict and watchful eye because I was regarded as the weakest, due to my frequent asthma attacks.

Education Background

My father attended the Kabaa Mission School, in Machakos County. Kabaa was founded in 1924 by a Catholic priest, Reverend Father Michael John Witte, of the Holy Ghost Congregation. The school offered tuition from nursery through primary, teacher training, technical training and secondary education. It also had a seminary section drawing students from all over East Africa, including Malawi. My father trained as a teacher but first worked with the meteorological department in Nanyuki and later at Kololo Hill in Kampala, Uganda before returning to the teaching profession.

Although a housewife my mother was literate having been taught how to read and write at the Aluor Catholic Mission School. My parents therefore valued education and we were encouraged to achieve all levels of education and to pursue careers along that line and excel. My father thus ensured that he paid fees and met other needs accordingly.

Our firstborn, William trained at the University of Nairobi in the early seventies and served as a teacher, retiring as Deputy Provincial Director of Education, in the former Nyanza Province. He passed on in 2009. John the second born, worked as a sales manager in many companies including African Tours and Hotels, East African Breweries and Total Kenya. The fourth born, Mary Magdalene trained as a nurse and later qualified as a clinical officer. Charles the fifth born, joined the police force and served as an officer, sales manager and later a pilot. The sixth born, Micheal passed on in 1971, just as he was about to complete his high school education. The eighth born, Richard Alex studied at Starehe Boys Centre and later, at the State University of New York. Currently, he is a professor in the United States of America. The ninth born, Joseph went to the University of Nagpur in India and the University of Lagos, Nigeria for graduate studies, and is serving as a senior administrator in the Office of the President of the Government of Kenya. Our lastborn, Pauline also studied at the University of Nagpur in India and the University of Jos in Nigeria for her graduate studies and is serving as a County Commissioner with the National Government of Kenya.

Primary School Education

I started my education at Jina Primary School, a Catholic-owned school, under the Mill Hill Missionaries. The school was located five kilometres from home. I had to walk about ten kilometres barefoot, every day, to school and back. For the first year, I wore a very long shirt and reaching almost to my ankles, without shorts, before graduating to a shirt and shorts in class two. At Jina, all the cleaning and other chores were done by the pupils. I learned my catechism and Christianity, and received preliminary preparation for confirmation at this school for which I was very grateful. Before my actual confirmation however, I went for residential training in catechism and the Bible at St. Peter Clavers Church, Yala. I was also taught farming techniques at this early stage which came in very handy when I was working with my mother and our farm worker, Sila Oluchiri, in the farm. I learned humility early in my life because whenever our farm worker was around, my father would always eat with him any meal brought out to the farm by my mother. One day, I asked him why he did it and he explained that all human beings are equal before God and that true Christian life requires that we practice what Jesus did – eat with others, as he was doing. This action has had a permanent effect in my life to date. I completed my standard four studies at Jina Primary School in 1963.

Relocation to Nairobi

I was only ten and half years when in December 1963, I moved to Nairobi to live with my second born brother, John Francis Obare and his newly wedded wife, Agatha Christine Obare. The reasons for my relocation were threefold. The most compelling one was the fact that one day while it was raining heavily, an older student had ran over me with a bicycle while I was on my way from school and fractured my left clavicle (collarbone). This was an emergency, and my father had to be called from the far off school that he was serving in, at the time. I could see the hopelessness in my parents' eyes as they frantically looked for a vehicle to take me to hospital in Kisumu, some 55 kilometres away. I was in so much pain, had difficulty in breathing and the swelling on my neck and chest was getting bigger. They must have thought that I was dying, and were praying loudly for the means to take me to the hospital. After one hour of standing in the rain, a good Samaritan offered us a lift, in his car to Kisumu. We were delivered safely at the hospital, where I received treatment. I wore a plaster of Paris cast across my neck, upper chest and shoulders for six weeks.

The other reason for relocating to Nairobi was that I had asthma and after the accident, the intensity and frequency of asthmatic attacks increased such that my mother, with the help of the local medical assistant at Marenyo Dispensary were unable to manage satisfactorily. On one of his visits to Nairobi, my father arranged for the famous chest specialist, Dr. James Angawa, the consultant in charge of the Infectious Diseases Unit of the King George VI Hospital (now Kenyatta National Hospital), to treat me. Dr. Angawa was from the same location as our family so my father knew him well. I was therefore very privileged to be treated by him. Within a few months of treatment, I had completely recovered. It is important to note that Dr. Angawa treated me free of charge. As a result of my early contact with him, I made a decision that I too wanted to become a medical doctor in order to help other suffering people. I felt like he had brought my life back.

The third reason for relocation was that since I was doing reasonably well at school, my father reasoned that I needed to attend a better school in the city to enhance my chances of success. Life in Nairobi was much better with less work, better food and I slept on a bed. We lived in Jericho Lumumba estate where nationalists such as J.M. Kariuki, Waruru Kanja, Bildad Kaggia, Senator Makasembo, and Onyango Midika lived. My brother, John was working with Sterling Winthrop Company Limited while his wife, Agatha Christine worked with Barclays Bank. They could therefore afford a reasonably good life, for that time. I joined Dr. David Livingstone Primary School, situated in Jerusalem Nairobi in May, 1964. It was about a three kilometre walk from where we lived, so I only had to walk six kilometres a day, to and from school.

At the new school there were very many teachers, each one teaching a different subject, and there were several streams of the same class. I noticed that the school had better teaching materials including blackboards, chalk of different colours, and many and better books. It was as if I had started learning all over again. We were taught metal work and carpentry, with practical work being conducted at the neighbouring Morrison Primary School in Bahati, two afternoons a week. Furthermore, there were extracurricular activities and clubs. I chose to join the Boy Scout Club, rising to the rank of a patrol leader. During the school holidays, I always went back to our rural home in Marenyo, to be with my mother and some of my siblings who were still staying with her. I left Dr. David Livingstone Primary School, in 1966 after sitting my final primary school examination.

I had joined different young teen age play groups within the estate, and would take part in them in the evenings and during the weekends. Some of these groups evolved into strongman groups, where occasionally we organised test matches to compare our strength with those of other young teen age groups from other estates such as Mbotela, Kaloleni, Jerusalem and Maringo. Members of these groups were aged between thirteen to sixteen years. There were strict rules of engagement, and one chose either boxing or wrestling the opponent. If the opponent declined the test then the challenger automatically became senior to the opponent. However, if the opponent was available, a neutral referee from a different group was appointed unanimously and his word was final. In wrestling, the match would be over once your back touched the ground. In boxing, except for an immediate knock out, most of the duels lasted between ten and fifteen minutes and you were disqualified if you hit directly at your opponents mouth, endangering his teeth. There were no weapons or hard drugs except for a few boys who smoked ordinary cigarettes. Personally, I did not smoke.

These encounters instilled courage and discipline in me and at the age of thirteen years, I rose through the ranks and file, to the deputy commander of our group. An older boy called Peter, remained the group commander until I left the group for high school in 1967. Apart from these groups, I was also a member of a band called 'L'Orchestre Lunna Success de la Capital', founded by Ochieng Kabbasselleh, and which later became L'Orchestre Lunna Kidi. Kabbasselleh was a student at Pumwani High School in Nairobi. Other members of the band included Boaz Divers and a Congolese known only as Hassan. All these members of the band have since passed on. I played the bass guitar for a year. My original interest in music commenced and was inspired by the Latin spiritual songs I used to sing during the Holy Masses at the St. Peter Clavers Catholic in Yala where I learned the catechism. I realized then that music enabled me to communicate more effectively with God. As we sang songs of praises to the Almighty God, I also enjoyed spiritual calmness and satisfaction beyond description.

Primarily therefore, I looked at music as a means of communication, expression and enhancing togetherness among human beings. I also imagined that through music one could make a stable career and become rich and popular as the likes of Elvis Presley and Cliff Richards. Our first recording led by the late Ochieng Kabasselleh was with Melodica Studios, and we were paid Kshs 300 after surrendering all the rights to the producer. My share of the proceeds was only Kshs 30.

On joining Starehe Boys Centre, I encountered strict institutional discipline which did not enable me to continue practising with the band as required. In order to cope with the order at Starehe, I opted out of the band and concentrated on my studies. However, my deep love for music continued albeit as a hobby and pastime. I was to benefit immensely from this love during my tenure as Vice-Chancellor of the University of Nairobi, as music played a pivotal role in the management of very difficult challenges.

Starehe Boys Centre

I was attracted to Starehe Boys Centre by the school band and the uniform; bright red shirt and deep blue shorts. Majority of the students at Starehe were bright but from poor family backgrounds and were sponsored through grants from generous organizations and individuals in Kenya and beyond. The rest of the students were sons of parents or guardians who could afford and were willing to pay in accordance with their means.

I was interviewed by the director of the Centre, the late Dr. Geoffrey Griffin, for one of the slots in the fee paying category. The interview was very difficult. I answered questions about my merit, honesty, diligence, commitment, uniforms and courtesy. I was very scared because there was a very huge man in the interview room whom I later came to know as Patrick Shaw, the deputy director in charge of administration, and a very huge bull dog called Prince. When the KCPE results were released I had passed well, and therefore admitted into one of the fee paying slots. The fees for a day scholar was Kshs 200 per year. Following my admission, I attended technical initiative tests at the Wilson Airport as a result of which I was placed in Form 1T, having done well in the test. After one term, I was transferred to Form 1A because I had politely and very clearly made my teachers understand that I wanted to be a medical doctor and not an engineer. My school admission number was 3466.

Starehe Boys Centre started in 1959, from the very humble beginnings of two tin-huts donated by Kenya Shell Limited. The founder, and then later the director, was Dr. Griffin, assisted by Geoffrey Gituro and Joseph K. Gikubu. The boys, selected at its inauguration, were mainly drawn from the Manyani rehabilitation camp. The Centre had no dining hall or bathing place and each day, the boys walked to Kariokor market. This was a very difficult moment for the boys but through diligence, they built themselves open sided sheds to serve as the first classrooms and workshops. The beginnings of the Centre were bedevilled by several other drawbacks, including that the director, as a civil servant was free to set up Starehe Boys Centre but was not allowed to request the government for any financial help.

By the time I joined Starehe eight years later, the school had completely transformed into a modern secondary school, with modern science laboratories, technical workshops, a library, dining hall, assembly hall and several boarding blocks. This transformation was certainly due to the single handed and most commendable effort of the director, who sourced assistance from Kenya Shell Limited, the Nairobi Round Table No. 1, the African Trust Fund, Save the Children UK, the Oxford Committee for Famine Relief (OXFAM), the Ford Foundation, Marlborough College, the Nuffield Foundation, Mrs. W. Kerr, and the post-independence Kenya Government among others. The government provided the Centre with qualified teachers. The Centre also attracted foreign volunteer teachers sourced from the American Youth Service Corps, the British Government and the Danish Government among others.

Dr. Griffin was also the inaugural director of the National Youth Service (NYS) in Kenya. Born on 13 June, 1933 in Eldoret, Kenya, he was only a few months old when the family relocated to Nairobi, where his father, was serving as a police officer. He spent the early years of infancy in a little house of wood and iron, located near the present day Fairmont Norfolk Hotel and subsequently, a stone house home in Westlands. He started his education at St. Helen's Kindergarten, the present day Westlands Primary School. From Nairobi, the Griffins moved to Kitale, and Geoffrey received his primary education at Kitale Primary School. In 1944, Dr. Griffin sat the Kenya Preliminary Examination, two years below the average age and obtained the third place in the examination nationally. This impressive performance took him to the Prince of Wales School in Nairobi, the present day Nairobi School. While at the Prince of Wales, he became the first Kings Scout in Kenya Colony. Dr. Griffin left the Prince of Wales School in 1949 in Form Five, and immediately was accepted as a cadet for training and service with the Survey of Kenya. This job took him to different parts of Kenya to work among the native Africans.

At the end of the State of Emergency, he was appointed to work on a rehabilitation scheme for young Mau Mau detainees. Many of these boys were housed in the notorious Manyani Camp, situated in the arid, inhospitable area between the coastal belt and Taita Hills. It was while serving at Manyani that he met Mr. Gituro and Mr. Gikubu, both of whom were destined to become his partners in the creation of the Starehe Boys Centre. After independence, Dr. Griffin was appointed the founder director of the National Youth Service (NYS) Kenya where he served diligently for 34 years (1964–1998). He passed away on 28 June, 2005.

The aim of Starehe Boys Centre is, "To mould a whole man, ardent in piety towards God, strong in patriotism and not petty tribalism, just in all ways, resolute and honest, and impregnable to any temptation of corruption, devoted to duty rather than stealer of employers time, willingness to go the extra mile, courageous in adversity, peaceful at temper but no coward, protector of the weak, prudent in decision making, temperate and honourable."

My entire stay at Starehe therefore was guided by the above aim. We were taught well, by qualified teachers with various subjects offered in the classrooms, laboratories, workshops and sports fields. In addition, my experiences at the Centre shaped and defined the rest of my life. The Centre had rules which had to be obeyed by all. We started the day at 7.45 a.m. with interdenominational prayers although occasionally, we had a Muslim prayer, head count and a military style parade and national flag hoisting, and a similar parade, head count and prayer, for lowering the flag at 5 p.m.

Our studies were of international standards to the extent that my teachers came from across the world. For example, I was taught Biology by Ms. Pamela Snethen, from the United States of America, while my Physics teacher, Mr. Nielsen was from Denmark. My Chemistry teacher, Mr. Harvey was from the United Kingdom, while my Religious Education teacher, Rev. Sister Christiana Sestero, was from Italy. Away from the classroom, I was taught about living a responsible and accountable life. At the end of the four secondary school years, I was supposed not only to have my form four certificate but also to transform from a boy into a responsible young gentleman, as per the aim of Starehe. One of the ways in which responsibility was instilled was through initiative test competition, which was regularly organised by Mr. Shaw. This entailed a boy using his extra instincts to follow different leads to distant but unknown destinations within Nairobi and its environs, on foot. The other was the volunteer service, where we worked, during the school holidays in hospitals, companies and government departments, among others. I volunteered several times at the Kenyatta National Hospital, a pharmaceutical company and often, to serve the poor and the less fortunate in our society. This volunteer service, particularly in health-related institutions, further encouraged me to work harder, in order to realize my dream of becoming a medical doctor.

Starehe used a baraza system to gauge and enhance participation. The baraza was some sort of students parliament, complete with immunity, and once a week, on Friday evenings after supper, the director, some of his deputies and teachers would come to the hall, for interactive discussion on any topic, opinion or problem. The boys were allowed to seek any explanations and complain about any issues including about the director himself. As I stated, there was complete immunity and thus no boy was ever penalized for whatever opinion stated during the baraza. During my stay at

Starehe, I attended many such barazas and the experience gained had tremendous influence in my later life. Starehe also had a Boy Scouts Troupe, and joining the troupe instilled further discipline in the boys and exposed them to endurance skills through various expeditions to many parts of rural Kenya. This was augmented by the President's Award Scheme, which tested the endurance and stress level of the members. I was both a Troop Leader in the Scout Movement and participated in the President's Award Scheme.

Starehe had many discipline systems, and the last and most important one was the prefects' system, under the guidance of the director, his deputies and the teaching staff. The prefects at Starehe were given a wide variety of punishments to choose from and the prefect was expected to exercise wisdom and fairness. They were supposed to serve their fellow boys and not be bosses. They were regarded as big brothers that the younger boys could turn to when they had a problem. The prefects were trained in effective leadership, teamwork and team building, standards, values and attitudes, action centred leadership and time management. They were also made to understand that the main aim of the punishment was to correct the offender and that if this was not achieved, then the punishment would be meaningless.

Some of the punishments for minor offenses included: cleaning any part of the school including toilets, and physical drill conducted during break (between 10.55 a.m. and 11.15 a.m.), Saturday working party given for moderate environmental offenses such as misusing electricity or water and littering the school compound, this involved working for three hours on Saturday afternoon. More serious offenses such as sneaking out of school, attracted up to a maximum of six strokes of the cane, commonly known as 'six of the best', given only by the director.

I used to perform very well in my class and most of the time I was number one, two or three. My best subject was History where my score remained between 95 and 98 per cent. My History teacher, Mr. Wanjohi was a Kenyan. Despite this excellent performance, I also played truant, sometimes skipping a lesson or two during my first year, borrowing a bicycle from wealthier students and riding to town then sneaking back. It was, I guess a case of youthful, early teenage exuberance, but my proverbial 40 days came one day when I was caught by Mr. Shaw, riding a borrowed bicycle in town, during class hours. He smashed the bicycle to smithereens, and took me back to school. When the director returned from his office at the NYS headquarters, it was 'six of the best' for me. This was another turning point in my life as I started being serious with my studies. The following year, I was appointed a prefect and therefore had more responsibility which included ensuring that the boys were well-dressed, with short and well-combed hair and nicely polished shoes before the morning and evening parades, in addition to other disciplinary duties.

Leadership and responsibility were certainly inculcated in us, and we were trained to serve in different areas. One way of noting this is to peruse a list of old 'Starehians' and where they are serving. The Centre being one of the best schools in Kenya has produced many prominent Kenyans serving the nation in different areas of the economy. For instance, in the media, Joseph Odindo headed the Nation Media Group as Group Editorial Director for many years, while Raphael Tuju of Ace Communications was also a government minister, among others. In the public service there is Julius Kipng'etich who performed a sterling job as Director of the Kenya Wildlife Service (KWS) before moving to Equity Bank as Chief Operations Office and later, Uchumi Limited. In the Industrial sector, there are: Solomon Waithaka, George J. Maara, David Gatama, and Ricky Aloysius, among others. In the health sciences there are many medical specialists including Dr. Ambrose Misore, Dr. George Ogonji and Dr. Robert Mathenge, to mention a few. In politics there have been many Members of Parliament including Phillip Galgalo, Mwandawiro Mghanga and Peter Kenneth. In the legal profession there are Joseph Anthony Obado-Adera and Jackson Barasa, among others. The head of the medical corps in the Kenya Defence Forces Dr. Brigadier General

Christopher Arrumm is also a Starehian, and so is Joseph Kamau who was Director of the Criminal Investigations Department (CID) in Kenya for a long time. In the University sector and by the Grace of God, I was the first Starehian to be appointed Vice-Chancellor.

I sat my form four examinations in 1970. When the results were announced, I had passed with a Division I. By the time I was leaving Starehe Boys Centre, I was a complete and totally disciplined eighteen year old young man already equipped with all that I needed to survive in life. In fact, the only reason I left Starehe was because at that time it did not offer science subjects at advanced level.

Strathmore College

It took the intervention of Dr. Griffin, to persuade me to apply to join Strathmore as he had been assured that I would be admitted, irrespective of the results. The competition for Strathmore was very stiff. Twenty boys were selected for the interview. The interviews were very involving and lasted about half an hour for each student. They were conducted by the Deputy Principal of Strathmore College, Mr. Peter McDermott.

At the end of the process, Ambrose Misore (a Strarehian) and I were selected to join the Strathmore A Level class. The interviews were done in June, long before the final examinations. So it came to pass that I joined Strathmore College in 1971. Strathmore offered advanced level courses for the science subjects, examined by the London GCE examinations syndicate. There was also a School of Accountancy, training students for the Association of Chartered Certified Accountants (ACCA).

On my first day at Strathmore, I was welcomed by Ertiman Gendia, a senior student, and Mr. Silvano Borusso who would later be my Biology teacher. I was taken to the cafeteria for my four o'clock tea and cake before being escorted to my new dormitory. My room was spacious enough for two students. It had a double-decker bed, a book shelf, two study tables and chairs. My roommate was a senior student, so I took the upper deck. Supper was a three course meal, the very first time that I had partaken of such a meal in my life. Unlike at Starehe, there was no uniform at Strathmore so for the first time in almost twenty years, I found myself free to wear whatever I wanted.

The following day we were addressed by the Principal, Dr. David Sperling, after introducing the teachers and other staff told us that Strathmore was a close family to which we belonged. Unlike Starehe, there was no prefect system because we were supposed to be mature enough to look after ourselves. My experience of being responsible, which had been honed by my stay at Starehe Boys Centre, came in very handy. Furthermore, Dr. Sperling assured some of us, that we were fully sponsored and therefore should not worry about tuition and examination fees. This was quite a relief.

The teaching at Strathmore was first class; I took Physics, Chemistry and Biology at advanced level and general paper at subsidiary level. We were few and the interaction with the teachers was very good. In the laboratories for instance, during various experiments, the teachers were able to interact and assess the students on a one to one basis. There were many clubs to choose from and there was also the Strathmore Students Association. I joined the debating club which was very refreshingly away from the sciences. In my capacity as the chairman of the debating club, we visited many other schools including: Kenya High, Loreto Limuru, Alliance High School, Mang'u, Lenana and St. Mary's School. I also joined the young farmers club, chaired by Chris Bichage. Furthermore, I contested and won the position of Vice Chairman of the Strathmore Students Association. At some point, I acted for six months as Chairman of the Association, when the substantive chairman, Mohammed Hamisi, an accountancy student was away. For sports, I played rugby, jogged and walked; I remember that in 1972, I took part in a walking competition from Nairobi to Naivasha.

On the other hand my spiritual life was also strengthened while at Strathmore. There was a Catholic Chapel and a resident Catholic Chaplain in the College, and both were available to students at all times. Interestingly many teachers including the Principal, Dr. Sperling were members of The Opus Dei and were instrumental in my spiritual nourishment. In this regard, I particularly remember my Biology teacher, Mr. Borusso and my Physics teacher, Mr. Hodge who served as my spiritual mentors, and encouraged me along the Christian walk.

During the school holidays, I worked in a pharmaceutical company in Nairobi. I opened my first bank account with the Postal Corporation of Kenya (Posta) at this time and started saving. The last week of my school holidays would always be spent with my parents and siblings at our rural home in Marenyo. During this week I would get involved in any work that was available, and also share with them my new farming knowledge gained from my experience as a member of the Young Farmers Club at Strathmore.

During my second year of study, the Principal became very instrumental in my continuing to study at Strathmore. What happened is that, as the workload became more I also had to read for more hours in order to cope with the workload. Consequently, I developed persistent headaches which were resistant to normal painkillers. For the first month, I was treated by a doctor without much improvement. My weekly academic performance started to decline and when my teachers reported to the Principal, he immediately summoned me to his office. After I narrated my predicament to him, he instructed me to get into his car, a Peugeot 204 and drove me to town to consult Dr. Binaguaiho, with whom he had made an appointment on my behalf. After my medical history and physical examination, the doctor, who was spot on in his diagnosis of an eye problem, referred me to an optician and by afternoon I was wearing prescribed lenses and my headaches were gone – thanks to the kindness and the wisdom of the Principal.

Strathmore College used to organize career talks for students with different professionals such as architects, pharmacists, medical doctors, engineers, scientists and teachers, being invited. During my second year of study, I attended one such career talk given by Professor Joseph Maina Mungai, the then Dean of the Faculty of Medicine at the University of Nairobi. His story about how he started the Faculty of Medicine, carrying cadavers in his personal car, a black Volkswagen, from Makerere University's Mulago Hospital to the University of Nairobi convinced me that I too was meant to be a medical doctor like him. He became my role model because of his thoroughness, patriotism, clear thinking and dedication to the duty of saving lives. At the end of the two years, I sat my London GCE Advanced Level examinations and when the results were announced in 1973 I had passed with three Principals, of grades A, B, E and a subsidiary pass in the general paper.

Strathmore College did not only offer a sound education, but also all-round skills and articulation. It is no surprise then that among prominent Kenyans who also schooled at Strathmore College include: the current Governor of the Central Bank of Kenya, Patrick Njoroge, Micah Cheserem, Chairman of the Commission on Revenue Allocation in Kenya, Sixtus Mwea a professor of civil and construction engineering at the University of Nairobi, Adam Mohammed Adam, a professor of medicine at the University of Nairobi, Dr. David Ndegwa a psychiatrist in the Lambeth area of England in the United Kingdom, George McOdawa a consulting engineer, Jim Mcfie who is a professor at Strathmore University, Chrisanthus Bichage a politician, Dr. Okello Agina, the Dean, Kenyatta University School of Medicine, Dr. Patrick Akuku Okoth a top-grade consultant neurosurgeon, and my cousin Justice Otieno Masime.

University Training

I had applied to the University of Nairobi's Medical School to study medicine and was accepted. However, shortly afterwards, the

Association of African Universities (AAU) Interaf scholarships became available. I was selected under this scholarship scheme to study medicine at the University of Zambia. Nonetheless, it happened that the daughter of Kenya's High Commissioner to Zambia, Mr. Leo Odero, had been admitted to study medicine at the College of Medicine of the University of Lagos, but he did not want her to go to Nigeria, and so he swapped my place with his daughter's. That is how I ended up in Lagos, Nigeria instead of Lusaka, Zambia.

Other Kenyan students from my Strathmore class who studied in Nigeria on the same scholarship include: Ambrose Ooko Misore who joined the University of Ibadan to study medicine and Patrick Akuku Okoth who joined the University of Ife, later renamed Obafemi Awolowo University, to study medicine. Two other students went to Ghana under the same scholarship. They were: David Ndegwa who joined the University of Ghana's Medical School at Legon, Accra, and Dickson Ayieye who joined the University of Kumasi School of Pharmacy.

Undergraduate Training

When I got the admission letter to the College of Medicine of the University of Lagos to study medicine, I was extremely elated and most thankful to God through whose grace and mercy I had achieved my lifelong goal. I therefore vigorously started looking for a Kenyan passport. In order to be issued with a passport, I needed to present my birth certificate. Since I had no birth certificate, I sought assistance from the Attorney General's chambers in acquiring one. The process was long and involved the provincial administration, including the chief and the local Catholic parish priest who was the custodian of my baptismal history. Eventually, after waiting for about two months, I was issued with a birth certificate to enable me apply for a passport. The process of acquiring a passport was even much more difficult, despite the fact that I was a fully sponsored student, nominated by the Government of Kenya. I applied for the passport and waited for about two months without any positive feedback. I therefore went back to the Ministry of Education at Jogoo House to report my plight. With only three days left before my planned departure for Lagos Nigeria, I still had not succeeded in acquiring a passport.

Although the Government had bought me the air ticket it took quick and compassionate intervention of a senior officer from the ministry, Mr. Jackson Wachira to enable me get my passport. Mr. Wachira camped with me at the immigration department for two consecutive days pleading the urgency of my case to the senior officers concerned in order for my passport to be released in time to enable me travel to Lagos Nigeria the following day.

Mr. Wachira went further and used his office at the Ministry of Education to alert the Vice-Chancellor (VC) of the University of Lagos Professor Ade-Ajayi, of the difficulties I was having in acquiring a passport, and the possibility that I might be late to take up my place, when the semester had commenced. Mercifully, the passport was released and I travelled on time to commence the semester. The impact created by the compassion exhibited by Mr. Wachira, to a young student whom he did not know, would influence the way I handled people for many years to come. As fate would have it, he was later destined to become the Administration Registrar at the University of Nairobi, a position he held for twelve years, until his retirement in 2001.

I left for Lagos aboard an Ethiopian Airlines flight on 22 September, 1973. In the same flight was Ambrose Ooko Misore, who was destined for the City of Ibadan, Nigeria to join the Faculty of Medicine of the University of Ibadan. At the Embakasi Airport (now Jomo Kenyatta International Airport) to see me off were members of my family, including my beloved mother, Joan Sarah Aloo, my brothers William, John, Charles and their families. Others were Mr. Shaw, who had become my mentor and Mr. Wachira. The excitement exhibited by my family about my departure was due to the fact that I was soon to become the first person in the family to board an aeroplane. What worried me most was that my mother thought she was seeing me for the last time.

She encouraged me but emphasized that if I did not return to find her alive, it was because she had been told that training to be a real medical doctor would take very long. Because of that fear, I ensured that I returned home to see her every year of my first five years of medical training. Her fears were however completely unfounded as I was able to take care of her for another thirty two years after the completion of my training as a medical doctor.

The flight to Lagos was delayed, and it took about six hours for us to arrive at Ikeja International Airport. The VC, Professor Ade-Ajayi, had sent a member of staff to pick me at the airport and take me to his office. The late arrival of the plane, coupled with very bad traffic in Lagos however resulted in my arriving at midnight, at the University of Lagos main campus at Akoka, Yaba where the VC's office and residence are situated. On proceeding to the residence, the staff found out from the security guards at the gate that he had already retired for the night and decided not to wake him up. They however left a message that I had arrived safely. The staff took me to one of the medical students hostels situated at Bode Thomas Street, in Suru Lere, Lagos. This was a senior student's hostel, for third and fourth year medical students. We arrived at 2 a.m. when all the students had retired for the night. One third year medical student, Boniface Oye Adeniran was woken up and to my surprise he gave me tea, bread and sardines, from the locker in his room. He further left his room for me for the rest of the night. I was particularly grateful because it was very hot and humid, but I could now take a cold bath and enjoyed cool air from the electric fan in his room.

The following day, the VC came to the Lagos University Teaching Hospital where the Faculty of Medicine was located and instructed that I should be allocated one of the rooms in the newly completed hostels situated in the hospital. That afternoon, he took me to his house for lunch. I was completely dumbfounded by his humility and simplicity, because despite his very high position, he had taken the time to receive me. All my life therefore, I have tried to emulate this, while dealing with all people.

The other student on the flight, Ambrose, had been accommodated at the Lagos airport hotel in Ikeja. The following morning, I went to see him off on the short local flight to the city of Ibadan where he was going to join the University of Ibadan's Medical School. I was accompanied by a third year medical student named Ositelu, who very kindly offered to accompany us to the airport. Ositelu was later to become a consultant physician.

On my first day at the University, I settled in my room in the newly constructed hostels at the Lagos University Teaching Hospital located at Idi-Araba in Suru Lere. My roommate was Clinton Nyamuriyekunge Masawa from Tanzania. It was very hot and humid so we contributed money to purchase an electric fan to keep our room cool. Everything else in the room was comfortable with two reading tables and bookshelves. There were also two lockable wardrobes and bedside tables. There was adequate lighting and sockets. The two beds were new, with new and comfortable mattresses and bedding. There were shared showers and toilets, for the 24 students per floor and there were four blocks of three floors each within the hostel.

There were a sizable number of international students at the College. For instance, there were three foreign students in my class: Thabo Mothebe from Lesotho, Chuchu Ongwachi from the United States of America and Francis Kwamin from Ghana. The class before us had my great friend Leonard Kileo Lema from Tanzania who later became a professor of cardio-thoracic surgery at the University of Dar es Salaam, Vanga Siwisa from South Africa and Asamoa and Otchere, both from Ghana. I also met Jeff Mbure who was a senior Kenyan student studying at the main campus at Akoka. The 1974 class that followed us had a quantum leap in the number of foreign students studying medicine. There were 60 students from Zimbabwe alone and many others from Guyana, Trinidad and Tobago, Uganda, Tanzania, Cameroon, Ghana, UK, South Africa, Lesotho, Angola and the Bahamas.

The welcome address to our class of first years was given by Professor Dosekun, a distinguished professor of Physiology and the Provost of the College of Medicine of the University of Lagos. Our class had about 160 students with 40 per cent being females.

On our way to the first lecture, Biochemistry, we were hijacked by senior clinical students. The first years were placed in the frontline of protest by the senior clinical students. The protest was about the poor quality of food served for breakfast. In my opinion however, the breakfast was very good. You had a choice of a traditional Nigerian breakfast, and a Western breakfast with bread, with something to spread on it, a choice of an egg, sausage, or beans, oats, and a choice of tea, coffee or chocolate. The cost at fifteen kobo was heavily subsidized by the Nigerian Government, the actual cost being four times more than that. My maintenance money was therefore more than adequate for me. The violent protesters blocked the main entrance to the hospital so that no patients could access the hospital. As a result of this, the Provost called in the police to break the siege. When it became difficult to restore law and order among the students, the College of Medicine of the University of Lagos was closed down indefinitely. The police immediately but politely ejected everybody from the hostels including the foreign students who had nowhere else to go. I was later made to understand that the soon to be held medical students' elections was the main reason for the riot and not the food as implied.

The closure was for two weeks. During this period I was hosted by two of my classmates Modupe Smith, a medical student, and her brother, Folarin, a dental student. When they spotted me walking aimlessly along Ojuelegba Street, they invited me to their home. They took me to their family home, a big house with many bedrooms. They were a strict Christian family and took very good care of all my needs for the two weeks that I spent with them. I had my own bedroom complete with a fridge and soft drinks, and the house help was available. The fridge and the freezers were full of many types of food stuffs.

My roommate, Clinton was hosted by another classmate called Ademiluyi. The Ademiluyi family did not live far from the Smith family, so we were able to visit with Masawa during the two weeks of closure. During this period Masawa and I took the opportunity to contact our High Commissions to Nigeria, based in Lagos and complained about the gap at the University which left foreign students exposed to danger during any abrupt closures. The Kenya and Tanzania Commissions approached the university and interceded for all foreign students. It is from that incident that arrangements were made from that time onwards, for the protection of all foreign students during such closures. Unfortunately, when we returned to the College after the two weeks, I found some of my belongings, including most of the newly purchased medical books, missing.

Our first lecture was on the history of medicine. The lecture was delivered by Olu Mabayoje, a distinguished professor of medicine, at the University of Lagos. This was followed by our first lecture in biochemistry, delivered by the Chairman of the department, Rev. Professor Sammy Ade Olaitan. Olaitan scared the hell out of us and made us believe that medical biochemistry was the most difficult subject in the field of medicine. He narrated horror stories of the many students who had dropped out of the medical school on account of failing biochemistry. From that point onwards, everybody took the subject very seriously, more out of a fear of failure, rather than a love for the subject. At a personal level, I actually developed a liking for biochemistry, especially because, I used it to perform certain diagnostic tests on my blood during the practical class. It was also very fulfilling to make acetylsalicylic acid (aspirin) in the laboratory. We had many professors and lecturers on the subject and I was lucky to pass biochemistry without a problem at the end of the two years of preclinical studies.

The Chairman of the Department of Medical Physiology was Professor Oyinade Elebute. Physiology, unlike biochemistry was very enjoyable to study. It involved the study of the normal functions of our living bodies. For example, we would take our pulse when resting, then after some exercises retake the pulse and record the rise in the heart rate. We also listened to our heart beat using stethoscopes and performed electrocardiography (electrical study of the heart function), on ourselves. I was particularly perplexed by the fact that alcohol was absorbed in the stomach while all other foods were absorbed in the small intestines. The laboratories were very well equipped and we also had many laboratory animals for various other experiments. We were taught different aspects of physiology, by a vast array of professors and lecturers, and it seems that all of us in my class enjoyed physiology. As a result, the majority of students passed this subject at the first examination sitting at the end of the two year pre-clinical period.

The most involving subject during the first two years was Human Anatomy. This is because the sheer volume of work in the subject was daunting. The chairman of the department, Professor Mohammed Muhiddin was from Pakistan. He was assisted in Gross Anatomy and Embryology by Professor Mohammed Lasi, and Professor Obuoforibo for Histology. There were also many other lecturers and practical demonstrators in Anatomy. The Anatomy laboratories were situated at Yaba, some five kilometres from the Lagos University Teaching Hospital at Idi-Araba Suru Lere so we had to be ferried in several buses. There were six students to one cadaver, on a dissection table. There was no danger of contracting disease from the cadavers because they were properly embalmed with formalin. Furthermore, each of the students was provided with protective gloves and each group had adequate dissecting instruments. We meticulously dissected the whole body using Cunningham's dissection manual, and starting with the upper limbs, chest, abdomen, lower limbs and finally the head and neck by the end of the second year. It is important for all aspiring doctors to thoroughly understand Human Anatomy because it forms the basis of the practice of medicine. I passed Human Anatomy at the first examination sitting and therefore proceeded to the clinical years which started in the third year.

Our class was now less by about ten students, because one student, Ngozi Erondu had performed so well in Biochemistry that he decided to continue with studies leading to the Bachelor of

Science (B.Sc.) in Biochemistry, before continuing with medicine the following year. The others had either dropped out or were repeating the year on account of unsatisfactory performance. In third year, we studied Microbiology and Anatomical Pathology, taught by Professor Odunjo; Haematology and Blood Transfusion taught by Professor Boyo assisted by Professor Akinnyanju; and Chemical Pathology, including immunology and pharmacology, taught by Professor Olu Mabadeje. Of all the above subjects, the most challenging one was forensic pathology aspects of Anatomic Pathology and specifically with regard to the performance of post mortems. Each student was required to perform a specific number of post mortems before being allowed to take the third year final examinations. Otherwise, the Anatomic Pathology laboratory was very well equipped with various specimens and there was a well-stocked museum with well-preserved and different human organ systems and parts.

During my third year, I was posted and completed my junior clinical clerkships in internal medicine and general surgery. The medical ward was headed by Professor Olufemi Falaiye, and my very first patient on call training, at the casualty department of the medical emergency room of the Lagos University Teaching Hospital, was a teenage female diabetic patient who was in ketoacidotic coma. Together with the medical officer intern and the medical officer (senior house officer), we managed this patient and after she stabilized, she was admitted in the ward where I followed her treatment and progress up until she was discharged.

For my junior clerkship in surgery I was posted to Professor Paul Omodare. My first surgical emergency patient was an eleven year old boy who was involved in a road accident. One of his lower limbs had been smashed just a few inches below the hip joint. I witnessed for the first time, and I had the first-hand experience of applying an emergency tourniquet to save his life. I also witnessed a situation where a registered medical practitioner signed the consent form for an emergency amputation in order to save the life of a minor, in the absence of the parents or legal guardian. If this was not done the patient would have died.

During my third year medical training, I boldly contested the position of the President of the Foreign Students Association, a university-wide based organisation. By this time, there were a sizeable number of foreign students drawn from many countries including the US, Canada, UK, Guyana, Bahamas, Trinidad and Tobago, France, Germany, India, Pakistan, and several African countries. I contested against Patrick Kuwong of Cameroon and won comfortably. This position of responsibility enabled me to work very closely with the VC and his office, on behalf of all foreign students. I had unlimited access to the VC, Professor Ade-Ajayi, who in turn instilled a lot of wisdom in me at that young age. One interesting aspect of my leadership was the invitation, twice, by the VC, of all the foreign students to his house for a reception. I also organized, with the assistance of the VC, a trip for foreign students to the republics of: Benin, Togo and Ghana, where we visited several universities. In Accra we were properly entertained by International Trade unionist, Dennis Akumu, then based in Accra, Ghana.

At the end of the third year, I passed all the relevant examinations and was able to proceed to the fourth year of study. Here, the subjects were Paediatrics, Psychiatry and Community Health (Public Health). The department of paediatrics was chaired by world renowned Professor Olikoye Ransome-Kuti. I was posted to his paediatric ward in the hospital. He was intelligent, thorough in his work and extremely firm in his management of other professors, lecturers and students. He supervised my very first research work on my paediatric project involving pyogenic meningitis in children at the Lagos University Teaching Hospital. He had a major and lasting influence in my later life, as he reminded me of the firmness of my mentor, Dr. Griffin. The department of community health was chaired by Professor O.O. Humponu Wusu. He was most humorous in the manner in which he delivered his lectures, because most of the time he dramatized his explanations in order to make the students understand better. Psychiatry was headed by Professor Anumonye, assisted by Professor Abua

Nwaefuna. Most of the Psychiatry lectures were given at Yaba, next to the Human Anatomy laboratories and not at the Lagos University Teaching Hospital lecture theatres.

I moved to the final year in 1977, having cleared the fourth year examinations satisfactorily. During this year, the three core clinical subjects were: internal medicine including Psychiatry (which was to be examined under Internal Medicine) chaired by Professor O. Johnson. Other professors in the department included: Olu Mabayoje, Prof. Femi Pearce, O. Elegbeleye, Olufemi Falaiye and O. Okuwobi, and many others since internal medicine formed a very significant aspect of medical training. My senior clerkship was unmarked, with no particular dramatic events. It was more of building on my earlier experiences, gained during the junior clinical clerkship. However I was also trained in medical specialities such as dermatology, cardiology and neurology, during my senior clinical clerkship. Training was thorough and involved outpatient clinics, ward rounds, medical grand rounds, lectures, tutorials, mortality reviews, emergency calls and radiology reviews.

The department of obstetrics and gynaecology was headed by Professor O. Akinkugbe, whose very firm leadership had a positive impact on my future. For example, when I camped at the Lagos Island Maternity Hospital for two days and delivered the required number of babies for my clerkship, he declined to sign off my logbook, insisting that I had to spread the experience for a longer period, preferably three weeks, in order to understand and be competent in the process of delivering babies. I appreciated that very firm leadership, which is what I needed, and which, eventually, I was to emulate in my later life.

Surgery included general surgery and specialities such as orthopaedic surgery, ophthalmology, ear, nose and throat surgery, cardio thoracic surgery, anaesthesia and intensive care medicine, plastic surgery, paediatric surgery, neurosurgery, urology, radiotherapy and oncology. This was a senior clerkship year, and it required detailed involvement of the student, in the art of patient management including history taking physically, physical examination culminating into a clinical differential diagnosis, followed by the choice of investigations that led to the final diagnosis. These were effected through surgical out-patient clinics, ward rounds, surgical grand rounds, radiology reviews, pre-operative preparation of patients, surgical emergency calls, surgical mortality reviews, surgical operations and surgical intensive care. After the diagnosis, surgical treatment was offered, and it was a requirement that, all students observe and assist in surgical operations. Furthermore, there was a logbook where students recorded these and different minor surgical operations performed by the individual students, under the supervision of a surgeon. One rotated through various units and students were placed on emergency call training and duties, in pairs.

Students were also free to do additional voluntary emergency call training and duties without restriction, as long as they were supervised by their trainers. The wards and surgical casualty were open and operational twenty four hours a day. It was therefore one's strength and determination that would determine how much additional clinical surgical experience one would acquire during the prescribed period of clinical clerkship. As a student, I was taught that there is no room for procrastination in the thinking process of a surgeon. This, coupled with the impact of the quick and visible results of surgical emergency operations, was responsible for my decision to become a surgeon.

In April 1978, I passed my final examinations and qualified to become a medical doctor. I had passed through the five years at the medical school, without repeating any examination. This could only happen through the grace of God, and I was most grateful to Him. To celebrate my graduation and becoming a medical doctor, I bought my first car, a Volkswagen Beetle. The car came in handy especially during emergency calls at night, on my internship. However, one night as I was serving my paediatrics posting under Professor Kuti, the car was stolen, right outside the paediatric casualty while I was on emergency duty. It was a very difficult period as it took me another six months to purchase another car. The Provost of the College of Medicine at this time was a world renowned cardio thoracic surgeon, Professor Ade Elebute. The chairman of the department of surgery was an accomplished and eminent professor of urology, Erete Offiong Amaku. These two men were to have a permanent positive influence on my future with their efficient, swift, and decisive management processes and actions.

I applied for internship to the Chief Medical Director of the Lagos University Teaching Hospital and was immediately posted to the medical wards to commence work as an intern. I was scheduled to spend three months each, in the four major clinical specialities of: internal medicine, surgery, paediatrics and obstetrics, and gynaecology. My surgical internship posting was to the urology unit of the department of surgery. The unit had patients in three surgical wards. The consultants in the unit were Professors Amaku, J.O. Esho and Dominic Osegbe. I thoroughly enjoyed my internship in surgery. I removed my first inflamed appendix under the watchful eye of Professor Osegbe. I was extremely keen during my surgical internship. Since I had already decided to specialize in surgery, I commenced during this period of surgical internship, the simultaneous study of the three core subjects of anatomy, physiology and pathology in greater detail for the primary fellowship examination in surgery. This study greatly enhanced my performance as a surgical intern, and I performed duties way beyond those that were expected of a surgical intern. I caught the attention of my consultant's because during surgical ward rounds, I would answer some questions which my senior surgical trainers (surgical registrars) did not know.

I performed many more emergency surgical operations even when I was not on emergency surgical call duty; this enhanced my very rapid understanding of the subject of operative surgery. My efforts did not go unnoticed because my professors were unanimous that I should immediately commence my postgraduate surgical training on completion of my internship. At this time I also had a part-time job as a demonstrator in anatomy to the first and second year undergraduate medical students. I had started to maximize the management of my time as instilled in me by Dr. Griffin while at Starehe. This was to my advantage as an aspiring surgical trainee and also worked to the advantage of the undergraduate students who were learning anatomy for the first time. It was during my stint in the anatomy laboratory, which had now been relocated to the Lagos University Teaching Hospital that I met Odudu Barbara Essien, a second year medical student, who would later become my wife.

Postgraduate Training

I successfully completed my internship in May 1979 after which I applied for registration as a medical practitioner with the Nigeria Medical Council. After registration I was recommended for surgical training by Professor Amaku, at the National Postgraduate Medical College of Nigeria. The training was to be undertaken at the Lagos University Teaching Hospital. Professor Amaku was later to influence my decision to become a urologist. Medical doctors always seem to hold two or more positions, and to be quite successful at doing so. For example, Professor Adesola, was both Vice-Chancellor of the University of Ilorin, and Vice-Chancellor of the University of Lagos until his retirement in 1988. Coming closer home, Professor Nimrod Bwibo, was the Principal at the College of Health Sciences and also the Deputy Vice-Chancellor (DVC), Academic Affairs, at the University of Nairobi.

Under normal circumstances, after one qualifies to become a medical doctor, they specialize in the clinical subjects such as internal medicine, paediatrics, obstetrics and gynaecology. One can specialize in a particular discipline either through fellowships or other equivalent certifications. Therefore, after my internship I simultaneously commenced my preparation for the Fellowship of the Royal College of Surgeons (FRCS) Examinations. The Nigerian part of the Fellowship took longer, and involved a one-year senior appointment in the developed western world and a thesis.

My first postgraduate training posting was to the Surgical Accident and Emergency Unit of the Lagos University Teaching Hospital. I took this opportunity to examine and resuscitate first-hand the victims of some very serious road traffic accidents, and other emergencies. Our casualty duties were rigorous and based on shifts but, I regularly and voluntarily performed duties beyond my shifts because I was very thirsty for surgical knowledge; after all, I had a lot of time at my disposal since I had no not started a family yet. Six months after my posting as a surgical casualty officer, and as a result of my good performance, I was released by the hospital to the University of Ghana's Medical School, at Legon, Accra, to attend a surgical training course organized by the Royal College of Surgeons of England, and conducted by Professor Selwyn Taylor and Professor Née Lomote Engman, among others. The training was rigorous with lectures and practicals in the subjects of surgical physiology, anatomy and all aspects of pathology. On completion of training I resumed my duties at the Lagos University Teaching Hospital.

In January 1980, I was granted study leave by the Lagos University Teaching Hospital to prepare for the FRCS examinations at the Royal College of Surgeons of Ireland in Dublin which I passed and returned to Lagos to continue with further training. I was posted to a general surgery unit, within the Nigeria National Postgraduate Medical College at the Lagos University Teaching Hospital. Later, as part of rotation, I served in other surgical specialities such as: paediatric, cardio thoracic, orthopaedics and plastic surgery, before proceeding to the University of Ibadan's Medical School, to sit another examination, within the Nigeria National Postgraduate Medical College. I passed the examinations, was promoted to senior resident in surgery and posted to the urology unit at my request. I resumed as senior resident in urology and reported to Professors Amaku, Esho and Osegbe in late 1981. These three professors would be my principal trainers for the fellowship in urology. The fourth trainer, Professor E.O. Nkposong was based at the University of Ibadan's Teaching Hospital in Ibadan. As part of my training for fellowship in urology, I was required to select a study topic in urology for my thesis; I thus selected a topic on prostate cancer, to be supervised by Professors Amaku and Osegbe. The study was titled "Primary carcinoma of the prostate in Nigerians as seen at the Lagos University Teaching Hospital." I submitted my very first peer reviewed publication in the postgraduate medical journal on prostate cancer in 1982. The paper was titled "The effect of rectal examination on the serum acid phosphatise levels in benign and malignant prostatic disease."

As a senior resident in urology, I was responsible for the training of the four junior surgical residents, together with the surgical interns rotating in urology. I found myself in charge of many doctors who had graduated many years before me such as the surgical senior house officers employed and deployed by the hospital. I was placed in this position of great responsibility because of my good clinical performance in the examinations. At the same time I started teaching clinical surgery, and continued to be a demonstrator in anatomy. I was very firm and fair in my management style which was issue-oriented. I was also a strict disciplinarian irrespective of who I was dealing with. I would march out of the ward or clinic, any student who was improperly dressed even if they were children of professors. It was my belief that every student or junior doctor must be responsible for their actions. I had learned this during my formative years in high school at Starehe. This firmness earned me enough respect of colleagues, that I was elected and served as national treasurer of the National Association of Resident Doctors of Nigeria. This position placed me in a professional leadership position, and as is destined, positively influenced my career on my return to Kenya.

It was a requirement of the National Postgraduate Medical College of Nigeria that all senior residents gain experience by working in the developed world for a period of up to one year. In this regard, Professor Ade Elebute, the Provost of the College of Medicine of the University of Lagos arranged with Professor L.H. Bloomgart of the Royal Postgraduate Medical School at

Hammersmith, for a post at the hospital. In 1983 I was deployed as a urology and renal transplant registrar, to work and be trained by Gordon Williams, a consultant urologist and transplant surgeon. Our team had a senior registrar, one other registrar and four senior house officers.

Before commencing duty as a urology and transplant registrar, I had to register with the General Medical Council of the United Kingdom. My duties involved outpatient urology and transplant clinics, ward rounds, grand rounds, urology and transplant theatres, intensive care, mortality reviews, emergency calls, and research activities. The most exciting part of my experience at Hammersmith Hospital was when I would be woken up at night to go and harvest a kidney from a card-carrying donor who had been certified brain-dead, while the other organs were kept alive. This was usually carried out in the other London hospitals. The kidney card was permission from the accident victim, for their kidneys to be harvested and transplanted to another patient in order to save life. After harvesting the kidneys would be tissue-typed against patients on the transplant waiting list. Two lucky patients would benefit from one accident victim. The transplants would be carried out immediately the tissue-typing was complete even if it meant waking up the recipients, for the emergency operation.

I was trained in the current trends in endoscopic procedures at that time and was able to use equipment that had not arrived in Africa yet. This was one of the purposes for this exposure and experience. I was placed in charge of the infertility clinic. I had the experience of managing patients from all parts of the world who had come to London for specialised treatment. This exposed me to the international diversity of various cultures. For example, one patient had travelled all the way from Shanghai, China, together with his brother and wife. His request was that we inseminate his wife with his brother semen, but of course there were ethical issues at that time. It was a requirement that donors remain anonymous in order to avoid future litigation or emotional attachment. This has since changed and even surrogate motherhood is practised worldwide.

While at Hammersmith, I was assigned the role of principal investigator, carrying clinical research on a renal transplant related subject. I decided to carry out a prospective study on "C-reactive protein on transplant patients". As a result of this study, I published, together with Mr. Williams and others, a peer reviewed paper titled "Measurement of C-Reactive protein concentration after renal transplantation" in the Journal of *Nephrology Dialysis and Transplantation*. My research capacity, methodology and acumen were greatly enhanced by my participation in this study, and indeed, enabled me to carry out other clinical studies on return to the College of Medicine of the University of Lagos, and later to the Faculty of Medicine of the University of Nairobi.

My consultant and trainer, Mr. Williams was always available even when called out at night. He was the last on emergency call duty, and was available and ready to advise and train me professionally. He taught me how important it was for a doctor to always be available: "the availability of a doctor is paramount, no matter how good and efficient a doctor is, if they are not available when required by patients or colleagues, then they are not efficient doctors and patients invariably die as a result of this". Williams was also very strict with the management of time and while I learnt many surgical techniques from him, I also learned how to efficiently manage my clinical and theatre time from working with him. These attributes would later come in handy when I managed the University of Nairobi as the VC.

On completion of my senior residency at the Royal Postgraduate Medical School in Hammersmith Hospital, I returned to the Lagos University Teaching Hospital, to continue with my research on cancer of the prostate leading to the fellowship in urology. I continued to teach surgery and anatomy to postgraduate and undergraduate students. I would also travel to the University of Ibadan's Medical School, to consult Professor Nkposong, a world-renowned urologist with long experience of treating prostate cancer patients among Africans. In 1985, after successfully completing my thesis, I was awarded the Fellowship in Urology, by the Nigeria Postgraduate

Medical College in Urology, followed later by Fellowship of the West African College of Surgeons. I became a consultant surgeon and urologist and in addition to my duties at the Lagos University Teaching Hospital, I became a consultant surgeon and urologist to the Duro Soleye Hospital, the First Foundation Medical Centre, the Motayo Clinic and the Shoreman Medical Centre, situated at Ikeja in Lagos Nigeria.

Courting Barbara

I first met my wife, Barbara (Née Odudu Augustus John Essien) when she was a second year medical student at the College of Medicine of the University of Lagos in the anatomy laboratories, located within the precincts of the Lagos University Teaching Hospital. I was engaged here as a demonstrator in anatomy in June of 1979 as I trained in surgery for the Fellowships of the Nigerian National Postgraduate Medical College and the West African College of Surgeons. Barbara is a really attractive woman, intelligent, strong and independent minded.

In the next few months, before I left for the University of Ghana for a six week intensive course by Professor Selwyn Taylor of the Royal College of Surgeons, I dated her and our relationship became serious as we kept in regular contact with each other through regular letters. I wrote very nice letters, and my communication was romantic albeit, serious. A Ghanaian Professor, Lomote Engmann was our point of reference or connection.

In January 1980 I proceeded to the Royal College of Surgeons in Dublin, Ireland for my primary FRCS examinations. On return to Nigeria, it became very clear to me that Barbara was meant to be my life partner. I therefore persuaded her to come with me to Kenya to meet my parents and the rest of my family.

I came to Kenya with her for the first time, in July 1980. I presented her to my parents and relatives. There was a world of difference between us because she came from a family of surgeons and engineers. Her paternal grandfather was a civil engineer, her father and three of her elder brothers were medical doctors, another elder brother an engineer, and the mother a chartered accountant. My father on the other hand was a retired primary schoolteacher and my mother, a house wife. This however did not affect our strong love for each other in any way. It blossomed in spite of our different backgrounds. After staying and interacting with her for two days, my parents and relatives gave me the go ahead to ask for her hand in marriage. This emboldened the two of us and we got engaged at the Mountain Lodge in Nyeri, in the same month of July 1980 before returning to Lagos. I was deeply impressed that she was quite down to earth and accepted my people with their very humble and simple lifestyle.

Upon return to Nigeria, I made haste to find Barbara's mother Evelyn Essien, to talk to her first before I could meet the rest of the larger family. Her father, Dr. Augustus John Essien had died when she was only thirteen years old. Her mother, an accountant was very friendly and understanding but was also emphatic that Barbara graduates and becomes a medical doctor first, like her three senior brothers before considering marriage. I was rather disappointed but still content that she did not reject me. She remained my steadfast friend in the family. The rest of the family were sceptical about my ability to satisfactorily look after Barbara in marriage. Barbara converted to a Catholic, and I was relieved and thankful to God that she had accepted to convert in order for us to get married in a Catholic Church wedding ceremony.

However, it was not until November 1981 that my family and I were allowed by Barbara's family to visit their home town in Ikot Ekpene Cross River State of Nigeria to traditionally ask for her hand in marriage. Cross River State has since been divided into two with my wife's State being the present Akwa Ibom State. I was accompanied by a very strong team of Kenyans which included the then Kenya High Commissioner to Nigeria, Alfred Machayo, among others. It was at this meeting that we were allowed to commence wedding preparations subject to her passing the final examinations in medicine due in April, the following year.

Barbara graduated from the Medical School in April 1982. On 15 May, 1982 we were joined in matrimony by Rev. Professor D. Schuyler, the University of Lagos Catholic Chaplain, at Our Lady of Assumption Catholic Church, Falomo Ikoyi, Lagos. My best man was my brother Joseph, our lastborn son. Our wedding was a colourful ceremony attended by many university, hospital and diplomatic staff, together with my inlaws family and representatives of my family, amongst many other friends. Immediately after the wedding we went for our honeymoon in the Republic of Togo. Our son, Michael Augustus Achianja Magoha was born on 18 March, 1985 at the Lagos University Teaching Hospital. A chip off the old block, Michael trained as a medical doctor and on graduation, pursued a course in neurosurgery, which he is about to complete.

Since my dear wife's father died when she was very young, she became used to broad and rational thinking from an early age. Coupled with the meaning of her name, 'Odudu' meaning 'God's power', and her strong Christian values, I found in her, a very strong and resilient, yet calm and composed character. She therefore became a strong pillar of support during my early career development and later in life. Her forthright and down-to-earth attitude was instrumental in shaping my very fast progress during my training as a surgeon, as well as helping me settle down in life. Naturally, these qualities have continued to endear me to her.

My grandfather Julius Ogola seated centre and my father Bernand Magoha standing left with his siblings, 1936

My maternal grandmother Veronica Akongo seated second from left, my mother Sarah Aloo, extreme left with her sisters Pauline and Elizabeth in the early thirties

My father Bernard Magoha seated left, at Kabaa School in early thirties

My father standing 3rd from left as part of Kabaa School football team in the early thirties

My father at Kololo Hill Kampala Uganda, 1936

My parents, in the centre at their wedding, 1937

First family photograph in 1960. I am seated on the ground, extreme left. Next to me in the centre is my brother Richard Magoha, with Michael Henry Magoha on the extreme right

My father Bernard Magoha, 1995

My mother Sarah Aloo Magoha, 2001

With members of the Journal Club at Starehe Boys Centre in 1970. Extreme front right Mrs Weisz (in charge of the club) next to Dr. Ambrose Misore, Dr. Brigadier General Christopher Arrumm, chief of medical services for the Kenya Defence Forces, 5th. 2nd back right Dr. George Ogonji a dental surgeon, Boaz Juma Otoya, 4th and myself

As a student at Starehe Boys Centre, 1967

As a student at Strathmore College with Mohamed Khamis on the left, 1971

As graduate of Strathmore College awaiting university placement, 1973

Seated on the chair extreme right with fellow students at Strathmore College, 1972

With my Siblings, in Nairobi, 1995. I am 4th from right

With my elder brother John Obare on the right at Falomo Ikoyi Lagos, on my wedding day, 1982

With my eldest brother William Ogola in Kisumu, 2001

Building a Lagos University Teaching Hospital Catholic Church at Idi-Araba, Suru Lere Lagos, Nigeria (extreme right back), 1978

With my brother Joseph Magoha, 2010

With my sister Pauline Anyango Dola, 2010

My brother Captain Charles Magoha, 2001

With my brother Richard Alex Magoha, 1981

After jogging at the Lagos University teaching hospital, 1977

As a Medical Student at the Lagos University Teaching Hospital, 1976

As a registrar at the Royal Postgraduate Medical School Hammersmith, London, 1983

On graduation as a Medical Doctor at the University of Lagos, April, 1978

Our wedding at Falomo Catholic Church Ikoyi, Lagos, May 15th 1982

Signing the register after the wedding in Lagos, Nigeria, 1982

My trainer Prof. Erete Amaku on my right hand side, 1982

Evening party after the wedding, May 15th 1982

My wife Odudu Barbara Magoha and the newly born son Michael Augustus Magoha, 1985

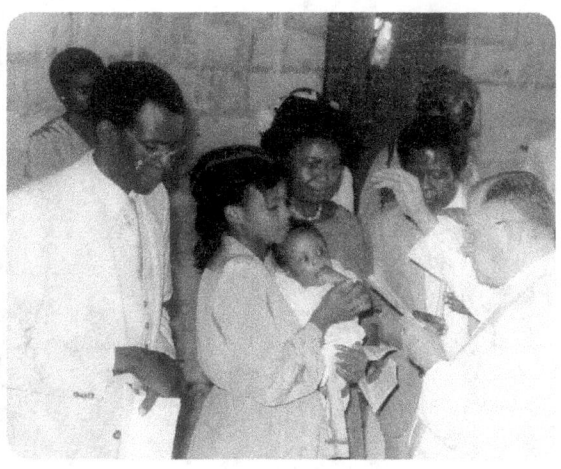

Baptism of my son Michael Magoha at the Lagos University Teaching Hospital Catholic Church, Lagos, 1985

My son at Chania Falls in Thika, 1989

My son as a student at Strathmore School, 1991

My son, third from right on the occasion of his confirmation at St. Mary's Catholic Church with God father Alois Otieno Kemo behind him, 3rd from right

My son squatting centre with Brookehouse basket ball team where he was captain, 2001

My son with Brookhouse basket ball team, squatting second from right, 2001

My son as a Medical Student at the University of Nairobi, 2006

Dr. Michael Augustus Magoha being congratulated by his mother Dr. Mrs. Barbara Magoha on graduation, 2009

With our son during his graduation, 2009

Our son on graduation with his cousins, 3rd from left, 2009

My wife and our son on his graduation, 2009

Myself as Vice-Chancellor of the University of Nairobi

My wife Dr. Mrs. Odudu Barbara Magoha

CHAPTER TWO

RETURN TO KENYA

The unfortunate demise of Professor Nelson Awori in a road accident left a vacancy in the Faculty of Medicine, at the University of Nairobi. Professor Ambrose Wasuna, whom I had earlier met in Lagos where he was an external examiner in surgery but was then stationed at the World Health Organization (WHO) in Geneva, encouraged me to apply for the job. He further introduced me to Professor Nimrod Bwibo, who was then the Principal of the College of Health Sciences of the University of Nairobi. Professor Bwibo wrote assuring me of his support and also encouraged me to send in my application for consideration for the post. I was a very strong candidate, because I had already published six papers in peer reviewed journals on the subjects of testicular torsion, breast cancer, cancer of the prostate, and C-reactive protein concentration after renal transplantation. As a result, I was appointed a lecturer, without an interview and told to report in June, 1987.

Since I had to give a six-month notice to disengage from my appointments in Lagos, I requested to report at the beginning of January 1988, and the University kindly obliged. The then Chairman of the Department of Surgery, Professor Julius Kyambi had the conviction that I had a lot to offer the department. Therefore, I returned to Kenya in December 1987, and started duty on the 06 January, 1988 with a salary of about Kshs 6,000. This was much less than the over Kshs 100,000 equivalent that I was earning from my teaching and consultancies in Lagos. Actually, I returned home out of patriotism and the desire to save the lives of our people; money gains were simply not my motivation, but rather I was determined to return home to my country having been away in Nigeria, United Kingdom and Ireland for 15 years.

After I had secured accommodation, my household possessions finally arrived from Lagos. By April 1988, I had settled down and was joined by my family. It however took a while before my family adjusted to the cold weather in Nairobi. I was posted to surgical ward 5A, at the Kenyatta National Hospital where the consultant in charge was Dr. Kagiri Ndirangu. This was a general surgical ward but it also had urology patients. My duties at the University included: teaching undergraduate medical students as well as postgraduate students studying general surgery and urology. This was effected through lectures and tutorials, outpatient clinics, ward rounds, surgical grand rounds, the operating theatre, mortality and radiology reviews and research methodology teachings. I noticed that the faculty was not as large as the one at the University of Lagos. There were fewer academic staff and that meant a lot more work for the lecturers. In urology for example there was only Professor Joseph Oliech, compared to four professors at the College of Medicine of the University of Lagos.

I quickly settled down to work and relied on all stages of my training, past and present in order to survive. I also paid a lot of attention to my original clinical research. I took on the supervision of students for the Master of Medicine (MMed) in surgery dissertations. Furthermore, I completed and published various studies whose data I had carried over from Lagos, Nigeria. As a lecturer, I embarked on clinical research on cancers of the prostate, penis and testis. I had noticed that no clinical research work had been previously carried out on these topics locally. I was given additional duties of selecting suitable patients for clinical examinations of the undergraduate and postgraduate students. The following year I was appointed one of the two examinations officers in the department, and also promoted to senior lecturer in surgery. In addition, I was appointed to represent the department in the library committee of the College of Health Sciences in the same year. My first three postgraduate Master of Medicine in Surgery students, graduated in 1990, and thereafter I took on many others as supervisor.

Having been given a part-time private practice license by the Kenya Medical Practitioners and Dentists Board, the University approved it on condition that I attend to patients only after work, on weekends or public holidays. I therefore opened a part-time surgical and urological consultancy clinic at Hurlingham, Nairobi which I later moved to the Nairobi Hospital. I was disciplined and therefore managed to balance my time well. I had gained patient admission rights to the Aga Khan, Mater, the Nairobi, and M.P. Shah hospitals. Consequently I was reasonably comfortable.

In 1995, my colleague, Dr. Ndirangu died after a long struggle with stomach cancer. He had been in and out of hospital for the past one year and travelled to the United States for further treatment. We rested him in his Othaya home. His demise affected me in two ways: first, it reminded me of my own mortality, since as doctors we always take death for granted; secondly, I now had to take charge of all of his duties, including being consultant in charge of surgical ward 5A at the Kenyatta National Hospital. This served to remind me of the great sense of loss that Dr. Ndirangu's death had on us.

In 1996, I was promoted to Associate Professor of Surgery. I qualified for the promotion because I had already supervised eight Master of Medicine in surgery students to completion, published twenty three peer reviewed scholarly articles in both local and international journals, in addition to taking part and presenting papers in many local and international surgical and urological conferences. This placed me way ahead of many of my professional contemporaries and seniors in the department, who had applied for the position. I was now poised to take up more leadership roles in the department. As professor, I was appointed in-charge of the examinations and timetable in the department and continued to discharge my clinical and other duties diligently.

In 1997, I was invited by Pfizer Limited to join their continental research team (on sildenafil or Viagra) in Africa and the Middle East, based in Johannesburg, South Africa. We held many consultative and research meetings in Cairo, Cape Town, Dubai, Kampala, Lagos, Dar es Salaam and Nairobi. As a result of the collaboration, I was appointed member of the international Erectile Dysfunction Advisory Council (EDAC). During this period, we launched Viagra in Kenya, Uganda and Tanzania. This international recognition was as a result of my earlier scholarly research and publications on erectile dysfunction.

In 1998, the substantive chairman of the department of surgery, Professor Michael Mbalu went on sabbatical leave. Another professor appointed acting Chairman of the Department of Surgery declined the position, which was accepted by the University. The University then appointed me acting Chairman of the Department.

However, the fact of the matter was that this appointment was almost by default, because I was not the first choice. On hindsight, I recognise it was God's hand in the appointment. The staff in the department of surgery became apprehensive because I had a reputation for being very firm in my management style. They had witnessed first-hand, the zeal with which I managed the examination and timetabling processes in the department. When I was appointed acting Chairman, there had been a history of a spate of burglaries in the department, with staff losing valuables. My first task as acting chairman was to commence discussion with industry to source funds for burglar-proofing the department. I easily and successfully completed the process and this simple act brought back staff confidence in my management style. They felt secure. As acting Chairman of the Department of Surgery, I became a member of the University of Nairobi Senate. The first time I met the then VC of the University of Nairobi, Professor Francis John Gichaga, was while I was supervising the installation of the burglar-proof grills at the department of surgery. He was on his usual tour of the University and was surprised that actual work was going on in the University, despite the fact that, the University had no money. He politely asked me where I had got the money from and why I was personally supervising the work. I answered that I had leveraged resources from the industry and I had to ensure that the money was used effectively and accountably, with the objectives being achieved. The VC then asked for my name, and made some notes in a small note book which he returned into his coat pocket and left.

In 1999, Professor Mbalu returned from sabbatical leave and resumed his chairmanship of the department of surgery. After a few months, he decided to take early retirement. As a result of this, another professor was subsequently recommended by the College of Health Sciences for substantive appointment as chairman of the department. However, I am the one who was eventually appointed substantive chairman, because the VC, recalled my fundraising capacity as exemplified by the metal grills sourced from industry and installed at the department of surgery. At a personal level I again saw God's hand in my appointment as I had not been the choice of the College. I humbled myself and settled down to work, and was always available. I brought discipline to the department. As a result, the academic staff was very satisfied with my leadership qualities. I had only served as chairman for one year when the vacancy for Dean of the Faculty of Medicine arose. Some members of the academic staff approached me to run for the position. I politely declined, but they would not give up. They sent Professor Zipporah Ngumi, a great friend of mine in the department, to convince me to contest, and I obliged. In 2000, I was elected Dean, Faculty of Medicine, unopposed. My new duties included being in charge of all academic programmes at the faculty in addition to being a member of the Senate and the Deans Committee.

It was at this time that an advertisement for the position of full professorship was put out, and I applied. I had supervised to completion over twenty two Master of Medicine Surgery theses, published thirty two peer reviewed publications in local and international scholarly journals, in addition to attending many local and international conferences. After the interviews, I was promoted to full professor of surgery at the College of Health

Sciences of the University of Nairobi. I strongly believed that it was by the grace of God that I had moved up the ranks from lecturer in 1988 to full professor in 2000.

On taking up the post, I was shocked to see the state of the Dean's office. To start with, there was inadequate physical space, filing space and cabinets and many files and documents lying on the floor. I gathered courage and sought audience with the VC to request for funds to enable me reorganize the office into a dynamic functional office. I was very warmly welcomed by Professor Gichaga and over a cup of tea he politely informed me that the University did not have funds for that activity at that time, but he authorized me to source for funds externally, if I could. I got in touch with several people from my list of external colleagues and contacts, and after two weeks I received a positive response from South Korea. They would send someone from their Embassy in Nairobi to verify the state of affairs, after which they would prepare a proposal. Within two weeks of this communication, the embassy sent a person to verify the status, and then offered me Kshs 15 Million to build and equip the Dean's office, and the registry.

I was elated and so relieved that I reported this news immediately to the VC. I was however disappointed because he insisted that in order to upgrade the Dean's office, I also had to provide funds for upgrading the Principal's office and boardroom, simultaneously. Undaunted, I got back to my friends from South Korea and passionately put the case forward regarding the need and justification for upgrading the Principal's office and boardroom. After thorough due diligence and inspection, our benefactors accepted to provide about Kshs 30 million, on condition that I and themselves be given authority to supervise the process. The VC approved the proposal and the conditions. Within two months a contractor was on site, adding a second floor to the existing College of Health Sciences main building. As the construction was taking place, we monitored and supervised the progress and were all satisfied and happy. The building was completed and furnished to the highest international standards, within eight months. During the construction the South Korean donor also regularly came to Nairobi to inspect the progress of the building and they expressed their satisfaction with the results that their donation had made to the Faculty of Medicine of the University of Nairobi. There was a big opening ceremony, presided over by the VC and the donors. I occupied the new office and reorganized it with pride and personal satisfaction.

What is important to note is that in this process, delicate as it was with expectations of results, and accountability in funding and resources expended, I had applied the resilience and wisdom that I learned from Dr. Griffin together with the compassion I learned from Mr. Sperling of Strathmore College and Professor Ade-Ajayi, the VC of the University of Lagos.

Normally, one serves as dean for one term of two years, and can be re-elected to serve another term. This however was not the case for me, because, as destiny would have it, I served as Dean in the magnificent new offices for only one year. It happened that a vacancy for a College Principal arose at the College of Health Sciences of the University of Nairobi in early 2001, and I was appointed in an acting capacity. This happened in a very simple way. One morning, the VC walked into my office and told me to go and occupy the Principal's office in an acting capacity, and to recommend to him a suitable person to act as Dean of the Faculty of Medicine. He further told me that my performance had earned me the job and that he would consult the Chancellor, His Excellency President Daniel Arap Moi, to confirm my appointment. I was happy but amazed. Here I was, the youngest Dean, with only one year in office yet both of the deans of the faculties of pharmacy and dentistry had been in office longer than me. In making this decision, he based it purely on measurable performance. Inevitably, Professor Gichaga left a lasting impression in me. He taught me that to get the best results, a leader needed to focus on performance, ability, commitment and passion. It is for this that I vowed to emulate throughout my tenure as Principal, Deputy Vice Chancellor (Administration and Finance) and VC.

I was appointed substantive Principal of the College of Health Sciences in March, 2001. My duties involved management of the three faculties of medicine, pharmacy, and dentistry. In addition to being a member of the University Senate, I joined the University Management Board (UMB) which was the top management decision making organ of the University. I also started attending the meetings of the University Council. As Principal, I was now involved in the total University management. In this capacity, I attended various strategy meetings of the University Management Board, chaired by the VC, and the Council, chaired by Professor David Wasawo.

In 2002, Professor Crispus Makau Kiamba, the Deputy Vice-Chancellor (DVC), Administration and Finance, was appointed VC. He took over from Professor Gichaga, who had rendered sterling service to the University during a very challenging time. The University of Nairobi Enterprises and Services Limited (UNES), was started, in 1997 through the wisdom of Professor Gichaga, to manage Module II academic programmes, provide consultancy services and carry out any other businesses in order to support the University's core business.

This was a brilliant idea, as the government funding had continued to drop, making it difficult for the University to fulfil its statutory obligations. The University of Nairobi Council, chaired by Professor Wasawo fully supported and approved UNES, which by 2002 was performing very well, under the capable management of Professor Kimani. The academic programmes in the faculties of commerce, medicine, law and arts were performing very well and could support key university functions such as teaching, research and community service. The financial woes of the University slowly turned round thanks, to UNES. Professor Gichaga served the University in that capacity for about eleven years, making him the longest serving VC.

With the appointment of Professor Kiamba, as VC a vacancy became available in the office of the DVC, Administration and Finance. I had been College Principal for only one year and some could argue that I was the least experienced and therefore the least qualified to be considered by the Council and Chancellor for that vacant position. There were five other college principals, more senior and experienced than I was. I was therefore completely surprised when, after he had served one month in office as VC, Professor Kiamba summoned me to his office and handed me a letter appointing me the next DVC, Administration and Finance. This is a position that I had not even dreamed of let alone lobbied for although I was aware that there had been intense lobbying at high levels for the position.

All my life, I have been trained to appreciate that it is only through diligent duty, hard work and proper time management that one could realise positive outcomes and be placed in a good competitive position for consideration to any position. I therefore recognize the impartiality and professionalism with which Professor Kiamba recommended me to the Council and the Chancellor, for appointment as DVC, Administration and Finance. At this point, I had no doubt that the Lord God Almighty had always planned for me to take part in the management of the University.

I took office as the DVC in April 2002. I immediately realized that the office was the most powerful in the University. It was in charge of finance, the budget and the general administration of the University, including all personnel issues and assets. Professor Kiamba, who was also the immediate past holder of that office was very instrumental in my settling down. He took the time to hand over to me in great detail. He further carried me through the University calendar, which outlined the duties of the office holder as per the law, and how the office related to his. Professor Kiamba's final advice was to be very diligent and prudent with financial matters and always to confirm that funds were available, before approving any expenditure. He confirmed his availability for consultation on a 24-hour basis, whether he was inside or outside the country. He believed in a decentralized, rather than a command and control system of management. He therefore enabled and supported me to operate the office freely without any hindrance whatsoever.

My first duty in office was to take an inventory of all University property including fixed assets. The second was to institute strict financial controls, including auditing the payroll. The University had just completed an exercise in rationalising staff (with some staff being laid off, while others were right-sized). Under the direction of the VC, it was my duty to ensure that the staff performed the duties for which they were paid. I therefore ensured that they were available for work during working hours without fear or favour. The procurement function at the University was a major challenge; a significant amount of money was still being lost through corruption and collusion. I paid particular attention to the establishment of new financial regulations and controls at the University. I performed thorough due diligence before purchase, delivery and acceptance of goods.

As a surgeon, I am used to making incisive decisions and getting to the point, and therefore it made it easier for me to go straight to the market and compare prices. I was surprised to realise that sometimes the differences between our purchase prices was as high as one hundred per cent in some cases. We designed an approach that made it possible for us to bring down the prices of goods substantially. Furthermore, we refused to receive or pay for the exorbitant goods. Soon we started getting value for our money. We started repairing the buildings including lecture theatres, computer laboratories, engineering laboratories, the Jomo Kenyatta Memorial Library, toilets, parking lots and roads in the main campus. I am grateful to the VC for providing the enabling environment of teamwork and team spirit.

At the beginning, the sceptics among the staff admonished me for beautifying the University; some even rudely referring to the beautification as taking place on the outside of a cup. But time would prove them wrong because our overall strategy and goal was to attract more students into our Module II programmes and underpin the sustainability of the University. I continued to raise funds for the University of Nairobi while occupying the position of the DVC. The most significant was travelling to Winnipeg and Toronto, Canada to compete with seven other Canadian Institutions for a grant of 2.4 million Canadian Dollars (CAD), equivalent to over Kshs 280 million. The competition for a grant from the Canadian Foundation for Innovation (CFI) was stiff, but the University's College of Health Sciences beat seven other Canadian Institutions and won it. The grant has since been utilized to construct an enhanced level 3 bio-containment laboratory, incorporating the University of Nairobi Institute of Tropical and Infectious Diseases (UNITID). The laboratory, one of the only two in sub-Saharan Africa, specializes in the management of haemorrhagic virus diseases research. Such viruses include the ones responsible for the Rift Valley and Lassa fevers among others. The location of this laboratory at the University of Nairobi has greatly enhanced the research capacity and international visibility of the University. I am proud to have led the University of Nairobi to the competition.

I cannot forget to mention the challenges caused by student indiscipline. While I was one of the principal assistants to the VC, the new government of His Excellency President Mwai Kibaki came to power in 2003, on a platform of increased civil liberties and freedoms. Soon thereafter, the University gave blanket amnesty to all student leaders who were on suspension. The Students Organization of Nairobi University (SONU) was reinstated. SONU had previously been suspended for indiscipline of its leaders. It was a very challenging time for the University top managers, especially DVCs. There was a very thin line between what constituted freedom and what was indiscipline. As university managers we had to be very firm while allowing increased freedom of expression and activity. Those students who crossed the line were disciplined according to our University regulations.

The latter part of 2003 witnessed a major change in the governance structure of the University. Previously, the sitting President was Chancellor of all public universities. This changed when President Kibaki appointed different chancellors for each of the public universities, except for Masinde Muliro University, where he remained Chancellor. For the University of Nairobi, he appointed a businessman and industrialist engineer, Dr. Joseph Barrage Wanjui. Dr. Wanjui was an accomplished entrepreneur. I must admit that at the beginning I had great difficulty dealing with the new Chancellor because of the business-like manner that he wanted things done.

I was very lucky that it was the VC who dealt with him most of the time. Dr. Wanjui was very clear in his mind that he wanted the University to be run as a business and had absolutely no time for public service bureaucracies. For a start, we could not perform tasks at the speed he required because we had chronic underfunding from the Government, which was a historical fact. Dr. Wanjui worked well with the University Council, chaired by Professor Wasawo, and the VC, Professor Kiamba.

Other members of the Council included Professor Juma Lugogo as Vice Chairman, Ahmed Yussufu as Treasurer, Professors Julia Gitobu and Miriam Were, Joseph Kinyua, the PS Treasury, Professor Karega Mutahi, PS Ministry of Education, Science and Technology, Simon Njau, PS Directorate of Personnel Management, Dr. Betty Gikonyo, Dr. Manu Chandaria, representing the Gandhi Memorial Academy, and Ms. Bella Ochola Wilson. There were representatives from the Senate, the University Management Board, the Convocation, Academic Staff Association and SONU.

I was therefore surprised when the Chancellor decided in late 2004, that the position of the VC was going to be advertised internationally and that the next VC was going to be competitively appointed, through a professional body. To the best of my recollection, the University of Nairobi Council had no problem with the VC, Professor Kiamba. Nevertheless, the Chancellor and the Council advertised for the position of VC internationally, with an insertion appearing in the *Economist Magazine*, in October 2004. The advertisement was also placed in a local newspaper, *The Daily Nation*, of 08 October, 2004.

The advertisement was placed by PricewaterhouseCoopers (PwC) who were contracted by the Council to manage the recruitment process. The title of the advert was, 'Leadership for Change'. This meant that they were looking for a VC to manage the change process at the University. Personally, I was not going to apply for the position. I was very satisfied serving the University as DVC, Administration and Finance, a position I had held for only two and a half years. However, Professor Kiamba encouraged and convinced me to apply for the position. He had earlier recommended me to the Council and the Chancellor, for appointment as acting VC. This he followed up with an elaborate and professional handing over of the office to me in my acting capacity. I had tremendous respect for him and we had an excellent and professional working relationship. I therefore found it difficult to disregard his advice, so I applied. There were more than 30 applicants, drawn from many countries including the United Kingdom, India, South Africa, Botswana, Nigeria and the East African countries.

The shortlisting was carried out by PwC and the relevant committee of the University Council. Only four candidates were shortlisted for the oral interviews. They were: Professor Richard Mwangi, a professor of Zoology at the University of Nairobi; Professor James Kirumbi Kimani, Managing Director UNES; Professor Jacob Kaimenyi, Deputy Vice-Chancellor, Academic Affairs, and myself. The interview was arranged and co-ordinated by PwC, through their Managing Director, Philip Kinisu. The seven panellists were members of the relevant Committee of Council with Mr. Kinisu serving as secretary. Professor Wasawo chaired the Panel. Other members were Professors Julia Gitobu, Julius Kyambi, Miriam Were, Karega Mutahi, PS Ministry of Education Science and Technology, Simon Njau PS, Directorate of Personnel Management, and Joseph Kinyua, PS at the Treasury. This panel carried out the interviews on 23 December, 2004. The first to be interviewed, was Professor Mwangi followed by Professor Kimani. I was called in the afternoon, followed by Professor Kaimenyi.

The questions they asked me were seemingly objective but actually quite difficult and one needed to think very quickly, articulate the answer and objectively engage the panel. The panel allowed an hour each for the rigorous interview. After the interviews, the University community was released early, to enjoy Christmas and the New Year holidays and festivities. Even with the release, there was some degree of unknown expectations and this inevitably led to some speculation among staff. This speculation was mainly due to the fact that the process had been quite lengthy; from October 2004 to January 2005.

In the New Year, the results of the oral interview were released and indicated that I had emerged first. The results were a complete surprise to me, because I had not even imagined that I would proceed beyond shortlisting and be interviewed, nor contemplated being declared the VC. Indeed, becoming the VC of the University of Nairobi was not one of my immediate goals in life, at the time. I had been trained all my life, to be satisfied with what I had at a particular time and therefore I was very comfortable and satisfied with the substantive position that I held. However, it turned out that I had been marked the best performer by all the seven panellists in the interview and it was therefore a rather testament of a solid and objective performance.

In the New Year, I was summoned by the Chancellor, Dr. Wanjui for a cup of tea. Present at this meeting were the Chairman of Council, Professor Wasawo, and Mr. Kinisu of PwC. We discussed my performance at the interview openly, as well as the terms of my engagement as the new VC. I was to be put on a performance contract, with specific measurable targets which had to be achieved on time, if I was to continue serving as the VC. It was stressed that only measurable outputs would matter, should I accept the appointment. I then asked if I was going to be given a free hand to run the University without outside and political interference and was answered in the affirmative.

It did not take long for me to begin to learn and appreciate there was no place for double standards in the life of Dr. Wanjui. He based my intended appointment on my impressive track record and performance at the oral interviews. I learnt yet another important lesson in my life; that only meritocracy, coupled with measurable performance outputs mattered, and all other factors were secondary. It was important for me to grasp that tribalism and political patronage were major hindrances to individual performance outputs leading to slow national economic development. These practices were still rampant in our country and even rife at the University, but with due diligence, the Council and the Chancellor, had ensured that these scourges are suppressed. I was therefore the first VC of the University of Nairobi and by extension the first senior public officer in the Republic of Kenya to be competitively appointed.

I was appointed the sixth VC of the University of Nairobi in a simple ceremony attended by the Chancellor, Dr. Wanjui, Professor Wasawo, Mr. Kinisu, and the Press. The ceremony took place in the Council Chamber, on the 05 January, 2005. I had opted for a simple ceremony, rather than an expensive inauguration ceremony, because the University was facing financial challenges. Soon thereafter, in mid-January, the University Council placed an advertisement in the local newspapers for the competitive recruitment of my replacement as DVC, Administration and Finance. The process ended with the competitive recruitment of Professor Peter Mbithi, with whom we would work cordially for the next ten years.

My first assignment as VC was to quickly build a synergetic team within the University Management Board, comprising the VC and his Deputies, College Principals and Deputy Principals, Academic, Planning and Administration Registrars, Director, Students Welfare Authority (SWA), Dean of Students, University Librarian, Managing Director UNES, Chief Finance Officer, Chief Internal Auditor, Chief Legal Officer, Chief Medical Officer, and Procurement Manager. In order to train the team, I contracted professionals to urgently train management board members in good corporate governance, team building, time management, among other management strategies. The first such management training was conducted at a Kisumu hotel. Many other sessions were to follow, during the early part of my tenure as VC. My goal was to create a lean and efficient team within the management board, with synergy teamwork and team spirit. I encouraged and embraced a decentralized system of management to the units, and discouraged command and control. This would later lead to a quantum leap in measurable outputs from various units of the management board leading to improved performance, throughout the University.

My Executive Management Board included: Professor Jacob Kaimenyi, DVC Academic Affairs, Professor Peter Mbithi, DVC Administration and Finance, Professor Isaac Mbeche, Principal, College of Humanities and Social Sciences, Professor Henry Mutoro, Principal, College of Education and External Studies, Professor Lucy Irungu, Principal, College of Biological and Physical Sciences, Professor Joseph Kitonyi, Principal, College of Health Sciences, Professor Francis Aduol, Principal, College of Architecture and Engineering, Professor Agnes Mwang'ombe, Principal, College of Agriculture and Veterinary Sciences, and Professor Peter Kobonyo, Deputy Principal, College of Humanities and Social Sciences. The expanded management team included the Chief Finance Officer, Mr. Michael Karue, Chief Internal Auditor, Mr. Peter Igiria, Chief Legal Officer, Ms. Rebecca Ngondo, Chief Medical Officer, Dr. Stephen Ochiel, Director Students Welfare Authority, Mr. Robert Lugwe, Registrar Academic, Mr. S. Mbalu, Administration, Mr. Awori wa Kataka, Planning, Mr. Wycliffe Asilla, University Librarian, Ms. Salome Mathangani, Dean of Students, Father Dominic Wamugunda, Procurement Manager, Mr. Henry Barasa and Estates Manager, Ms. Sarah Ngugi.

With this team thoroughly trained, we set out to tackle the major problems affecting the University together. It is significant to note that we did not start from nowhere, but we recognized and built on the groundwork laid by the previous VCs: Professors Francis Gichaga, and Kiamba especially with regard to the establishment of UNES. On settling in the office as VC and the CEO I signed a performance contract with the University Council, involving specific measurable targets. The most urgent target was to formulate the first-ever University of Nairobi Corporate Strategic Plan. The Chancellor's first firm instruction was that I must develop a strategic plan within four months as he believed that the University was going nowhere without it. In fact he did not understand how the University had existed for all those years without a strategic plan. The plan was required very urgently in order to enable the University Council to sign another corporate performance contract with the government, through the Ministry of Education Science and Technology, by June 2005.

I immediately appointed a committee of the University Management Board (UMB) and Senate to develop the Corporate Strategic Plan, (2005–2010). The committee was chaired by Professor Francis Aduol, and had many experts on strategic planning from the School of Business and the School of Computing and Informatics. I managed the process and it did not take long before the Committee developed and tabled the draft Plan for discussion, input, ownership and ratification by UMB, and Senate for input and ownership. Subsequently, a special meeting of the University of Nairobi Council held on 06 May, 2005 approved the first ever, University of Nairobi Corporate Strategic Plan (2005–2010). This was on time to enable the signing of the corporate performance contract between the Council and the Government through the Ministry of Education, Science and Technology. The Plan would henceforth determine the way I managed the University as the CEO. In order to facilitate its implementation, the UMB determined the need to restructure and rationalize the University's functions for the purpose of streamlining operations and with a view to enhancing efficiency, effectiveness and productivity. This restructuring and rationalization of functions would inevitably lead to the collapsing of departments, sections and units in order to minimise the duplication of roles.

The restructuring saw the collapsing of departments and creation of schools from faculties. At the College of Health Sciences for example, the three departments of clinical chemistry, haematology and blood transfusion, and anatomic pathology were merged into one Department of Human Pathology. In the College of Biological and Physical Sciences, the two departments of botany and zoology were merged into the School of Biological Sciences.

The Faculty of Arts, located at the College of Humanities and Social Sciences in the main campus had duplicate departments at the College of Education and External Studies located at Kikuyu campus. These departments were collapsed and rationalized, and an associate Dean selected to manage the activities at Kikuyu. At the College of Architecture and Engineering, the School of the Built Environment was created to incorporate the departments of land economics, architecture and HABRI. This strategic restructuring and rationalization of academic functions resulted in the reduction of the number of operational units across the University by about twenty five per cent, and subsequent reduction of the financial expenditure of the units. The Senate had significant input in the restructuring, and subsequently, the final approval by the Council was received well as it was in conformity with the University's approved Strategic Plan.

As the CEO I had to deal with financial challenges. Indeed, financing the University was a major challenge because government funding had continued to dwindle. The funds received from government was not even adequate to cover the gross payroll, covering only seventy three per cent of the payroll. Furthermore, the University had statutory and other debts, to the tune of Kshs 2 billion. Therefore, one of my top priorities was to control the expenditure, and grow the income with the strategic goal of settling debts, and placing the University on the road to world class excellence.

The University did not have an alumni association, which would have been one way of growing income. Together we embarked on the establishment of the alumni association. The

University management and the Council launched the University of Nairobi Alumni Association (UONAA), on 05 February, 2005 with Dr. Betty Gikonyo, an eminent paediatric cardiologist and entrepreneur, serving as the inaugural chairperson. Since then, the Association has opened professional and discipline based chapters and has made a significant positive financial contribution and impact at the University of Nairobi.

Because of the long recruitment process for the VC, the 32nd graduation ceremony, originally planned for February 2005, was shifted to March 2005, with the approval of the Chancellor. The University at this time had 25,000 undergraduate and 5,000 postgraduate students. It became clear that the sheer number of students graduating could not be handled in one ceremony. Indeed, a select committee to recommend on the future of graduation ceremonies concluded the need for two graduation ceremonies; the first one would take place in August of every year for the Colleges of: Education and External Studies, Agriculture and Veterinary Sciences, Architecture and Engineering, and Biological and Physical Sciences. The second graduation ceremony would be held in December of every year for the Colleges of Humanities and Social Sciences and Health Sciences. On completion of my ten-year tenure as VC, I had presided over the 52nd graduation ceremony making a record total of twenty one ceremonies, without any loss of time.

The Transition Period

The transition period was most challenging. I knew for a fact that one of the greatest challenges to our nationhood and by extension the University of Nairobi was tribalism. I had risen at the University through the ranks, from lecturer to full professor of surgery in 12 years, and from Chairman of Department of Surgery, to Dean of the Faculty of Medicine, then Principal of the College of Health sciences, DVC in charge of Administration and Finance, and finally to VC, within a space of six years.

This rapid advancement was based purely on merit. I did not have strategically placed influential personalities to ensure my career progression. For the record, among my professional mentors from high school up to this time, none was my relative or from my community. I had been treated fairly and given an opportunity to serve. This would form the basis of my administration, where meritocracy was core. All staff were treated equally based on merit and with regard to measurable work outputs without fear or favour. I further ensured that throughout my ten-year tenure as VC, the University of Nairobi was not turned into a tribal enclave. This was one of my practices that would endear me to all staff and ensure my success. I chose to give all staff an equal opportunity.

I also opened up to receive advice from all wise professors in the University willing to offer the same. One such professor, Godfrey Muriuki, had been a member of the University of Nairobi Senate for over 30 years and perhaps it is his wisdom and ability to assess a situation, which in many ways acted as guard and caution in my dealing with issues during the transition period. The term of the Council, chaired by Professor Wasawo came to an end in March 2005, at the expiry of the second three-year term. This was followed by the appointment of a new Council chaired by Dr. John Nyangeri Simba.

This Council was appointed by the Chancellor, through a consultative process. He sought my opinion about certain people before appointing them. One of the people he asked me for an opinion about was Dr. Simba, an accomplished lawyer with tremendous industrial experience having headed a commercial bank for many years. Simba had also been Vice Chairman of Kenyatta University for many years and thus was appointed the Chairman of the Council. For the Vice Chairman, Dr. Wanjui suggested another experienced entrepreneur Nicholas Ng'ang'a, Chairman of Safaricom. Mr. Kinisu Managing Director, PwC, was nominated the treasurer. Other members of the Council included: Samuel Kamau Macharia, Chairman of Royal Media Services, Isaac Awuondo, Managing Director, Commercial Bank of Africa,

Terry Davidson, Managing Director of Kenya Commercial Bank, Dr. Betty Gikonyo, an eminent paediatric cardiologist and Chief Executive Officer of the Karen Hospital, Bella Ochola Wilson an entrepreneur, Tom Mshindi, a top manager at the Nation Media Group and Dr. Manu Chandaria an industrialist. These members of the Council, and the Chancellor were external to the University, and were all from the private sector with a business background. The University therefore was now poised to start doing business efficiently and on time as was the practice in the private sector. My challenge was therefore to change the mind-set of staff to think in conformity with the goal and strategy of the Council.

Having trained the UMB, I now embarked on the training of the University Senate, by corporate experts. The main goal of this training was to inculcate private sector thinking and a more business-like approach to the performance of tasks. The Senate received training on good corporate governance, time management, performance contracting, procurement of goods and services and record keeping, among others. The Senate was a large body, with about 200 members representing all units within the University, including chairs of departments, deans, and directors of faculties, schools, boards and other units, along with the members of the expanded UMB. It was extremely important for the Senate to understand and own the newly formed Council along with their goals and strategies which were incorporated in the Strategic Plan.

Over the years, especially with dwindling capitation and austerity, a culture had pervaded the University, this old culture needed to be politely discarded through very firm persuasion and training, and a new business-like culture adopted and implemented. This was the only route to turning around the University to the road to world class excellence. After all, culture can kill even the best strategy. Therefore, we had to increase our financial base by attracting more students. One way of achieving this would be through offering quality services. Even though we had the necessary human resource capacity in terms of adequate and dedicated lecturers, professors and administrative staff, it was not going to be easy to achieve quality given the dilapidated infrastructure and lack of essential equipment in place at the time. Indeed, even after restructuring and rationalization, which helped in reducing expenditure, we still had to urgently improve the infrastructure. This, coupled with the presence of a sizable number of sceptics in the Senate and the political interference from those who thought I was the wrong candidate, became bottlenecks during the transition period.

I had to use the wisdom and patience of a saint, rather than intelligence, to successfully deal with these challenges. One of the strategies we decided to use was to invest in the completion of stalled projects which had been started and abandoned 20 years earlier. Consequently, we completed lecture theatres and laboratories, equipping them to the best international standards. As a result, the enrolment numbers increased and there was a gradual improvement in the financial base of the University. Further, we purchased a strategic building in Kisumu to enable us expand the popular business, law and education courses in the western region. Again this helped in increasing the financial base and enabling us to implement our strategic plan.

My next focus was on the personnel managing the finance department. The Chancellor and the Chairman of Council were quite emphatic about the professional qualifications required for the personnel managing this finance department. They insisted that all accountants must be fully qualified, chartered and registered active members of their appropriate professional bodies. The finance officer, Mr. Michael Karue was holding that office in an acting capacity. We advertised for the position externally and competitively recruited him as the Chief Finance Officer (CFO), because of his qualifications, experience and proven track record. This was followed by the external advertisement of twelve positions for professionally qualified and chartered accountants to manage finances at the six colleges, SWA, and at the central finance department. Most of these critical positions, such as the college bursars, were occupied by officers at various stages of accountancy training, rather than professional accountants.

Once qualified staff were recruited and assigned financial management duties, the other officers, previously holding the accountancy positions were redeployed to less strategic areas of the University without any loss of income. Some were encouraged and those who were able to continue, received sponsorship from the University to complete their training in accountancy. There were loud protests about this activity, coupled with attempted political interference, but I remained firm and steadfast and stood my ground, supported strongly by the Chairman of Council, John Simba, and the Chancellor Dr. Wanjui.

The second stage was to acquire a Financial Management Information System (FMIS). Dr. SK Macharia, himself a chartered accountant and who was Chairman of the University of Nairobi Tender Committee, advised me to float an international tender for this. He was quite sceptical about the capability of local firms to deliver a suitable system that would turn round the University's financial management style, ensuring prudent implementation of financial regulations and controls. The University duly floated an international tender and procured the System from ACCPAC, London. This was followed by the University sending ten senior accountants, including the CFO, Michael Karue and Chief Internal Auditor Peter Igiria to London, to undergo thorough training in the management of the recently acquired system. The training was intensive and lasted three weeks.

I was indeed very fortunate to have someone of Dr. SK Macharia's calibre and experience in my Council. I was to learn much more from him during his tenure as Chairman of the Tender Committee. The sceptics had by now reduced in numbers; most of them had realized that I had been recruited on the platform 'management for change' and that I was proceeding well on the course of change management at the University, as per my performance contract and terms of engagement. The acquisition, training and implementation of a strict financial management system marked a turning point in my management of University affairs. As the VC, I now had absolute control of the University finances, with a very competent and well trained team of qualified accountants and a functioning financial system.

The management now instituted new fiscal regulations and stricter financial controls which resulted in the University getting value for money. We had succeeded in preparing the University to be run efficiently, as a private entity, devoid of public service bureaucracies.

Specific Painful Incidents during the Transition Period

On being appointed VC, I found out that the Kenya Revenue Authority (KRA) had temporarily frozen all the accounts belonging to the University of Nairobi, in all banks. This was due to non-remittance of Pay As You Earn (PAYE) statutory deductions as required by the law. This situation had been occasioned by the fact that over the past ten years, the exchequer remittances to the University of Nairobi had been chronically inadequate to even cater for the monthly gross payroll, resulting in cumulative debts to KRA of Kshs 1 billion. This chronic underfunding by the exchequer commenced during the reign of Professor Gichaga as VC and continued through the reign of Professor Kiamba. What I did not quite understand was why KRA decided to freeze all the accounts soon after my appointment and assumption of office. This move was quite painful and distressing for me as a newly appointed and relatively inexperienced VC. As a result, I was not going to be able to pay the mandatory monthly staff salaries as per the staff employment contracts. I therefore sought swift advice from the Chancellor, who however curtly advised me to wake up and start performing my duties competently as the VC and CEO of the University.

At first I was surprised by the Chancellor's action but quickly snapped out of it as soon as I realized that it was for my own benefit and a form of training on the job. I was at Egerton University in Nakuru County attending a VC committee meeting with vice-chancellors of other public universities when I learned that all accounts of the University had been frozen by KRA. They were to remain frozen until the University paid the statutory debt in full. The Chancellor's action emboldened me and gave me a fighting spirit. I was not going to take this lying down, after all the University belonged to the government. I therefore constituted an emergency *ad hoc* committee of management consisting of myself as Chairman, the DVC, Administration and Finance, Professor Mbithi, the Managing Director UNES, Professor Kimani, and the Principal of the College of Humanities and Social Sciences, Professor Mbeche, a management scientist, to urgently deal with this perennial problem once and for all. This team employed a three-pronged approach in order to quickly solve the problem. The first one was direct engagement with senior KRA officers concerned, including the Director General. The second tier of engagement involved full briefing and firm request for urgent support from the Permanent Secretary in the Ministry of Education, Professor Mutahi, who was fully supportive of our endeavours. The third and perhaps most important tier involved the direct engagement of senior Treasury officials including the Director of Budget, a Mr. Ngugi, and the Permanent Secretary Mr. Kinyua. These engagements bore fruit as our accounts were unfrozen on time to enable us pay staff salaries without any delay. The engagements also further formed the basis of our future negotiations with the government, that eventually led to the government repaying the statutory debts in full to KRA on behalf of the University. The university on its part made a firm undertaking and commitment to KRA to always pay, timely and in full, all future statutory deductions, a feat it has implemented diligently to date.

My other very painful episode was in regard to the Kibwezi research farm, where after demarcating the borders and planting trees on the firm, a local politician incited the residents against the University. The residents, through the politician petitioned the government for the repossession of the land yet it legally belonged to the University of Nairobi.

The University was carrying out extensive research at the farm, through the two colleges of Biological and Physical Sciences, and Agriculture and Veterinary Sciences. It was also actively used for training by the College of Agriculture and Veterinary Services for its agriculture and range management programmes. In this regard, the University had constructed adequate boarding facilities for the small groups of students to be trained there at any one time. The University also kept large herds of livestock at the farm for training purposes, and provided community service to the local population by running a primary school, and a well-stocked, equipped and staffed health centre. In addition, the University trained the locals in farming and a wide range management techniques.

One morning I was summoned to the office of the Head of the Public Service for an urgent meeting regarding our Kibwezi farm. As a Public Servant, I was very stressed because I did not like mixing politics with my professional work. At the office I met Professor Mutahi, the Kibwezi politician, the Head of Public Service, and other staff from the Ministry of Lands. The topic for discussion was how to surrender our Kibwezi farm back to the locals because we were supposedly not utilizing it for anything. This was not true and I clearly stated the University position with evidence to back it up. I was strongly supported by Professor Mutahi, while the local politician insisted on repossessing the farm. Therefore, the meeting did not achieve much. I referred the matter to the Chancellor who swiftly interceded at presidential level and saved our Kibwezi farm, much to our delight.

CHAPTER THREE

INFLUENCES IN MY LIFE

Certain people have influenced my life in one way or the other. While I may not always have understood what they were telling me, and even fighting off some, they ultimately instilled the roots of transformative change in me. They persuaded, encouraged and even trained me.

The most significant influence in my early life was that of my mother, Joan Sarah Aloo (*nyar gi opere*), meaning daughter of the Catholic priests – a name she acquired due to the fact that she lived most of her early life in the Catholic missions of Aluor, and later Yala. Mother moulded me to be God fearing, teaching me right from wrong, at a very early stage in my life. She also taught me the possible consequences of wrongdoing. I was asthmatic and perhaps because of this, she was closer to me than any of my other siblings. She always ensured that I kept warm to avoid asthmatic attacks. My father, Bernard Magoha was a strict disciplinarian, who did not hesitate to cane us when we went astray. He was a 'hands-on dad'. During my early childhood, my parents taught us that we must be responsible for our actions. Just thinking about this early influence, I believe that it stood me in good stead much later in life, as I dealt with indisciplined students during my tenure as VC of the University of Nairobi.

When I was a child, I wanted to help people get well. I wanted to 'treat' people just like my paternal grandmother, Maria Akumu did. Grandma would prepare concoctions from some plants to clear my chest and improve my breathing, especially during the cold weather. She looked after me, whenever my mother was away. The fact that she prepared the medicine herself impressed me a great deal, and no doubt would later influence my decision to become a medical doctor. However, my decision to become a medical doctor was more substantively influenced by two physicians during my early life: Dr. James Angawa, a consultant chest specialist had the first impact in my life as a western-trained medical doctor. He successfully treated my asthma with the kindness, compassion and dedication that I could only compare to my mother's. I was only 11 years old during my encounter with him but it was in that episode that I made a firm decision to become a medical doctor. This decision would be reinforced many years later by Professor Joseph Mungai, Dean of the Faculty of Medicine of the University of Nairobi, in 1972. Professor Mungai had come to give a career talk at Strathmore College. He was smartly dressed and very clear in his thinking and decision making processes. His commitment to serve humanity for no gain at all resonated well with what I had been taught earlier at Starehe Boys Centre. I saw my future self in him.

The greatest influence in my teenage years occurred at Starehe Boys Centre and was impacted by two great gentlemen: Dr. Griffin, and Mr. Shaw. I met Dr. Griffin for the first time in January 1967, during the interview to consider me for admission to the Centre. He instilled great fear in me through the questions he was asking. Initially, I did not like him because he interfered with my teenage freedom and happiness, which to me were sacrosanct. I imagined that he was a dictator, sent to Starehe to torment young boys at the prime of their life. I could not have been more wrong in my imagination and judgement. I discovered that after all, it was him who was destined to be my saviour by teaching me about the challenges of real life situations and instilling discipline in me. Soon enough, I was carried through the rules and regulations at Starehe; rules which had to be obeyed by all. To start with, one had to stand up and at attention, military style, whenever the director or any of his deputies was passing by. This was the first time I understood the obedience of a properly constituted authority. We were taught to obey rules and willingly and happily accept punishments for dissent. A student was alright until a school rule or regulation was broken, when some form of punishment was meted down at him.

If it was caning, it could only be done by Dr. Griffin. He took the time, immediately after the punishment, to invite you to his office for a cup of tea. During this session, he would explain why you had been punished, in the hope that you would learn a lesson from the session. He further assured one that he would not be judgemental about your wrongdoing and subsequent punishment in future.

This attitude and teaching by the director has remained with me for the rest of my life and it certainly influenced the way I managed staff and students during my tenure as Dean of the Faculty of Medicine, Principal of College of Health Sciences, DVC, Administration and Finance, and most significantly as VC of the University of Nairobi. His approach involved training all students in responsibility and leadership. The director was the master strategist and tactician while Mr. Shaw was the implementer of strategy. Our thinking and reasoning power was enhanced through the free participation by students and staff in the weekly barazas, chaired and coordinated by the director. During the barazas, there was great interaction between students and teachers that enabled raising issues which would be discussed and debated thoroughly before a common and binding decision was reached. In addition, there was immunity and therefore no participant was penalized for the issues raised, no matter how grave. These barazas would later positively influence and inform my decision making process while dealing with staff and students during my ten-year tenure as VC. I learned to close issues already discussed and finalized, and not keep on beating down an opponent who was already on the floor. I also learned, for the first time, that in order to receive maximum output from people, one needed to empower them and give them space to perform their duties, without undue interference. By the time I was leaving Starehe, I had learned all that I needed to survive in life as an older teenager.

Professor Jacob Festus Ade-Ajayi, Vice-Chancellor of the University of Lagos, and David Sperling, Principal of Strathmore College, influenced my life in regard to how I viewed compassion and simplicity in human life. Professor Emmanuel Adeyemo Elebute, Provost of the College of Medicine, University of Lagos, and later Chief Medical Director of Lagos University Teaching Hospital, and Professor Olikoye Ransome-Kuti, Chairman of the Department of Paediatrics, College of Medicine, University of Lagos, directly personified the Hippocratic Oath administered to all medical doctors and impacted on me the seriousness of professional discipline in medical practice.

Professor Gichaga, was Vice-Chancellor of the University of Nairobi when I became Principal of the College of Health Sciences. It was his boldness in conceptualizing, implementing, monitoring and evaluating the Module II academic programmes at the University which ensured sustainability of the University. This commendable strategic effort was later to be adopted by all other public universities in Kenya and the East African region and has by extension ensured national and regional sustainability of public university education. His non-tribalistic influence and impact on my administrative career at the University of Nairobi is described elsewhere in this book.

I first heard of Professor David Peter Simon Wasawo from my father in 1962, while I was in primary school in Jina. I was informed that he was the most learned black man in Kenya at the time and was therefore the pride of our country which was approaching independence. We were all supposed to study hard and emulate him. But it was not until the late eighties that I first met him, albeit briefly as a patient, just after my return from abroad. After that short encounter, he left the country to work for the United Nations. I did not meet him again until he was appointed Chairman of the University of Nairobi Council in 1999. He was one of the first indigenous lecturers at Makerere University in Uganda, where he started lecturing in the early fifties. He was also the first indigenous Deputy Principal of the University of Nairobi College of the larger University of East Africa. Professor Wasawo was not only an eminent professor but also an accomplished top-grade scientific researcher. He was a sophisticated, intellectual sage, yet very down-to-earth and extremely simple in life. He was an astute negotiator, diplomat and an academic statesman of incomparable abilities with a very large capacity to listen attentively before commenting on issues. Usually, he would allow everyone to make their contributions before commenting very wisely and intellectually with advice, support, dissent or sanction.

As Chairman of the University Council, he presided over the initial transformational change strategy at the University and together with professors Gichaga and Kiamba, implemented the Module II academic programmes through UNES, then led by Professor Kimani as Managing Director. He was a constant companion of my predecessors Gichaga and Kiamba, during some of the most turbulent and challenging periods in the management of the University. He strongly supported the University management during the initial resistance to the implementation of Module II academic programmes by students and other stakeholders, who erroneously associated Module II programmes with a fall in the quality of academic standards. On the contrary, the quality of academic outputs improved drastically as a result of this strategy.

I worked with Professor Wasawo in the University Council from 2001, when I was serving as Principal of the College of Health Sciences, and then later as DVC for two and a half years, Acting VC for three months, and substantive VC for three months until March 2005. During this period, he proffered wisdom and knowledge, and impacted on my thinking and decision making. His love and compassion for students was unparalleled, despite his firm belief in discipline. He was firmly of the opinion that the punishment should be corrective, resulting in better behaviour. A practical demonstration of his love and compassion for students was when he invited the entire Executive Committee of the University of Nairobi Women Students Welfare Association (WOSWA) to his home, at Fort Ternan, for a two-week holiday, at his own cost. Little did I know that later on, as VC, I would not only adopt but actively apply this principle. As a result, many students reformed, completing their studies and later in life, contributed to the social, political and economic development of our country.

Dr. John Nyangeri Simba, a distinguished University of Dar es Salaam educated lawyer, became the next Chairman of the Council in March 2005 replacing Professor Wasawo who had completed two terms. Dr. Simba simultaneously became the Chairman of UNES. He had wide experience in government, having first worked in the Attorney General's Chambers, and later the Industrial Commercial Development Corporation (ICDC) where he served in various capacities from deputy corporation secretary and chief legal officer, corporation secretary and chief legal officer, executive director, and finally the CEO. As Chairman of the Federation of Kenya Employers (FKE) Dr. Simba was very conversant with labour issues affecting the University, and was consequently very instrumental in the solution of myriad industrial relations disputes affecting the institution, during his tenure as the Chairman of Council.

I therefore enjoyed working with him, because of his rich private and public sector experience, which came in handy during the transformative leadership and change management experience. He strengthened my understanding of the legal interpretation of our student management rules and regulations. Most importantly, the Council gave me free hand to run the University without undue interference, while providing the necessary oversight role. I discussed the initial concept of the University of Nairobi Towers with him and the Chancellor, Dr. Wanjui. The professional advice he gave me, impacted on the confidence with which I continued to pursue and plan for this mega project. I discussed the strategy of academic expansion with him and he assured me of the Council support which led to the purchase of two properties, in Kisumu and Mombasa. This enabled the University to expand its academic programmes without compromising the quality of education. He further provided invaluable advice during the restructuring of the University of Nairobi Pension Scheme in 2007, which led to the turnaround of the scheme. The financial returns for members from the pension scheme have improved tremendously, averaging twenty per cent per year over the past three years.

The University of Nairobi honoured Dr. Simba with a degree of Doctor of Laws LL.D (*honoris causa*), for his distinguished contribution to the Council, and his transformative leadership, change management and best practices and corporate leadership skills. He was specifically recognized for his role in the exponential rise in the international rankings of the University due to the practice of good corporate governance, provision of quality education, internationalization of the University and significant increase in research output by individual academic staff members.

The Vice Chairman of the Council was a Makerere University trained entrepreneur, Nicholas Ng'ang'a. He had a very rich mix of public and private sector experience which was relevant to the transformational change at the University. Mr. Ng'ang'a had served as Permanent Secretary in the Ministry of Finance and was therefore very conversant with government systems of funding the public universities in Kenya. A prolific administrator, he had also served a stint in the Ministries of Foreign Affairs and Health; had been past Chairman of the National Bank of Kenya, and Chairman of G4S Security Company Limited, Kakuzi Limited, and is currently Chairman of Safaricom Limited. At the University of Nairobi, he was appointed Chairperson of the building committee; the organ that was instrumental in approving the completion of numerous buildings in various campuses, which had stalled at foundation levels in 1992. Mr. Ng'ang'a handled the committee deliberations efficiently and professionally, without the usual bureaucracy in the public service resulting in significant improvement of the University's infrastructure.

Phillip Kinisu, a University of Nairobi graduate, and London trained chartered accountant was the Treasurer to the University Council. He headed PwC for many years, operating in Kenya, Uganda, Tanzania, Angola, Ghana, Mauritius, Zambia, Nigeria and Rwanda. His extensive management experience enabled him to competently lead the delivery of his firm's professional services to a broad range of clients in the public and private sectors of the economy including but not limited to financial services, manufacturing, transport and government. As a senior partner and CEO of PwC, Mr. Kinisu and his firm together with the University Council managed the process of the first competitive search for a public university VC in Kenya, which resulted in my recruitment. His appointment as Treasurer to the Council, three months into my appointment, was therefore a great relief to me. As CEO of the University, I consulted him regularly on matters pertaining to financial management of the institution. This anchored and professionally emboldened my financial management style. From the foregoing, it was obvious that I had a very competent Council capable of helping me navigate management for change at the University.

Dr. Betty Gikonyo, a highly respected professional colleague and entrepreneur, was the longest serving member of the University Council, where she served for more than 11 years. She was in Council for the whole ten-year period that I was VC. She was elected the inaugural Chairperson of UONAA in February 2005. She steered the Association to greatness by strategically expanding its professional branches to the colleges, schools and faculties of the University. She competently increased the international visibility of the University during her tenure as chairperson. She mobilized funds to provide bursaries for the numerous intelligent but needy students. This she achieved through the assistance of Professor Muriuki, the University special students advisor, who meticulously performed background checks to ensure that only genuinely needy students benefited from the bursaries. Dr. Gikonyo replaced Mr. Ng'ang'a as Chairperson of the building committee of the University. She was destined by history to preside over the consideration for the construction of the University of Nairobi Towers building, providing professional approval before forwarding to the Council for consideration and final approval. I was indeed very lucky to have her as Chairperson of the building committee because, in her capacity as CEO of Karen Hospital, she had just completed the construction of one of the most modern hospitals in Nairobi, the Karen Hospital.

I was also quite lucky to work with very qualified and experienced 'hands-on entrepreneur', Dr. SK Macharia who a was appointed to the University Council, in March 2005. He was already a very successful entrepreneur with a distinguished career as an industrialist and media mogul. One of the key players in the Kenyan media sector, he is the Chairman of the Royal Media Services Group, which controls Citizen Television Station and a significant number of radio stations in the country. He was trained in the United States of America at Seattle Pacific University, and the University of Washington, graduating with a Bachelor of Science degree in accounting and two Masters degrees in accounting and finance, in addition to being a chartered accountant. He had endured a very challenging childhood, and surmounted hurdles on the road to achieving his dreams of a good education. On return to Kenya, he had a stint in government at the Industrial Commercial Development Corporation, the Kenya Industrial Estates (KIE), Agricultural Development Corporation (ADC), and later the International Finance Corporation (IFC), which is the private sector arm of the World Bank Group.

It was on the basis of these distinguished qualities that in April 2005, I proposed Dr. SK Macharia to the University of Nairobi Council for appointment as Chairman of the tender committee. I urgently needed to learn from his very rich industrial and accounting experience in order to successfully manage the procurement process at the University and eventually succeed as VC. At that time, the tender committee would meet as per tradition either at 9.30 a.m. or 2.30 p.m. At his first meeting, he would hear none of this. He convinced me about the significance of time management in any serious venture and strongly advised against waste of time. We agreed to change the time of the tender committee meetings to 7.30 a.m., This immediately translated into faster and better results from the tender committee. There was initial resistance to this strategic change by academic members of the tender committee, but after a while it was adopted with relief since by 9.30 a.m. the tender committee meetings would be over, leaving the rest of the day for other planned commitments.

The lesson I learnt from this would be the most significant during my tenure as Vice Chancellor. This is because I not only took the cue, but went further and started all University management and Senate meetings at 7.00 a.m. and occasionally at 7.30 a.m. This new culture cascaded down to the colleges and units, and resulted in a sustained and exponential improvement of the University's performance, due to the completion of more targeted tasks, within less time. It was Dr. Macharia who guided me in the establishment and implementation of the Computerized Financial Management Information System that has saved the University billions of shillings since its installation in 2006. His significant contribution to the visibility of the University of Nairobi is underlined by the fact that for the ten years of my tenure as VC, his television company, Citizen TV, covered all the twenty one graduation ceremonies (from the 32nd to the 52nd) live, and free of charge.

He also regularly gave me invaluable financial management advice throughout his tenure as a University of the Council member and after. This contributed significantly towards my running the University efficiently as both a public and a private enterprise resulting in the current very favourable rankings locally, regionally and internationally. Dr. Macharia was honoured by the University, through the conferment of the degree of Doctor of Letters *(honoris causa)*. This was because of his immense support to the University of Nairobi, his philanthropic and charitable work to the Kenyan community, his business acumen and efforts at expanding the media industry in Kenya and the region.

One other member of the University of Nairobi Council who significantly impacted on and influenced my administrative style as VC was Mr. Isaac Odundo Awuondo, the then Group Managing Director and CEO of Commercial Bank of Africa. A University of Nairobi graduate and professional chartered accountant, Mr. Awuondo had extensive experience in the banking and financial industry. He was also non-executive director of Kenya Hospital Association (Nairobi Hospital), Rhino Ark Trust, Bata Shoe Company and Deposit Protection Fund. He was therefore a financial entrepreneur and a key player in the Kenyan banking and financial sectors. He was appointed by University Council to the University Pension Scheme, as a Trustee. The Board of Trustees of the Pension Scheme appointed him Chairman of the strategic and most important, investment committee. As Chairman of the investment committee, he brought in his very rich accounting experience. He steered the Pension Scheme to profitable but non risky investments that resulted in significant growth and returns. Being a major player in the financial industry, there are many instances he professionally advised the Board of Trustees against risky investments which would otherwise have resulted in losses. The Scheme benefited significantly by posting healthy financial returns during his tenure.

It is important to note that these high-flyers dedicated a share of their time to serving the University, not out of coercion or desire for monetary gain or recognition, but they willingly supported me and the management. For instance, Terry Davidson, a Kenyan-born banker, entrepreneur, philanthropist and consultant educated in Kenya and England, was yet another such support. Mr. Davidson had wide experience in both public and private sectors of the economy having spent over 30 years with Citibank in various parts of the world including being the regional head for East and Southern Africa, and CEO of the largest bank in Kenya, the Kenya Commercial Bank. He was a founder member of the Capital Markets Authority, and past Chairman of the Kenya Bankers Association. He was also a non-executive director of the deposit protection fund and Faulu Kenya. He was an independent consultant and board member in various organizations including the publicly listed Kenol-Kobil Company Limited; KK Security Group, Prime Bank, and First Capital Bank of Zambia. He was a Trustee of Gertrude's Garden Children's Hospital. At the University of Nairobi Council, he was appointed Chairman of the audit committee and brought in his vast experience, assisting the management to implement financial regulation as per international accounting standards. I enjoyed working with him because he enriched my understanding of the audit process and my role as CEO.

In addition, I had the privilege of working with Dr. Manu Chandaria, an engineer, industrialist, entrepreneur and philanthropist. Dr. Chandaria was the longest serving member of the University of Nairobi Council, having represented the Gandhi Memorial Academy Society for several decades. He had the institutional memory of the previous Councils and this was instrumental in their smooth transition. He was chairman of the Comcraft Group of Companies, and served on many boards including industrial manufacturing plants, the Kenya Association of Manufacturers, East African Business Council, Kenya Private Sector Alliance, Bank of India Advisory Committee, Kenindia Assurance Company Limited and East African Reinsurance Company Limited, among many others. He was director of many boards and member of numerous committees, both in the public and private sectors of the economy at local and international level. These included Standard Chartered Bank, UNES, the National Council of Science and Technology, Capital Markets Authority, Insurance Advisory Board, Investment Promotion Centre, Joint Industrial and Commercial Consultative Committee and the New Partnership for African Development (NEPAD). He was also appointed by the then President to the National Economic and Social Council.

Dr. Chandaria was extremely active on social and philanthropic fronts. For instance he served as chairman, trustee, and member of numerous social welfare and charitable organizations such as Watoto Kwanza Trust, Chandaria Foundation, Kenya Ear Foundation, and Mahatma Gandhi Memorial Academy Society. He was therefore a productive Council member, improving the output of the Council through his very rich industrial and management for change experience. Dr. Chandaria regularly attended and contributed to Council meetings and usually analysed the University's budgets in great detail, improving them with his in-depth input and experience before onward transmission to government for consideration and approval. He never shied away from commending me on any positive achievement, and was readily available for consultation.

What impressed me most was his humility, despite his vast experience, knowledge and wisdom. He actually initiated most of these consultations himself, because of his passion for freely sharing his knowledge with others. I benefited greatly from his experience and motivation during my tenure as VC. The Gandhi Smarak Nidhi Fund which he ably chaired, annually awarded multiple postgraduate scholarships to the University of Nairobi to strengthen programmes in science and technology including engineering, building, life, physical, biological and computer sciences; good corporate governance, among others. Dr. Chandaria and his foundation contributed Kshs 50 million towards the construction of the University of Nairobi Towers. He impacted great influence in my style of management for change at the University. Imagine this great engineer industrialist and a man of enormous influence, experience, and wealth, always very busy and extremely committed elsewhere, humbling himself to look out for the VC in order to share his management experience with him for the greater interest of the University.

Dr. Joseph Wanjui an American-trained engineer, industrialist and entrepreneur was appointed Chancellor at a time when the University needed someone with experience in both the public and private sectors of the economy. Apart from being trained as an engineer up to the master's level, he further attended the Stanford University Graduate School of Business Executive Program which was critical in establishing University-industry linkages. He was very well versed with management for change as he had been in charge of several such changes in his career in both the public and private sectors. Indeed, on his return to Kenya from the United States of America, he first worked with Esso Limited as a management trainee and later East African Industries, one of the subsidiaries of Unilever. He joined as technical director, progressing to Managing Director and finally Chairman. He had joined East African Industries after serving at the Industrial Commercial Development Corporation where he served as CEO and member of the national advisory committee. He also initiated and concluded negotiations for industrial and commercial firms such as Panpaper, Kenya Industrial Estates, Union Carbide, and ICDC Investment Company (Centum), among others. He was on the board of Kenya National Trading Corporation (KNTC), International Finance Corporation business advisory council an affiliate of the World Bank Group, Commonwealth Africa Venture Capital Fund, Kenya Institute of Management, and Hillpark Hotel, among others.

Initially, I had a lot of difficulty understanding and working with him. It was not until he reconstituted the University Council in March 2005, to be chaired by Dr. Simba that I started embracing his management style. I was encouraged, empowered and impressed when, while reconstituting the Council, he asked for my opinion on some of his nominees. He went further and requested me to suggest some names to be considered for appointment to Council and two of my nominees were approved.

This taught me a great lesson at the commencement of my tenure as VC, as I immediately adopted the consultative and inclusive approach with members of my UMB with tremendous positive and synergistic outcomes. The newly reconstituted Council was his greatest gift to me as the incoming VC. All the external members were from the private sector with extensive industrial and managerial experience as illustrated throughout this chapter.

At a personal level I developed a close working relationship with the Chancellor. We consulted regularly at either his or my request and he was available all the time. These meetings took place either in my office or in one of his offices. He even convinced me to attend the Stanford University Graduate School of Business Executive Program, which he had attended earlier. This was extremely useful and contributed immensely to the transformation of the University. Furthermore, he did not interfere with the management of student's affairs and referred all appeals back to my office to deal with, through the Council. This very quickly sent a clear message to students that there was only one centre of power; that of the VC's office. I was able to stabilize the University very quickly because of this empowerment and lack of interference. As a result, the University never lost any academic time due to student unrest, during my ten-year tenure as VC.

CHAPTER FOUR

TRANSFORMATIVE LEADERSHIP

At the time of my recruitment, the University of Nairobi was one of the largest institutions of higher learning in East and Central Africa. The undergraduate student population was 25,000 while that of postgraduate students was 5,000. The University staff population was 5,000 including 1,500 academic staff.

Founded in 1954, the Royal Technical College of East Africa first transformed to University of Nairobi College of the University of East Africa, which in turn became the autonomous University of Nairobi in 1970. In subsequent years, the institution, student population, academic programmes and infrastructural facilities have expanded dramatically. During the eighties and nineties the University faced mystical challenges as it strived to ensure that adequate physical capacities, quality and availability of academic staff and relevance of academic programmes were not outstripped by the increasing demand. These comprehensive and complex challenges required an individual with exceptional personality and proven leadership qualities.

Transformative change however is not an easy concept to grasp. Looking back, I encountered some challenges to get the University community to embrace the concept and to practice it in their everyday activities. The individual to be VC, and CEO of the University was defined as one who should be able to manage participatory planning processes and to set long and short term strategic visions and goals; to promote efficiency and good order including the welfare, conduct, and discipline of staff and students. The person appointed was to be an innovative, visionary leader capable of building a dynamic and motivated management team. Of particular importance in the equation was the ability to formulate and execute a change management programme to ensure the sustainability and transformation of the University on the path to world class excellence. This was a long-run expectation, and therefore the individual appointed was supposed to apply the highest degree of ethical standards, integrity and professionalism, demonstrating a track record of success and performance characterized by clear vision and strategic thought.

According to the advert, a long one indeed, the ideal candidate was to be in charge of management for change team, with the ability to translate strategic ideas into valuable performance outputs and capacity, and to motivate and influence people. Most significantly the candidate was supposed to secure and manage financial support of the University and direct the fundraising activities for the development plans, and a team leader who would work very closely with the Council and its committees, the Senate faculties, institutes and departments and all staff and students.

As I have already mentioned, I was the first public university VC and by extension the first public officer in Kenya to be competitively recruited, after an international advertisement. From the onset, I knew it was not going to be easy as the job required someone that would drive what was being called 'management for change' at the University of Nairobi. This was a break from the traditional strategy employed in universities at the time. As I took over, I was immediately aware that I had taken on an onerous task. I had to manage change and elevate the dwindling, nay a tottering university that was almost collapsing due to the chronical underfunding by the exchequer. It had dilapidated infrastructure which included poorly equipped science and computer laboratories, inadequate and poorly maintained lecture theatres and tutorial rooms lacking basic ICT facilities and a financial management system that was still manual and therefore open to manipulation and possible financial loss. Staff morale was very low due to poor remuneration. Consequently, there was a huge exodus of academic staff to universities in the developed world. Furthermore, the majority of academic staff, seconded to other external universities for further studies, failed to return to the University on the completion of their training. There were also frequent disruptions of University academic programmes due to frequent student unrest.

This was most certainly a depressing state of affairs, and whoever was appointed the VC was required to possess the requisite skills and competencies to successfully carry out the necessary management changes in order to move the University towards world class excellence.

At this juncture, it is important to elaborate, from my own understanding what transformative change is. It is a word that in the first five years of my tenure, was bandied about, baptized all sorts of names, and even despised. It was a struggle for many to embrace and seek to make it work.

Transformative leadership is a management style where the leader is charged with identifying needed change, and creating a clear vision to guide the change not only through inspiration, but also execution of the change in tandem with the organizational needs. Transformative leaders also motivate and raise the morale of the team members by using several methods, that connect the leader, team members and workers to take greater sense of self identity and self in the organization and the collective identity of the organization. The transformative leader should be a role model for the workers, in order to inspire them and raise their interest in the organization and be able to challenge them to take greater ownership of their work.

The leader should understand the strengths and weaknesses of his staff and align their skills to the tasks that enhance their performance and output. Transformative leaders make their teams advance to higher levels of morality and motivation. Through the strength of their vision and personality, these leaders are able to inspire their colleagues to change their expectations, perceptions, and motivations to work towards greater common goals. Transformative leaders possess the ability to make measurable changes, lead from the front by demonstrating strong examples, and by formulating and articulating energized visions along with challenging goals. They are usually moral examples in the organization working towards the benefit of staff and the organization.

Transformational leaders have high expectations for the team members, believing that they can bring out their very best performance. As a result, they inspire, empower and stimulate to much higher levels of performance. They are charismatic leaders who challenge the team to be innovative and creative allowing them freedom of choice and thought.

They also demonstrate genuine concern for the needs, feelings and well-being of staff by providing individual coaching, support, encouragement, and mentorship. This personal attention to each team member and workers is a key element in bringing out the best performance of staff. Transformative leaders use only persuasive means, based on reason, promoting cooperation and harmony using only authentic and consistent means and promoting an ethical climate among them. They encourage team members and workers to share their ideas so that the leaders can recognize and appreciate their unique and diversified individual contributions in the organization. The team members and workers achieve extraordinary outcomes and in the process develop their own leadership capacities which are critical to the improvement of the organization.

Transformative leaders avoid the top-down approach in communication when dealing with their team members and workers. They are generally energetic, enthusiastic and passionate about their work. They take control of situations with a clear vision of the set goals and many times challenge the status quo; for them, failure is not an option.

From the foregoing it became very clear to me on appointment as the sixth VC of the University of Nairobi, that if I was going to have any measurable impact during my tenure, then I had to effect change management through a transformative process. The change was to be incremental, in order to be meaningful. As the transformative team leader, I would be responsible to the University Council, the policy making oversight body, but would be in charge of the UMB, Senate and other workers in the colleges, departments and units.

I was to be in charge of the students and therefore work through the SWA, and the Dean of Students. Power would therefore be devolved from the UMB to the Senate and then to colleges, with college principals fully empowered to run the colleges without undue interference. In order to successfully manage the change, the Chancellor, Dr. Wanjui appointed a new Council, which had personalities with rich experience, as earlier explained.

This was a blessing for me – I had a very competent oversight team to guide me in terms of policy. My first task was to develop the first-ever Corporate Strategic Plan, of the University. This task was completed and approved by the Council within five months. The second most important task was to build synergetic teams, starting with the UMB. This board was chaired by the VC. The members included the DVCs, college principals, and their deputies, UNES Managing Director, Chief Legal Officer, Chief Finance Officer, Chief Internal Auditor, Chief Medical Officer, University librarian, the registrars, SWA Director, estates manager, dean of students, procurement manager and Director ICT.

When I took over as VC, university officers were members of the UMB, but we were not working as a team. Indeed, we were working as if to maintain the status quo. But I did not effect change or replace any of the managers that I had the power to. What I did instead was to give everybody an opportunity to serve, with me as the team leader. I did not need to be surrounded by sycophants or 'loyal' tribesmen. The most important thing was meritocracy and ability to perform certain tasks and deliver prescribed performance outputs on time. Given my competitive recruitment, and my performance contract, I very firmly but methodically passed on the message that the status quo was not an option and that 'transformational change' was the only constant.

To begin with, I created a synergetic team, empowering the members and making them feel that they were valued and respected. I then outsourced various professional organizations for experts and assistance in conducting a series of training sessions for the management team, which was to be responsible for transformative change at the University. At first, I attempted to hold the training sessions in hotels within the Nairobi metropolis, including the Kenya College of Communications. However, this did not work out well. I remember one or two training sessions where a significant number of managers failed to reside in the hotels, preferring instead to commute from their homes. They reported late and left early before completing the day's training. The fact that I had led by example through staying at the hotels did not persuade them. I therefore abandoned this approach and adopted a different training strategy, deciding to carry out the sessions in various government and parastatal owned hotels across the country, as was permitted by government then. This was more productive and team members were persuaded to board in hotels away from Nairobi. It also had an added advantage because it enabled us to have extra training sessions after supper and fostered bonding.

We were professionally trained and inducted well into various management courses including financial management, human resource management, integrity, performance contracting, ISO certification, student management, time management, public procurement, industrial relations, good corporate governance and team building, transformative leadership, results based management and public sector reforms, among others. Some of the earlier and very useful team building exercises were carried out by the FKE in Kisumu. These sessions were instrumental in empowering the managers within the UMB to feel appreciated as valuable members of the team whose contributions and input was appreciated. During the sessions, all team members were encouraged to contribute without fear or hindrance. My responsibility to lead from the front demanded that I perform the same way that I was firmly persuading them to do. I had to walk the talk in order to be emulated. For example, I expected the college principals to be fully in charge of their colleges at all times, providing any required information promptly. I knew that I had achieved my goal of creating an empowered synergistic management team when I witnessed with pride that 95 per cent of them were enjoying their work and performing far beyond their set targets.

Having achieved a synergetic team within the UMB, I set out to train the next most important management organ, the University of Nairobi Senate. The Senate had a large membership in excess of 160 members, and the success of our transformative change management strategy largely depended on whether or not they understood our set goals and strategies. The Senate is chaired by the VC and had members drawn from the UMB, deans and associate deans of faculties and schools, directors and associate directors of institutes, directors of statutory boards, chairmen of academic departments, and student representatives. On my appointment, I worked with all members of the Senate that I inherited. I did not see the need to replace them just because they were appointed by my predecessors. This inclusion empowered and encouraged them to feel valuable, wanted and appreciated as members of the larger management team of the University. At a personal level, I believe that everybody should be empowered, given specific performance targets and appreciated on successful completion of such targets.

It was easier to train the larger Senate because a sizable number of senators were also members of the UMB and had already been trained, enabling them to actively assist in the training of the rest. They acted as role models to other senators while explaining some of the new strategies to the lager membership of the Senate. The Senate was also trained in various hotel locations outside Nairobi in order to maximize their participation and bonding. The same concept of transformative leadership change was utilized whereby individual members were empowered to participate by contributing and feeling free to offer their views without fear or hindrance. This consequently enhanced their bonding and team spirit. The training was carried out by a wide range of professional experts from both the public and private sectors, including the Kenya Bureau of

Standards (KEBS) for training related to ISO Certification. As a result, the University was ISO Certified in 2008.

I successfully engaged FKE who assembled a wide range of professional experts in the fields of industrial relations, human resource management including time management, synergetic team building, financial management, public procurement management including the application of public procurement rules, regulations and challenges; and good corporate governance, among many others. A very competent government department in charge of performance contracting, together with performance contract experts from the corporate private sector trained the Senate on the process and managerial aspects of performance contracting. The Senate was also trained in transformative leadership; results based management and public sector reforms, and ICT skills for development.

In order to improve delivery of course content efficiently and by various means, teaching staff in all the colleges were retrained by pedagogy experts drawn from the College of Education and External Studies. After this series of training sessions, a staff appraisal evaluation tool was introduced, which among other things empowered the students to directly assess their lecturers. Furthermore each lecturer was required to display outside their offices, the times when they would be available for consultation by students.

The entire elected student leadership of SONU and its parliament were trained along the same lines with the UMB and the Senate. Emphasis was placed on dialogue, team building and teamwork rather than confrontation and destruction of University property with consequent loss of academic time. The student leadership was sensitized on the rules and regulations relating to student discipline, the disciplinary process and specifically advised against cheating in examinations and the consequences thereof. The students were encouraged to actively contribute to the training process by freely offering their views, without any fear or hindrance. They would henceforth be part of the management team, as far as student affairs were concerned, by actively engaging members of the UMB and the Senate for speedy and peaceful resolution of issues. The student training was very effective because as I have already mentioned, no academic time was lost on account of University closure related to student indiscipline during my tenure as VC.

After successfully training the UMB, the Senate and the student leaders, the stage was now set to devolve the process to the colleges and units. It was envisaged that once all staff and students were trained, I finally would be a transformative team leader for the entire University community. The college principals, deans, directors and chairmen of departments were empowered to collectively or individually train the rest of the staff and students. It is interesting and also encouraging that while the college team leaders were carrying out the training, they were so empowered that they acted as role models for others. The devolved training was similar to that carried out earlier for the UMB and the Senate. For example, ISO training was done to all university units with the assistance of the KEBS personnel, the college principals and the SWA Director.

The journey towards transformative change was not easy. The University, driven by the strategic plan had started the process of transformative leadership and change management in earnest but there were a few sceptics, some of whom outrightly resisted any form of change. I ignored these, choosing instead to focus on our strategic objectives and goals. A significant number of staff had formed a habit of reporting late and leaving early. Further, there were some who were away for most part of the day, and yet expected to be paid. The absenteeism and absconding resulted in the loss of many man hours. However, after we developed a Service Charter and utilized the training gained from the ISO Certification team, we firmly put policies in place to ensure that every worker reported to work on time, and performed their targeted tasks to completion.

The performance contracting process acted as a catalyst enabling the colleges and units to compete in meeting their targets. The college principals for example, signed a performance contracts with the VC on specific targets to be achieved. The principals were empowered to give specific performance targets to different members of staff, who at the end of the year would be appraised based on the measurable outputs. Any staff who underperformed would in the first instance be counselled and disciplined by the college authorities, according to the University regulations and the terms of service. Only very difficult staff members would be referred to the DVC, Administration and Finance, and finally to the VC, where necessary disciplinary action would be taken in accordance with the law. Individual staff rights would be guaranteed by allowing the staff union officials to be in attendance at every stage of the disciplinary process. Some senior academic staff including professors had their contracts terminated after due disciplinary processes. The reasons for termination included absconding from duty, losing examination scripts, chronic alcohol abuse and theft of university assets.

The recognition of minority opinion energized the University community into one large synergetic team that enabled us to rise to the best University in Kenya and the region. Indeed, everyone was listened to without discrimination; this is best exemplified by the freedom which members enjoyed during the restructuring and rationalization of the University academic units. Majority of faculties accepted to rationalize, restructure and even in some cases downsize and rename schools. This was after thorough deliberations and approval at the UMB, the Senate and the Council. Some faculties however had very strong arguments for the retention of their identity. Although they were in the minority, their wish was granted and were retained as faculties. These included the Faculty of Arts, Faculty of Veterinary Medicine, and the Faculty of Agriculture.

We sent a very clear message to the rest of the staff, that it was not going to be business as usual and the status quo was definitely not going to be maintained. Change was inevitable and was the only way to ensure future sustainability. The University Council chaired by Dr. Simba, as the oversight and policy making body fully supported the decisions of the management. After a short while most of the sceptics were won over, and for the first time most of the felt empowered and responsible for, and proud of the positive changes. I noticed that they were enjoying their work and performing way above their targets, enabling the changes to be noticed by external stakeholders.

Student behaviour improved greatly as a result of the regular engagement between their leaders and the University management including the offices of the Dean of Students and the special students advisor. The office of the Dean was devolved to the college level, with an office of assistant dean of students in each college. This behaviour improved further, upon the establishment of the office of the DVC in charge of Student Affairs. Student disciplinary proceedings were attended by students' union leaders, in order to ensure fairplay and protection of students' rights. Punishment was given according to the severity of the offence. For example, any student who was found guilty of cheating in examinations was discontinued but with an opportunity to appeal. Those whose offenses could not be proved beyond reasonable doubt during the disciplinary proceedings were counselled and allowed to return to class.

Change is always resisted. To say that I did not meet opposition to my transformative change agenda at the University would not be true. For instance, at the beginning of my tenure I encountered considerable opposition from a small section of staff which almost progressed to open rebellion. This opposition was especially with more vitriol and hostility from a sizable number of very senior academic staff, mainly professors who rightly thought they were the custodians of the University's ethos and culture. How could I even dare to effect any such drastic changes? Who did I think I was? After all to them I was truthfully much younger and relatively inexperienced as compared to their many years of 'professorship and experience'.

Indeed, I had only been a full professor for five years as compared to 10 to 15 years for most of them. Furthermore, other VCs supposedly more 'senior and superior' than me had served their terms at the pleasure of the Chancellor and left. In the same vein therefore I would also serve my term and leave. In other words they believed that VCs come and go, while they remained permanently stationed in their academic and administrative positions until they retired. In their opinion therefore, I had absolutely no right whatsoever to divert them from the known, proven, comfortable and culturally acceptable path that they were very familiar with. I had no business trying to chart for them a new path leading to the unfamiliar and unknown future. After all, I had no political godfather, and so they saw me as just a passing cloud full of steam which would soon fizzle out.

My transformative change agenda had however come to stay and failure was definitely not going to be an option. I decided not to be combative but firmly persuasive and resilient. In addition to relying on lots of prayer, divine guidance and intervention, I went back to basics and remembered what I was taught by my parents in my formative years. But what formed the backbone of my confidence and resilience was what I was taught at Starehe. I recalled vividly, the aim of Starehe which I applied to the letter in my management of the opposition from staff and students. First of all I gave them due respect by listening to their opinions before very firmly putting my case across. Inevitable change, in my view was the only constant. I incorporated their positive opinions in our change strategy, and this empowered them, while making them feel part of the change team. Since I humbled myself before them but remained strong and resolute in my strategy for positive transformative change, their opposition mellowed down and eventually fizzled out completely. For example, the fact that I personally went to the students' hostels on many occasions to repair, paint and clean the deplorable toilets definitely softened their resistance. I also insisted on timeliness and availability for duty without fail, fear or favour. They began to understand that I just wanted a better University, and was therefore more of a servant leader. Unknown to them, I was simply going the 'extra mile' and applying what I had learned at Starehe. Eventually, this successfully changed their mind-sets, making us one big transformative team.

Whenever I had challenges in making very difficult decisions with far-reaching consequences, I would sleep over them, and consult widely from senior university professors such as: Professor Muriuki who was the longest serving member of the University Senate and therefore had acquired tremendous and useful experience in dealing with students, staff, and academic matters; Professor Kyambi who had served in the University Council for many years, Professor Joseph Oliech, and Professor Mutahi who was then the Permanent Secretary in the Ministry of Education. Professor Oliech was particularly useful as he had previously served as the Director of Medical Services, at the Ministry of Health, placing him in very good stead to offer useful advice based on his practical experience in dealing with many different categories of health workers, patient stakeholders countrywide and the general public. I also regularly consulted the three available former VCs; Professors Mungai, Gichaga, and Kyamba who had invaluable practical experiences for me to learn and emulate. Professor Gichaga's experience was particularly instrumental with regard to my successful management of Module II academic programmes which was his brainchild.

My great mentor, Dr. Griffin also advised me regularly until his death in 2005. In addition, I always prayed and regularly listened to classical music especially by Wolfgang Amadeus Mozart. Music always had a way of calming me down. I would also regularly brisk walk, and occasionally jog in order to clear my mind before making any major decisions. Once in a while I played basketball with my son Michael in our home in Lavington, Nairobi when time allowed. Being a father helped me relax and have a clear thinking and decision making process. In fact, sometimes I retreated to my rural home for a few days, where I would tend to my cows and plant some trees to clear my mind.

The Stanford Experience

In 2006, two years after I had assumed office as VC, the Chancellor, broached the idea that I enrol in an executive programme at Stanford University. Because it was just a suggestion, I did not immediately take it up. However, Dr. Wanjui was persistent. He had also attended the programme in 1983 and believed that I would gain value from attending it.

The Stanford programme brought together leaders and Chief Executive Officers from all over the world, not only to learn new things but also to share experiences, good corporate governance and best practices. Indeed, Dr. Wanjui narrated the advantages of the programme and how it improved his management skills beyond his expectations, impacting a positive shift in the trajectory of his career. He emphasized that many successful leaders, who wanted to transform their thinking and that of their institutions had attended this programme with measurable results. I therefore applied for the June 2009 intake. The programme was very expensive and I am grateful to the University for covering the costs.

Before travelling to Stanford, I read several books on finance, accounting, operational and production chain management, and supply chain management in preparation for the programme.

I was well received at Stanford University in the US. The accommodation was very comfortable with a wide range of food available. The facilities for academic, sports and extracurricular engagement were also excellent. The daily schedule was very tight requiring that one manages their time optimally. The daily activities commenced at 6 a.m. with a session of physical exercises for about an hour. We were divided into two groups; one could choose to join the jogging group, or the brisk walking group. I chose the brisk walking and physical exercises group. Breakfast was served from 7 to 8 a.m., followed by lectures from 8 a.m. to

6 p.m., with lunch and tea breaks in between. This was followed by evening receptions where we were encouraged to network not only with our groups but also with the professors and various speakers, just before dinner at 7 p.m.

The climax of a typical day would be group discussions. It is from these discussions that I learnt and benefited most. We were divided into smaller discussion groups of 10 participants each to reflect a diversity of backgrounds and experiences. The primary purpose was for the group participants to discuss cases and readings in smaller face-to-face set ups, in preparation for the larger classes the next day. The groups also provided participants with an excellent informal setting in which to learn from each other, and share experiences and best practices. Learning from the experiences of others was one of the most important benefits that I gained from attending the Stanford Executive Program (SEP 2009). My goal was to return to the University of Nairobi and run it efficiently as a business entity. Everybody's viewpoint was considered and discussed equally in these groups. The take-home point for me was to listen equally to all my managers, team members and staff with greater attention in order to understand their viewpoints and reap maximum benefits from their contributions as 'might does not always make right'. My practice of not being the 'boss' or a technical star, but rather a first among equals in the management team emanated from the discussions and had a phenomenal impact on my transformational role at the University. The four problem solving steps involved: determining that there is a problem, and accurately defining it; exploring various alternatives and evaluating them; making a decision; and implementing the solutions, formed the core of our learning from each other's experiences.

The Dean of Stanford Graduate School of Business, Professor Robert Joss had roots in industry, having worked in diverse corporations in various positions including: Vice Chairman Wells Fargo Bank in San Francisco, Chief Executive Officer and Managing Director of Westpac Banking Cooperation. The faculty of the Stanford Executive Program comprised exclusively of senior staff of the Stanford Graduate School of Business, consisting of 30 full time professors, 17 guest professors and speakers from the industry. Outside of their normal duties as researchers, many actively engaged in the management and mentorship of some of the world's leading companies and industries. They included: Robert Burgleman, David Kreps, George Foster, Charles O'Reilly, Jeffrey Pfeffer (all professors of management), James Patel, professor of supply chain management and public and private management, William Barnett, professor of business leadership, strategy and organizations, Francis Flynn, Roderick Kramer, and Hayagriva Rao, professors of organizational behaviour, Edward Leazar, professor of human resources, management and economics, Kathryn Shaw, David Saloner, professors of economics, and Margaret Neale, professor of organizations and dispute resolution, among others.

Guest lecturers included: George Shultz, professor of international economics who also served as the sixtieth, Secretary of State, of the US, William Perry, professor of engineering and an expert in US foreign policy, national security and arms control who also served as the nineteenth Secretary for Defence in the US, and Condoleza Rice, professor of political economy and public policy who also served as sixty sixth Secretary of State of the US.

My group consisted of 88 accomplished participants, at the peak of their careers, from across the world. All were top managers, most of whom had earned their MBA degrees, and included Chief Executive Officers of various companies, industries and organizations. They also came from very diverse professional backgrounds including ICT, corporate development, operations production, finance, accounting and banking, human resources, research and development, universities among others. For purposes of effective teaching, we were divided into three equal groups and taught separately by an excellent group of professors.

Our morning exercise programme was linked to a series of four lectures entitled, 'The effect of health on successes'. This was applied to the various organizations and individuals represented with a main emphasis on the significance and impact of good health on the performance of CEOs and their institutions. I was particularly excited by the elaboration on business simulation laboratory, capacity management, business process designs and delay, congestion and delay in business processes. I believe that these are all critically relevant to the improvement of service delivery at the University. Indeed, when I applied the details to the University of Nairobi, I could immediately see where the bottlenecks were and what needed to be effected to correct them.

The discussions on accounting for valuation and control, and managerial accounting were critical because financial management was one of the critical areas at the University that continually needed attention. We also discussed various options and derivatives in modern corporate finance, coupled with sound financial management, and the creation of value and shared experiences and best practices. Lectures on strategic leadership in dynamic environments and global growth strategies impacted new knowledge to me that would later be very instrumental for the achievement of the mission and vision of the University of Nairobi. For instance, the lessons and discussions on the global context of management, profiting from evidence based management, executive decision making, and how leaders use power effectively, were relevant in the management of the University. As a CEO, it was refreshing to listen to and discuss the lecture on 'winning through innovation'. Perhaps it motivated my decision, when I later returned to Nairobi, to convince the Council to create the position of DVC in charge of Research, Production and Extension. It is no accident therefore that the University of Nairobi's digital repository and policies on research, innovation, plagiarism, open access, intellectual property, communications, extension and outreach, and human resources were developed as a result of this training.

At Stanford, it was emphasized that a CEO should pursue a sound market strategy and the delivery of customer value through marketing. From discussions centred on customer-based brand equity, brand strategy, and strategic brand management leading to strong branding and the building of market focus through tough times, we shared best practices and personal experiences on the values of a strong brand and the concept of global branding. This was very critical because when I returned, I embarked on redesigning the University flag which I had created two years earlier. I also settled on the University logo to be embedded on our colour to form the University standard which would fly alongside the national flag. I further focused on the quality of products and graduates by ensuring adequate improvement in infrastructure and equipment necessary for their production. The most tangible result of this is the actualization of the University of Nairobi Towers.

My experience at Stanford, especially on the concept of attracting and retaining strategic core staff was particularly pertinent and useful to the University. For example, on return I immediately embarked on identifying, recruiting and retaining the core staff that I deemed essential for our vision and mission, and development strategies. Further, I retrained and ring-fenced other staff already within the institution. The concept inspired and encouraged me to re-hire the very efficient and strategic senior staff who had retired, on contracts of one or two years, renewable, based on performance outputs. Employee relationships and particularly empowerment, trust and motivation were key to attracting and retaining staff.

The concept of the University of Nairobi Alumni Centre also emanated from my experience at the SEP. The idea was adopted well by the chairperson of UONAA, Dr. Betty Gikonyo who vigorously pursued the strategy. All the architectural drawings are complete and the process is at the fundraising stage with the University having donated the land upon which the Centre will be built.

CHAPTER FIVE

SERVANT LEADERSHIP

What is leadership and who is a leader? Are leaders born or made? Leadership is a position of authority and influence which enables an individual to exercise power and control in the entities that they guide or control. Leadership can either be democratic through plebiscite; competitive through advertisement, shortlisting and interviews; selection by private and public entities or professional consultations; and by civilian or military dictatorships, for example, the case of military *coup d'états*.

One could become a leader by choice through either competition or selection. Leadership could also be forced on an individual as the case where junior army officers carry out a coup and thereafter install an unwilling senior army officer to lead them. In both instances, the leader exercises authority, power and control over his juniors. Whether one is a team leader depends on whether he or she is able to form a team. The question is, were the team members voluntarily sought or just conscripted thereby leading to the formation of a group rather than a team?

A dilemma that faces leaders is if the position of leadership has been imposed on them, can they lead without knowing what to do and how to work with their followers? This leads us to the big question of whether leaders are born, made or both.

The job of leading an organization such as a university is quite challenging and complex. Inevitably, it is rational for one to argue that it is unreasonable to expect any individual to be born with all the requisite leadership qualities to enable him or her become an effective leader. Therefore, some of the leadership qualities may actually be acquired through nurturing and development, while others are acquired through experience.

There are those who argue that an effective leader must have some innate characteristics and qualities. Indeed, the concept of extraversion is consistently associated with how to get strong leaders into positions and with the leader's effectiveness. Certain personality traits including authority with high energy, possession of exceptional intelligence, assertiveness and self-confidence, extreme persistence, boldness and risk taking, high general IQ, and physical attractiveness, and demeanour have been strongly associated with smart and effective leadership. Other innate characteristics such as vision, honesty, humility and empathy are deemed critical for strong and effective leadership. Such leaders must also possess the initiative and smartness for analysing complex management situations and making informed decisions and possess an innate desire and drive to lead. Such a leader must be accepted by their followers and have the ability to listen to team members and recognize their contributions in a natural and an unpatronizing manner.

In reflecting on whether leaders are born or made, I believe that while possessing the genes for leadership provides definite advantages on leadership, on its own it is insufficient for propelling one into strong and effective leadership. Holistic leaders in addition, are developed or honed through hard and consistent work. This means that leaders can be taught or learn their duties as long as the innate minimum requirement is present. Leadership can be learned and nurtured through skills development and commitment, role models and personal experience. The title 'leader' alone does not make one a leader. I am convinced that while there may be a bit of leadership traits everyone, it does not necessarily make them leaders. I strongly submit that effective leaders are both born and made, in equal measure. Lawrence J. Peter, a Canadian writer, formulated the Peter Principle in 1969. His assertion was that in a hierarchy where there is learning, training and experience, every employee tends to rise to his level of incompetence. This suggests that leadership is not possible for all despite their desire or training. The question is, can everyone lead given the opportunity? My answer is no. Not everybody has the innate intelligence, the desire and the drive to lead. That is, despite all the learning, training and experience the individual may possess, without the innate component of leadership, he cannot be a strong and effective leader.

When I was appointed VC I considered myself a holistic leader, possessing the innate characteristics necessary to lead in addition to the acquired and learned requisite experience. As the team leader, I immediately embarked on the process of building a formidable team. I encountered numerous challenges especially at the beginning. The challenges were mainly due to institutional culture. Culture can kill even the best strategy. I found in place large groups of managers in the UMB and the University Senate. My first challenge was whether or not to reconstitute the membership of the two management organs or to work with the staff I found. The organs functioned like two large groups rather than teams, and were used to the 'status quo' attitude. For example, Senate meetings would usually take a whole day commencing at 9.30 a.m. through lunch break, to about 3.30 p.m. or even later. Currently, Senate meetings start much earlier and business is completed by about 10.30 a.m., enabling the managers to perform other equally important University duties, for the remaining part of the day.

After all considerations including wide consultation and prayer, I decided that it was in the best interest of the University to work with the teams that I found in place. Since I already had clear strategies and goals to where I wanted to take the University, I felt that in order to build an effective transformative team I had to change the mind-sets of the individual team members in both the Senate and the UMB. I had already been exposed to the reality that leaders have a big role to play in changing mind-sets. However, I must admit that at the beginning it was quite difficult to change the mind-set of managers. For example, to request members to commence management meetings at 7 a.m. instead of the usual 9.30 a.m., and to complete the meetings by 10.30 a.m. was not easy.

I arranged for systematic training of the managers in groups and individually by various professional experts. Further, we empowered individuals to feel that their views were as important as those of the team leader. I frequently explained to the team that I was just their colleague, 'a first among equals'.

The University community is an academic community used to debate and therefore I accorded them ample time to air their views without hindrance. If I had not gone this way, perhaps I would have been viewed as a conspirator and a prejudiced individual. These actions invariably softened their hard stands and we started functioning as an effective transformative team rather than groups.

It is important to note however, that there were a few members who proved very difficult to convince to join-in. They represented only about five per cent and it would have been easy to just ignore them. Nevertheless, I continued to listen to their opinions without prejudice and adopted those that were constructive to management decisions. Unfortunately, most of the time, their views were directly at variance with the strategic plan. It was as if they did not want the management team to move forward successfully. A secondary challenge arose as to whether they should be replaced. I decided against this and continued to work with them to the completion of my ten-year term. After all, diversity is the hallmark of Kenya.

I can recall a very painful incident in which I needed to routinely replace a chairman of an academic department. It happened that the said chairman had completed the mandatory two of the three-year terms. The college principal and dean of the relevant faculty had strongly recommended another professor for appointment to the chairmanship of the department as was practice. I proceeded to appoint the nominee chairman, but he dramatically declined with no valid reasons. On further investigations I discovered that he was working on private consultancies outside the University, utilizing University time and therefore could not spare time to serve as an effective chairman of a department. We asked him to either substantially reduce his private consultancies to a level that would enable him work at the University as the main employer, or leave altogether. He did neither and after due process, was removed from the University service for neglect of duty.

Normally, teaching staff are allowed to engage in part time private practice or consultancies so long as these are carried out in one's free time as they benefit the staff as well as the University. However, this must always be balanced and ultimately the University should derive the greatest benefit.

One may argue that I was either dictatorial or coercive in my management style. However, my strategies and goals for the change management at the University were directly opposite. I strongly believe that I was neither dictatorial nor coercive in this situation or any other during my tenure as VC. What I did, which was part of my defined duties as the chief academic and administrative officer of the University, was to use my very firm but soft persuasion skills to ensure that staff carried out their assigned duties. This method was very effective in many other instances. It is only when a staff member refused to learn from their mistakes that firm disciplinary process and removal from the University was effected.

Outside the established University management teams, few staff actually actively resisted changes to the status quo. These were used to doing very little work, seemingly spending most of their time working elsewhere and thus did not feel accountable to anyone. It was common for some to show up at the University for their lecture hours after which they would disappear. They were therefore not available to mentor the students as required. When we insisted that they must be available and that they pin on their office doors the days and hours they were available for consultation, they resulted to name calling. They went as far as blackmailing me through writing petitions to the government and other external stakeholders.

This state of affairs was totally unacceptable and we ensured that it stopped. In order to deal with it effectively, I retreated to the UMB and the Senate. It was extremely important for my team members to fully understand and own the intended tough action plan in firmly dealing with such staff. At the UMB, there was consensus that firm action had to be taken as long as it was within the University statutes and terms of service. The University was definitely not going to turn round unless I rallied everyone on board. The Senate was very supportive of our intended actions. Having secured the full support of my top management organs, we firmly proceeded with decisions which objectively instilled institutional discipline and eventually propelled the University to its current world class excellence status.

The students and SONU were known for all the wrong reasons including rioting, blocking major highways, destroying public property and sometimes even commandeering public transport vehicles. The greatest downside for the University was the habit of some students while on legitimate academic or social expeditions outside Nairobi, to loot from shops, restaurants and hotels. In other instances students would mount illegal roadblocks, stone and extort money from motorists just because of temporary power blackouts, some of which ironically were occasioned by their illegal connections and unauthorized cooking in the halls of residence. This behaviour resulted in disruption of academic calendars. This uncontrolled indiscipline by students had to stop.

The management therefore set out to train all the incoming student leaders including SONU Executive and Congress on good corporate governance, financial management and accountability and the University's vision, mission, core values and strategic plan among others. During these interactive trainings, students were told in no uncertain terms that their behaviour was not only unacceptable but also was giving the University a very bad image. They were also warned that in future, there would be severe disciplinary consequences as per the statutes. This dialogue approach was further strengthened by the establishment of the office of DVC Student Affairs, to specifically mainstream and address student affairs at the University. The effects of all this firmness in dealing with students was phenomenal. There was tremendous improvement in student behaviour which resulted in the restoration of public confidence in the University. Most important was the fact that the University never lost any academic time as a result of closure during the ten years of my stewardship as CEO. As a matter of fact, I held 21 successful graduation ceremonies, graduating over 95,000 graduands in ten years. This number was greater than the total number graduated from the University during the previous 40 years, which was only 70,000.

Dealing with the three staff trade unions: the University Academic Staff Union (UASU), the Universities Non-Teaching Staff Union (UNTESU) and the junior staff, the Kenya Union of Domestic, Hostels, Educational Institutions, Hospitals and Allied workers (KUDHEIHA) separately was also a substantial challenge to my leadership acumen and style. We had valid and legal discussions and signed Collective Bargaining Agreements (CBAs) with them separately. This challenge was made worse by freedoms brought by the new Kenya Constitution 2010, which protected all manner of picketing under the law. I had therefore to continuously engage the three trade unions separately in negotiations. I had earlier been trained in negotiating skills by FKE, and the International Labour Organization (ILO) in Geneva, Switzerland. These skills came in handy as we were able to negotiate fruitfully over the years despite the several short strikes called, which fortunately did not affect the University's academic calendar.

However, one of the most trying times of my leadership was when I had to make a decision as to whether or not to forcefully break up the noisy picketing that involved the violent flushing out of University workers from their work stations and offices. Sanity and restraint prevailed upon me and my managers and continuous dialogue prevailed with good results. But perhaps the most difficult decision which I had to make as a University leader and VC was not to close the University after I had been given the go-ahead to do the same by the Senate and the Council, and government.

An effective leader must at times make the final decision by biting the bullet. This happened to me on several occasions, but the most memorable one is when there was a nationwide strike of all public universities as a result of industrial action by staff. Although other universities had closed, I kept the University of Nairobi open and operating normally, due to the continuous dialogue with staff. I insisted that all staff had to sign in on reporting and on leaving work. This worked very well and we decided not to punish the few staff that did not report to work. I learned that wisdom and tolerance, together with tough decision making were great virtues in leadership.

A common ploy used by leaders is having a political godfather, to assist them in every move. I was different. I strongly believed that I did not need a godfather to carry out my duties, as they were clearly defined by University statutes and the Council. In order to exploit my full leadership potential, I needed to operate with a reasonable degree of autonomy. This environment was provided by the government through the Ministry of Education, Science and Technology which did not unduly interfere with University affairs while exercising its legitimate oversight authority. I worked very well with Professors Mutahi as Permanent Secretary and Kiamba. However, the attempts by some government officers to influence the running of the University were vigorously resisted.

I survived the ten years despite having served under seven Cabinet Ministers. Both Presidents Mwai Kibaki, and Uhuru Kenyatta did not interfere with the running of the University. The government judged me on the basis of the results of impressive measurable outputs. Indeed they recognized my change leadership potential and was awarded two State Honours: Moran of the Order of the Burning Spear (MBS in 2005), and Elder of the Burning Spear (EBS in 2006), during the first two years of my tenure as VC.

From my point of view, I was taught the significance of servant leadership right from my early years as a prefect at Starehe and a student leader at Strathmore. I was also an international student leader while studying medicine at the University of Lagos and doctors' leader of the Nigerian Resident Doctors Association while at the Lagos University Teaching Hospital. Therefore, I had a reasonable stint at leadership albeit at lower levels before being appointed the VC. Furthermore, I had moved through all the ranks of leadership having been Chairman of the Department of Surgery, Dean of the Faculty of Medicine, Principal of the College of Health Sciences, and DVC, Administration and Finance. I was therefore not entirely new to leadership and management by the time I was appointed VC. I found it prudent in my leadership role to accept my mistakes and absolutely normal to be corrected by team members. This is because I learned, over the years that strong and effective leaders accept their mistakes and learn from them.

As a transformative team leader, the ability to involve all staff eventually endeared me to the members of my core management teams, the UMB and the Senate. This was extremely significant as we had to cascade the new leadership style and team discipline to all the six colleges, SWA, and Central Units of the University. Within the colleges, cascading was to be effected to faculties, institutes, schools, centres, departments and other administrative units. The cascading was to be effected by members of the UMB and the Senate including college principals, deans of faculties and schools, directors of institutes, centres and SWA, chairmen of academic departments, and heads of non-academic units of the University.

I thoroughly enjoyed my job and despite its challenges, at no time during the ten years did I regret taking it up. What is important also is the fact that my team members, workers, stakeholders both local and international, professional colleagues and the public at large regarded me as an effective transformative leader based on the measurable outcomes of my leadership. My leadership style succeeded because it was always based on consultation. I had two formidable management teams that owned all my decisions: the UMB, and the Senate. I also regularly consulted the Council on whose behalf I managed the University, and occasionally the government, through the Ministry of Education. My success was as a 'team leader and not as an individual'.

Did my leadership style succeed? Yes it did because the University of Nairobi has transformed to world class excellence. I attribute this success to our staff, students, and other stakeholders who understood that we meant 'University business and not personal business'. My parting message as a leader was very clear – that all staff and students irrespective of their rank, ethnicity, colour or creed played significant roles in transforming the University to its current status. A leader must not be judged by the number of years in leadership, but by the tangible achievements attained irrespective of the leadership period.

CHAPTER SIX

My Ten-Year Agenda as Vice-Chancellor

The University of Nairobi is mandated to provide tertiary education and training in Kenya in addition to research, innovation, transmission, preservation and extension of knowledge, and community service. My immediate agenda after being sworn in as the VC included the formation of cohesive and formidable management teams.

My teams and I embarked on the difficult and challenging process of transforming the University. Inevitably, our work culture had to change in order to use the laid out strategies to achieve the set goals. Firm and objective persuasion, inclusion, perseverance and role modelling by the already trained members of the change management teams, were some of the strategies that we used to change the University culture. Hard tackle was only applied to less than five per cent members who took more time to be convinced that change management had come to stay, and that the status quo was not an option.

Since its inception, the University of Nairobi had not developed a strategic plan. After my appointment therefore, one of the most urgent tasks given to me by the Council, was to urgently formulate the strategic plan. From the beginning, we realised that we could not effect any tangible and meaningful changes without a plan. We therefore vigorously pursued this task for three months and by the beginning of May 2005, we had the plan approved by the Council and ready for implementation. By the time I was completing my tenure of service in January 2015, the plan had been reviewed twice to cover the period up to 2018.

Another important organ that was missing at the University was an alumni association. The prominent and top-grade paediatric cardiologist and entrepreneur, Dr. Betty Gikonyo agreed to serve as the founding chairperson of UONAA. She worked very hard and established many professional Alumni Chapters, in the six colleges of the University. UONAA became a very significant stakeholder and partner in the change management process during the ten years of my stewardship. The association established an annual prize award as well as a Bursary Fund of Kshs 2 million to assist needy but bright students.

Restoring Institutional Discipline

As part of the challenge to achieve world class excellence, I focused on institutional discipline for successful implementation of the strategies and goals. This was because the University is blessed with excellent academic staff with the ability to carry out some of the best cutting-edge research in this country and beyond. However, the challenge was that some lecturers were missing classes and unavailable for consultation. It was important therefore to address this matter. We insisted that all lecturers follow the timetable, and be available for staff meetings. We also ensured that there were no more rescheduled or make-up lectures. Institutionalising statutory timelines assisted in ensuring that slacking lecturers reduced while missed lectures became a thing of the past.

While it is true that no other University in Kenya has even a third of the professors and associate professors at the University of Nairobi, when I took over the mantle of leadership it was also true that the numbers were not adequate. It became urgent therefore to sort out the matter by implementing the already existing statutory staff levels. At the time, there were 95 full professors and 126 associate professors at the University. On the completion of my term as VC, we had increased the numbers to 154 professors and 253 associate professors. With the presence of this kind of excellent locally and internationally trained academic staff, all that was required was a firm, objective and transformative leader to persuade them to be part of the larger team implementing the University's strategic plan.

We effected this process by providing the beacons and then encouraging and empowering staff to actively participate. As a result, more staff were available for academic duties beyond the statutory prescribed time. I am proud to state that we started to see many academic staff working well beyond the official working hours in order to complete specific academic and research related tasks. What inspired me further was that the majority of staff were happy and enjoying their work.

Majority of the non-teaching staff were qualified and suitable for their different tasks. However, they were also not available for duty. There was late reporting, leaving early, and some even employing underhand tactics such as disappearing but leaving coats, ties or handbags in the office as a guise that they were around. They seemed to be carrying out personal businesses, during University's time. To curb these tendencies, we essentially set firm and strict compliance measures with established timelines for different cadres.

In terms of professional capacity and general attitude, there were, in a few critical areas such as the finance department a few people in management who were not qualified. Many in this group had abandoned their accountancy training either shortly after enrolling or midway, and therefore did not understand the current international accounting standards. Such staff were redeployed to positions requiring less professional accounting responsibilities without any financial disadvantage. This enabled us to competitively seek, employ and retain some of the best accountants.

I also took the opportunity to confirm the appointment of the Chief Finance Officer, Mr. Karue, and the Chief Internal Auditor, Mr. Igiria, both of whom were in acting capacities. The new look finance and audit departments were mandated to urgently revise and implement the University fiscal regulations which would form the basis of all future financial and procurement transactions. The financial regulations would ensure that the University was run professionally, according to the University of Nairobi Act of 1985, the Universities Act of 2012 and the University of Nairobi Charter 2013, the Exchequer and Audit Act, and the State Corporations Act, and other government financial regulations and guidelines as issued from time to time as well as international accounting standards. Simply put, there would be no more expenditure without proper justification and availability of funds. There would also be authority to incur expenditure executed by the account holder and no goods and services would be procured without strict adherence to the Procurement Act of 2005 and the Procurement Regulations of 2006. Furthermore, goods would no longer be received prior to professional inspection, and payment would be made only after ascertaining the delivery of quality goods and services.

Proper financial discipline would not have succeeded without the establishment of an audit committee of Council for fiduciary oversight. For nine out of my ten years as VC this committee was chaired by very competent members of Council, who were accounting professionals with long experience. The first Chairman was Mr. Davidson, the next one was Mr. Awuondo, the third one was Mr. Kitili Mbathi, and the fourth Mr. Hamisi Dena. The audit committee whose membership also included the University's Chief Internal Auditor, Mr. Igiria, provided very competent oversight and ensured that the University was managed professionally.

When I was appointed the VC, the University had dilapidated structures, due to lack of or poor maintenance mainly as a result of severe fiscal constraints. The constraints were occasioned partly by chronic underfunding by the exchequer, inability by the University to raise enough money from the full fee paying Module II programmes, and inadequate financial controls. Further, the University was in debt of about Kshs 2 billion, and also lacked adequate, accurate, timely and reliable financial data to assist the management in effective decision making. The institution operated on a rather scanty and multiple software programmes that had little impact on its quest to implement the strategic plan. It became necessary therefore to restructure the finance department into an efficient and functional unit, with the capacity to provide reliable financial data that would assist in decision making processes. One of the first challenges I faced was devising a strategy to electronically monitor financial transactions and grow earnings from Module II students through a planned strategic expansion of market driven courses including business, law and medicine; encourage consultancy; mainstream research; and continue lobbying the government for increased capitation.

In order to implement the strategy of electronically monitoring all our financial transactions, we had to search for a suitable financial system. We embarked on an international tender to procure a computerized FMIS. It is important to note that we had floated a local tender and the offers presented were three times higher than the cost of the same system acquired through an international tender. Dr. SK Macharia was the Chairman of the tender committee then and he advised us to go for an international tender. The advice was approved by the Council and implemented by management.

The University consequently implemented the FMIS in 2007. This is a system that computerizes the financial and accounting functions, and manages all aspects of budgetary, general ledger, accounts receivable and payable, bank reconciliation, cash flow management, inventory control, and the preparation of the annual final statement of accounts. The system was integrated with the in-house programmes such as: Students Management Information System (SMIS), and the Human Resource Management Information System (HRMIS) to make the process of data harnessing and collation as smooth and transparent as possible. Prior to acquisition, of the FMIS, staff from the finance department and the ICT Centre were sent to London for training on how to use the software. In order to enhance its performance, the software was upgraded in 2013 after seven years of application. The new version allowed for integration with other University in-house software, and enabled upgrade of the database to a higher version for easier administration. This therefore enabled the University to merge main data and financial data resulting in substantial savings for the institution.

The University accrued many other benefits from the financial programme. The system for instance, tremendously improved the financial operations and the quality of reporting framework within the University. It also eliminated the risk environment associated with financial malpractices as it had inbuilt control systems. The system also resulted in faster and efficient processing of financial documents and payments within a strong and flexible financial management of both income and expenditure functions. It also greatly improved and enhanced bank reconciliation processes in the University, and enabled efficient and prompt preparation of University end of year audited accounts among many other functions. Consequently, the University evolved to be among the top institutions with an effective and efficient finance department in the country, and the East African region.

With the successful implementation of the computerized fiancial system I, the accounting officer of the University was finally able to electronically monitor all financial transactions from anywhere.

One of the most important and guiding documents for the University is the calendar which contains all relevant annual information about the University, including the Almanac. The calendar was being produced once every two to three years. This situation was occasioned by financial constraints. I observed that if I wanted adequate planning, local and international visibility, I would have to ensure that the calendar was produced every academic year, with a revised Almanac for every year and any other important changes and events in the University captured at the same time. As a result, there was enhanced staff confidence and strict adherence to the Almanac.

While the HRMIS was developed in 2000, six upgrading enhancements took place during my tenure as VC. This system which was the first computerized information system to be developed and implemented under the Oracle Relational Database

Management System (RDBMS) improved the decision making processes at the University, enabled efficient management of University personnel records, enhanced the timely production of University budgetary estimates, and enabled efficient and effective processing of the payroll and payslips. This directly resulted in reduced expenditure on operational costs on payroll processing and overtime which was immensely beneficial to the University. It also enabled and enhanced the production of P9 forms for submission to KRA, and for the staff, the efficient processing of leave applications.

During my first term in office, we developed and implemented the University of Nairobi Service Charter. The principal aim of the Charter was to guide and enable the University to excel in teaching, research, scholarship, consultancy, community service, good governance and management. This was the first Service Charter to be developed by the University of Nairobi and it was a commitment to deliver high quality service to staff, students, research collaborators, donors, other stakeholders and the general public. It was a holistic and very important document which the university community was expected to actualize and fully comply with in the performance of their duties. For instance, it addressed the management of time by staff thereby solving the chronic lateness and early departures from work.

Previously, the University had experienced the loss of many man hours and reduction of productivity leading to poor performance. One feature of the Service Charter was the introduction of the annual Staff Performance Appraisal. This appraisal, conducted between October and March of every academic year, ensured that all staff were accountable for their work on a yearly basis. The lecturers would not only be appraised by their peers and management, but also by their students. Another feature of the Charter was that staff and student clearances were to be finalized within two working days, and the finance department ensured strict adherence to all financial regulations and procedures, budgetary provisions, and processing approved payments within three days.

The Charter also provided for routine correspondence to be replied to within seven days, and all telephone calls to be answered to within 20 seconds. Its implementation added new impetus and further invigorated the University as it started functioning efficiently devoid of the usual public service bureaucracy. The Charter also provided for feedback, particularly important with regard to external stakeholders including research collaborators, donors, industry and linkage partners, universities, UONAA, trade unions and government departments.

The ISO 9001:2008 Standard Certification

In 2007 the University embarked on the ISO Certification process and identified KEBS to lead the process. All staff were sensitised by ISO Standard professionals from KEBS, followed by the training of 64 Internal Quality Auditors. After due process, KEBS awarded the University the ISO 9001 Standard Certification in July 2008. The University developed a Quality Management System (QMS), which has been rectified twice, as per the requirements of the ISO 9001 Standard. In April 2009, the University reviewed its QMS in order to comply with the ISO 9001:2008 Standard. In April 2010, an assessment of the long term sustainability of the QMS was undertaken while its comprehensive review was done in March 2011. Over the last seven years, the QMS has gone through pre-certification; two re-certifications and nine surveillance audits conducted by KEBS, and 13 internal quality audits. This is in addition to training 114 internal quality auditors.

The implementation of the ISO 9001:2008 Standard resulted in increased and significant benefits, identified through regular internal surveillance and certification audits conducted by KEBS, surveys and feedback within the University, and ranking by external bodies such as Webometrics and the government through Performance Contracting assessments. The achievements of the University as a result of ISO 9001 Certification are in relation to improved effectiveness on service delivery, operational performance, and use of automation, among others.

Key growth areas over the period that the University has been ISO 9001 certified include: increased student enrolment and graduations, increase in the diversity of curricula offered, content and delivery; revenue enhancement; staff retention; increased research funding and output; improved international ranking; new collaborations and linkages; and increased asset base. For instance, the fixed asset value of the University at the time I was leaving office in January 2015 was Kshs 120 billion, compared to Kshs 20 billion when I assumed office.

Some of the other achievements include: the inculcation of a culture of quality in both staff and students; improved staff competence, morale and ownership, improved work environment for both staff and students; improved work environment satisfaction index from 66 per cent in 2010 to 96 per cent in 2014, increased use of ICT as a prime mover for performance; consistency in documentation with improved document and record management across the entire University; increased customer satisfaction; improved student satisfaction index improved from 77 per cent in 2010 to 91 per cent in 2014; increase in the employee satisfaction index from 64 per cent in 2010 to 79 per cent in 2014; improved infrastructure and facilities; effective and efficient maintenance of various equipment in laboratories, workshops and theatres with regular calibration; and servicing, across the entire University.

The institutionalization of quality into the University processes saw it win various international awards and recognitions including recognition and award of the Commonwealth for the University of Nairobi Calendar, and Website in 2010; declaration of the College of Health Sciences as a Centre of Excellence in health training institutions in East Africa in 2013; and the School of Law's victory at the Africa Moot Court competition in 2014.

The ISO 9001 Certification also resulted in improved branding, visibility, ranking and benchmarking with other local and international universities. By the completion of my tenure, the University had achieved improved rankings locally, regionally and internationally, for example being ranked number one in Kenya and East Africa; number seven in Africa, and 855 globally among 23,000 Universities. The ranking was done by the Webometrics.

Reports submitted to the National Ethics and Anti-Corruption Commission indicated the significant contribution that the QMS had made towards promoting integrity, combating and preventing corruption within the University of Nairobi. From the foregoing, it is very clear that one of the most important key drivers of the change management process at the University, and which led to my success as a transformative VC and CEO was the certification and successful implementation of the ISO 9001:2008 Standard.

Performance Contracting

Performance Contracting was introduced by the government in 2004, as one of the tools for enhancing service delivery in the public sector. The University of Nairobi has been on performance contract since the 2005/2006 financial year, meaning that for nine of the ten years of my tenure as VC, the University was on performance contract whose features include alignment of performance management system with national policies and development strategies which include institutional strategic plans. Other features include: performance measurements involving monitoring and evaluation; performance reporting; and a feedback mechanism including a reward and sanctions system.

The University Council has been on performance contract with the Government since 2005/2006. The practice up to 2012/2013 was that they would sign the performance contract which would then be passed on to the VC. During the implementation process, the VC and management would cascade the performance contract to the six colleges, SWA, and the central units within the University. These had their individual performance contracts which fed the management and Council targets, providing quarterly reports. All together they formed the Council's institutional quarterly reports to the government through the Ministry of Higher Education. This method improved performance at the University because the six college principals would actively compete among themselves and thereby surpass their set targets. They are ranked by management and rewarded or sanctioned during each performance cycle, depending on their performance.

The University of Nairobi has had a sterling performance during the performance contract evaluations and rankings by the government since commencement of the contracts. To start with, in the 2010/2011 performance contract results, the University emerged number 1 out of 178 state corporations and became the first public entity to attain the grade of 'Excellent' in the entire public service since the inception of performance contracting system in the public institutions. In the year before that, 2009/2010 the University occupied the third position, and in 2008/2009 it occupied position two in the state corporation category overall. In all the three years, the University consistently maintained first position among public Universities, and was the university of choice. Therefore the University of Nairobi has sustained excellence in the performance contracting process, resulting in tremendous benefits and efficiencies. Some of these benefits effected during my tenure as VC include the introduction of the Authority to Incur Expenditure (AIE) to effectively and efficiently control and manage the budgetary process; efficient fuel management through an electronic card system; implementation of Enterprise Resource Planning (ERP) system in finance; improved fees collection through implementation of Student Management Information System (SMIS); and the development of over ten new bean seed varieties by the College of Agriculture and Veterinary Sciences; reduced turn-around time for issuance of transcripts; ISO 9001:2008 Certification; the review of University of Nairobi Strategic Plan 2008–2013 in 2010; automation of various processes such as online hostels booking by students; provision of hotspots to eliminate physical data points; online leave application and approval; establishment of a drugs management system; increase in electronic library resources for both students and staff; and introduction of the use of power factor capacity banks to curb leakages in power consumption and reduce costs. The use of CCTV cameras in the University libraries and the central examination centre was introduced as a direct result of the performance contracting process, together with the use of Voice over Internet Protocol (VoIP), and the Very High Frequency (VHF) radio system for security and health services staff. Streamlining the management of motor vehicle repairs and partial outsourcing of cleaning and security services were also as a result of the performance contracting process.

Rapid Results Initiative (RRI)

The University underwent two Repid Results Initiatives (RRIs) during my tenure; one in 2007 and another in 2013. The RRIs were part of the government initiated Public Sector Reform Programme that emphasized high quality Results Based Management (RBM) within the shortest possible time. It was a result-focused approach that breaks down long term goals into 100 days results' commitments. In line with the University's of Strategic Plan 2005–2010, and as part of performance targets, staff were trained notably in the field of RBM. The process commenced with identification of critical thematic areas that required radical transformation to improve output and increase customer satisfaction. These areas included streamlining procurement by creating prompt and efficient processes; improving communication between staff, students and stakeholders; streamlining the issuance of transcripts; providing responsive student records; improving the use of ICT facilities; and revenue collection enhancement. These areas were critical to the University and were associated with serious drawbacks that impacted negatively on efficient service delivery. At the completion of the first 100 days RRI cycle, all objectives were achieved. The RRI therefore had three key benefits: improved performance results; new ways of accomplishing and sustaining results; and skills and confidence to scale up the initial results. All these benefits were crucial in my change management strategy.

The second 100 days RRI phase carried out was on the role of University in the implementation of the Kenya Constitution

(2010) and sensitization of the University community on the Public Service Integrity Program (PSIP). It was carried out from August to November 2013. This was done in partnership with the Commission for the Implementation of the Constitution (CIC), Ethics and Anti-Corruption Commission (EACC), and UONAA. Phase one of this RRI involved massive publicity including a high profile official launch by all the three participating entities and training of "Integrity Champions". Phase two involved college-based intensive sensitization, reporting, monitoring and evaluation. All staff, students and a sizable number of alumni participated and provided the necessary support that led to the successful implementation of the RRI.

On completion of the second RRI cycle, the University had made major strides in embracing the new Constitution. Over 200,000 hard and soft copies of the Constitution were distributed to all members of staff and students as a first step towards sensitization followed by alumni and other stakeholders.

University Open Day

The first open day for the University of Nairobi was held in 2008, at the Great Court. Since then, it has been held annually, with the last one in my tenure being in 2014. The principal aim was to create open forums of interaction between the University, its clients and stakeholders and accorded academic units including faculties, schools, institutes, centres, and departments an excellent opportunity to showcase their products, goods and services to stakeholders and members of the general public.

This day was also set aside for the University to give an account of itself, and strides taken since its inception. Other departments that exhibited during open days were those that play supportive roles in the achievement of the core functions of the University. They included admissions, library, bookshop, and welfare departments such as the dean of students, health services, accommodation, sports and games among others. This opened up the University to public scrutiny, and provided a channel for feedback. Some corporate organizations were invited to market their products and services and give career talks and opportunities.

The Examination Process

The examinations were perhaps the most important and challenging duties of a University lecturer. The students had to be adequately prepared before sitting an examination. However, there was definitely something wrong with the examination process at the University. The space allocated for examinations at the central administration block at the main campus of the University consisted of three small rooms which were later converted to the office of the DVC, Student Affairs. This space was grossly inadequate to allow sitting for examinations for about 30,000 students at the time I was appointed VC, and about 80,000 students at the end of my tenure.

The University had over 300 academic programmes and one can only imagine the congestion occasioned during the examinations. This was aggravated by the fact that professional proofreading of the examination scripts by teaching staff who are examination officers or coordinators is supposed to be camera-ready in order to avoid any leakages. Because of this inconvenience, some academic staff irregularly delegated the handling of examinations to non-teaching staff, including the proofreading process. This resulted in examination leakages. To deal with this, definite and urgent remedial action had to be instituted.

The other challenge within the examination process was that lecture theatres were not suitable for carrying out examinations for the large classes which had between 300 to 500 students. These large theatres were constructed in such a way that a student sitting behind another was at a higher pedestal and could therefore see what the one sitting in front was writing. The solution to this problem required the construction of a large flat examination room where students would sit far apart from each other and individually concentrate on the examination. As an immediate measure, I insisted that only academic staff with at least the rank of lecturer be appointed examination officers to enable them handle examination scripts from the setting, through proofreading to the actual examination. This important duty was not delegable unless under exceptional circumstances. This improved only one aspect of the challenges while the congestion and its consequences persisted.

Central Examination Centre

As a permanent strategy, management proposed to the University Council, the construction of a comprehensive four storey building to serve as the Central Examination Centre and to be located at Chiromo Campus. This building would provide a permanent solution to all problems associated with examinations. The Council approved the construction of the centre which was completed and put to use within one year. The building had a secure floor with two large reinforced fireproof strong rooms for storage of all confidential examination related materials and certificates. The same floor had two very large well-equipped rooms with up to ten carefully selected and vetted secretaries for proofreading purposes. Lecturers coming to proofread examinations carried out their tasks on time and in reasonable comfort, without overcrowding as was the case in the past. We also increased the number of senior and junior staff at the centre and sent them for relevant training in order to enhance operational efficiency.

Another two floors comprising of four large halls were specifically built to accomodate students from all the six colleges of the University, during examinations. The two floors could sit a maximum of 700 students sitting on desks fixed to the floor at intervals of three feet each. This eliminated the possibility of some students copying from others during examination. The building was very secure with 24-hour physical and electronic surveillance including CCTVCameras. Particularly, the CCTV cameras reduced incidences of students smuggling unauthorized material including cell phones into the examination halls.

Students caught cheating in the examination either by the invigilators, CCTV cameras or reported by fellow students were punished. The punishment involved immediate suspension from the University followed by a disciplinary hearing. Those found guilty of cheating were expelled but with an option of appeal. It is gratifying to note that examination cheating at the University reduced by about 90 per cent, largely as a result of these measures.

In order for the University to rationalize and maximize the utilization of teaching space, the two floors at the centre used for examinations had to be booked in advance throughout the year, according to the examination Almanac. Since examinations are taken periodically, the 700-capacity room was strategically utilized for lectures by the School of Business. The handling of examination scripts after sitting the examination was also a challenge. Although the identity of every student is ascertained on entry and exit of the examination hall, some students would sign the exit register but fail to hand in their examination script especially if they had not prepared adequately. Such students would later claim that their marks were missing and there was evidence that they had actually sat the examination, as per the attendance records. This proved to be a very serious challenge to effectively deal with. However, one day a student confessed the whole scheme and how it worked to me in a plea bargain. Henceforth, we meticulously ensured that students handed in their scripts before signing the exit register.

Nonetheless, the problem of mishandling student scripts still prevailed due to carelessness of lecturers. There was a case in point where a lecturer had carried many scripts of different examinations to his home for marking – while drunk. After three months he forgot about them while the affected students in their final year of study were about to graduate. Efforts by the relevant Dean and the DVC Academics to recover the scripts was met with unwarranted vitriol and rudeness.

Almost five months later the unmarked scripts were forcefully recovered from his home and marked by another lecturer in time for the affected students to graduate. The lecture's engagement with the University was terminated. Since this happened just after my appointment as VC, it sent a very strong message to the rest of the staff on consequences of failing to perform allocated duties.

I would like to appreciate UASU for playing a prominent role in maintaining high academic standards as exemplified by their firm support for justice and fair play in this case. In order to maintain the sanctity of the examination process, the handling of results was improved by ensuring that all scripts were marked by the correct examiners on time and the results released in a twimely manner to students.

Student Management Information System (SMIS)

Professor Kiamba launched the SMIS in 2002 when I was the DVC, Administration and Finance. The system kept records of all undergraduate and postgraduate students. It capably managed their registration including application, registration and nominal role reports and also enabled fees remittances, captured examination and transcripts, and produced student graduation lists. During my tenure the system was further developed and enhanced nine different times with the last one in 2013. These enhancements included the incorporation of the Hostel Administration Management Information System (HAMIS), Online Students Clearance and Course Registration Modules, Online System for Interfaculty Transfers and production of Online Graduation Lists. Other enhancements included an online students' portal that allowed students to access examination results and accommodation details, online integration with the banker's systems, online receipting of fees payments, and Customer Relationship Management system (CRM) which enabled the production and issuance of transcripts within one hour, among other important functions.

The University has therefore reaped significant benefits from utilization of the SMIS. These include increased efficiency in the examination marking process, and the integration of examination rules for each degree programme into the system which ensures knowledge memory for the department resulting in faster processing of the examination results. The system also enables the University to perform a quick online counter-check of students information before the issuance of a transcripts and degree certificates, and ensures that only students without fee balances are cleared. This important feature of the system enabled the University to effectively collect all outstanding fees from students which was a major challenge in the past. The system also enabled the University to save money by reducing operational costs which was previously done manually.

Streamlining the teaching, examination and management processes together with enhanced numbers and total dedication of the academic and non-academic staff, and the increasing number of academic programmes resulted in a very positive impact of student numbers, graduation statistics and visibility. There were 300 academic programmes when I became VC, which had increased to 584 by the time I was leaving. There was a student population of 30,000 in January 2005, and in January 2015, the number had grown to 79,000. When I took over as VC, 74,500 alumni, but at the end of my tenure the number was 165,400. This indicated a phenomenal and consistent growth of both undergraduate and postgraduate enrolments. The number of graduates per year increased from 5,000 in 2005 to 14,300 in December 2015. The number of PhD graduates increased from 28 to 123 over the same period.

Policy Documents

In order to entrench good corporate governance at the University, the management debated and approved the development of various important policies. There were 20 policies developed and implemented during my ten-year leadership. These policies provided management, staff and students with suitable professional policy frameworks to guide them in the running of the University. In addition, they played a significant role in the improvement of all aspects of the University activities resulting to excellent performance.

The University of Nairobi Research Policy

The University of Nairobi Research Policy document is anchored on the 2008–2018 Strategic Plan of the University of Nairobi, the Kenya Constitution 2010, the Kenya Vision 2030, and the Government of Kenya policy documents and guidelines. It outlines the general vision of the University with regard to the utilization of cutting-edge research knowledge, targeted at the current national development needs and demands in the future. It also constitutes a baseline for the participation of academic units in research career development, within the University. It further ensures the conformity of research with international best practices in order to facilitate, implement, disseminate and foster research linkages with other institutions locally and internationally including grant awarding organizations.

The policy was deliberately designed to enable the institution fully contribute towards the development of Kenya, the East African region and the world at large. It provides a clear policy framework to facilitate all research-related development and review, and the planning and implementation of all research activities at the University.

Furthermore, it ensures that all research activities have a clear purpose; drawn from the vision and mission of the University and that all resources mobilized for research activities are directed towards fulfilling strategic institutional goals. The research policy also provides minimum standards for implementation of research and research related activities that encourage efficient and effective communication, efficient ethical and honest research, and availability of all essential human and material resources. It ensures that research activities underpin educational activities of the University of Nairobi, thus facilitating the development of sufficient numbers of highly-skilled human capacity necessary for sustaining the University and Kenya's national development.

The University of Nairobi Intellectual Property Policy

The University of Nairobi Intellectual Property Policy was formulated and implemented in 2006. It was aimed at guiding management, teaching staff, students and associates on the development, ownership and management of intellectual property. The principal objectives of this policy included: protection of the rights of the University, its innovators, research sponsors, other stakeholders including the general public; promotion of creativity and innovation; and ensured fair and equitable distribution of all benefits accruing from all innovators and inventors. The Intellectual Property Policy was also designed to eliminate infringement, improper exploitation, and abuse of the University's intellectual assets. It targeted to optimize the environment and incentives for the creation of knowledge, and promote linkages with the industry. In addition, it stimulated research through developing and utilizing novel techniques and creative modes for commercialization, with plough back of resources to the University and other interested parties.

The University of Nairobi Plagiarism Policy

Being the largest University in Kenya and East Africa, the University of Nairobi produces massive academic output. To ensure scholarly excellence and ethical practices in teaching, learning, research and consultancy, and to maintain academic integrity of both students and staff, the University committed to curbing plagiarism by developing and institutionalizing a Plagiarism Policy. This policy established the framework for detecting, deterring, and dealing with plagiarism. It was the product of a thorough review of a number of policies drawn from international and regional practices. The policy also strived to strengthen two core values highlighted in the Strategic Plan 2008–2013; these are innovativeness and creativity.

As much as the policy was intended to promote, educate and protect student and staff interests about academic integrity, it also targeted to protect the interests of students, faculty and the University. The policy outlined the general vision and commitment of the University with regard to integrity requirements in the execution of academic programmes, the creation and dissemination of research knowledge, targeted at promoting excellence in scholarly output. Furthermore, the policy set out strict rules and regulations for detecting, preventing and addressing plagiarism in order to promote academic integrity. It therefore established mechanisms for reporting plagiarism and prescribed procedures for dealing with such cases.

The University of Nairobi Open Access Policy

The University took practical steps to preserve and disseminate knowledge through the provision of a conducive environment for conducting quality education and research. In December 2012, the University management developed and implemented the Open Access Policy, and signed the Berlin Declaration on Open Access to knowledge in the Sciences and Humanities as evidence of its commitment to the global Open Access initiative.

This policy, in particular played an enhanced role in anchoring the institution into world class status. It ensured long term preservation of the University's research output, increased visibility of the University's research and enhanced its collaborations with the global research community. This policy also enabled open access of scholarly output resulting from academic activities undertaken at the University as well as promoting high standards in the management of research outputs.

The Open Access Policy provided scholars the opportunity and platform to promote their academic work by enhancing access to research outputs and undoubtedly anchored the University in the national, regional and international arena for global visibility.

The University of Nairobi System of Websites Policy

The University of Nairobi management developed and launched a System of Websites Policy in 2012. The main objective of the policy was to ensure accuracy, consistency and integrity of the web content and protect the identity and image of the University regionally and internationally. The policy also provided a set of mandatory guidelines of the University's system of websites and guidance on the maintenance of the web content to ensure continued reflection of the true status of the University within the web space.

The University of Nairobi Communication Policy

One of the most important policies formulated and implemented during my tenure as VC was the Communication Policy which stipulates how the University handles communication between its internal and external stakeholders. The policy was anchored on the Strategic Plan 2013–2018 and emphasizes communication between University and its stakeholders as a two way process with open communication between the governing organs and stakeholders. Policy outlines the principles, guidelines, practices and processes that the University shall embrace while fostering excellent communication. It puts in place a solid communication structure giving every facet of the University adequate visibility. It also ensures that academic and research activity and communication relations anchored on different communication platforms reach the targeted stakeholders.

The Policy demonstrates that the institution is among the top organizations that have embraced best practices in communication. Through implementation of the policy, the University realizes its vision, mission and core values. The University chose this path in order to realize its vision of moving firmly forward towards world class academic excellence, thus emphasizing the centrality of stakeholders in its communication web.

The University of Nairobi Alcohol and Drug Abuse Policy

This policy prohibits the selling and use of illicit drugs within the University premises and ensures that all University employees and their dependents, and students are fit to carry out their duties. It also ensures that the University community and the wider society are educated on alcohol abuse, prohibited drugs and substance abuse. The policy also puts in place mechanisms for counselling and treatment of alcohol and drug abuse patients within the University.

The University of Nairobi Recruitment and Selection Policy

The Recruitment and Selection Policy was developed and implemented by the University management in order to competitively attract, identify, and hire the most qualified and suitable applicants available, in line with institutional established criteria. It also ensured that vacancies, were filled within the established time scales and in a cost effective manner, enhancing gender equality and national cohesion. The Policy ensured that the recruitment process complied with all national laws on hiring practices in the public service and the applicable Collective Bargaining Agreements (CBA).

The University of Nairobi Records Management Policy

The University initially lacked an organized and efficient records management system. Implemented in 2007, the policy enables the University to facilitate and apply standardization to procedures and practices in the management of all records at the University of Nairobi. It also provides a suitable institutional policy framework to support efficient and effective management of records and to ensure that records management guidelines are consistent with national records management policy's, systems and procedures.

The University of Nairobi Gender Mainstreaming Policy

The Policy was operationalized in 2008. The policy aims to create and sustain a fair and just academic environment where men and women have equal opportunities to realize their full potential and contribute within a community of scholars, and in a culture of mutual respect.

The University of Nairobi HIV/AIDS Policy

This Policy was established in 2003. The Policy provides an institutional policy framework through which to address the HIV/AIDS scourge. The Policy was revised during my tenure to contribute to the prevention of HIV transmission and mitigate against social, economic and health impact of HIV/AIDS. It was important in conducting advocacy, prevention, control and mitigation against the impact of HIV/AIDS impact on the university community.

The University of Nairobi Policy on Training and Development
This policy provides clear procedures for identifying, prioritizing, planning and monitoring staff training and development within the University. The policy on Staff Training, Promotion and Establishment (Kagiko Report) provided guidelines on selection, promotion and development of all university staff.

Other Policies
Other policies developed and implemented during my tenure include: the University of Nairobi Anti-Corruption Policy, which set out management, staff and students firm commitment to zero tolerance to corruption within the University; the University of Nairobi Disability Mainstreaming Policy, which promoted and ensured full inclusion of students and staff with disability into the life of the University; the University of Nairobi Maintenance Policy set the standards on to which the University would adopt techniques for maintaining its physical assets; and the University of Nairobi ICT Policy, provided guidelines for the developers and users of the University ICT resources on the appropriate standards to be adopted.

Good Governance and Standards Enhancement
In order to further enhance good governance at the University, the Council approved a proposal to appoint two new DVCs: one in charge of Student Affairs and an other in charge of Research, Production and Extension. This was effected at the beginning of 2011 and saw Professors Mbeche and Lucy Irungu appointed.

The duties of DVC Student Affairs include planning, organizing and managing work study programs, sports and games, catering and accommodation, community service, recreation, health and security of students. He was also expected to develop and implement programs such as leadership and training that support students' educational experience and wholesome life.

The duties of the DVC Research, Production and Extension include mainstreaming and advancing the research profile of the university, in order to enhance its scholarly publications, innovation and intellectual property functions; planning, organizing and managing research infrastructure development; appropriate policy planning, coordinating; administrative and logistical support for research at all levels; quality control and capacity building. The ability of the University's innovation and incubation centre such as the Science and Technology Park, in conjunction with the Intellectual Property Management Office to transfer research outcomes to commercial outlets is a highly commendable effort and benefit to the University, and is attributed to this office.

In 2012, the University launched the Digital Repository, an in-house online archive established for the purpose of collecting, preserving, and disseminating digital copies of scholarly and intellectual property output of the University. The content includes: journal articles, academic reports, research papers as well as theses and dissertations. It also includes digital assets generated by academics, course notes, learning objects, speeches, presentations and conference proceedings.

The launch of the online Open Access Digital Repository, approval of the policy, redevelopment and revamping of its staff personal profile websites resulted in significant improvement of its openness. Indeed, in the Webometrics, the University's world ranking greatly improved from position 4057 in July 2012 to position 855 in January 2015, out of 25,000 Universities; and from position 26 in Africa in July 2012 to position 7 in January 2015, out of 1,500 Universities. The University maintained the top position nationally, and the East, Central and West African regions. Only a few South African and Egyptian Universities were still performing better than the University of Nairobi at the completion of my tenure.

The University also revamped the content of the digital repository between January 2013 and December 2014, by adding 74,100 items in the repository. In January 2013, the Webometrics introduced ranking criteria for repositories and the University of Nairobi digital repository was ranked position 1,176 in the world and 31 in Africa. This improved significantly to position 257 in the world and six in Africa in January 2015.

Internationalization of the University

In order to increase efficiency, local, regional and international visibility, and transform into an international research and innovation hub, the University of Nairobi management and the Council embarked on a well-organized programme to internationalize the University. As a first step, we systematically strengthened the office of the Centre for International Programmes and Links (CIPL) and its activities. The Centre, established within the University is responsible for initiating, facilitating and coordinating international programmes and links, students and staff exchange and mobility, collaborative research projects, and worldwide networking. Through it, the University has continued to strengthen its ties with other international Universities around the world.

Indeed, Universities in Asia and the Far East, Europe, North and South America, Australia and New Zealand, participated in these activities. The Centre was also responsible for the welfare of international visiting academic staff, scholars and researchers, coordinating the activities of the University of Nairobi staff and students visiting other international universities, and collecting and disseminating relevant information on international programs and links, among other functions. The University thus recognized that an education with international standards is necessary to equip students with knowledge and skills for survival and growth in a competitive labour market.

I am proud of these activities, which resulted in a great increase in the number of international students at the University, necessitating the establishment of an annual International

Students Day at the University. The international standards of the University drove countries such as Liberia to send large numbers of their students to our School of Business.

During my stewardship as VC many international guests visited the University. These included Angela Merkel, Chancellor of the Federal Republic of Germany; the Prime Minister of the Republic of South Korea, Kim Hwang-Sik; Niccolò Rinaldi, a member of the European Parliament; former American Secretaries of State Hillary Clinton and Madeleine Albright; former (American Senator) and President Barack Obama.

In 2005, Chinese President Hu Jintao was entertained by students from the Confucius Institute of the University of Nairobi, and in recognition of the excellence of our Confucius Institute, I was appointed to represent the African continent in the Confucius Institute Council, in Beijing, China in 2007 – a position I hold to date.

In addition to the above-mentioned visitors, there were also numerous visits by renowned international academics from all over the world who shared with me their experiences and best practices while others were research collaborators, and yet others came to benchmark with the University. They include: president of the University of Manitoba and Vice Presidents of Universities of Toronto, Alberta, Western Ontario, and Prince Edward Island all in Canada; Tony Frank president of Colorado State University in the United States of America; President of Linkoping University in Sweden; and President University of Helsinki in Finland, VCs Universities of Sydney and Adelaide, and DVCs Curtin University all in Australia, VC of University of Coventry in the United Kingdom, presidents of Yonsei University and Hankuk University of Foreign Languages in South Korea, President of University of Turkish Aeronautical Association in Turkey, Maharishi Markandeshwar University in India, Presidents of Yokohama, Soka, Shiga Medical and United Nations and Vice President of Kanazawa Universities all in Japan, Presidents of Tianjin Normal, Zhejiang Normal, Tongji, Xiamen, Shanghai Finance, and Peking Universities all in the People's Republic of China.

There were also many scholars from our principal research collaborators including Universities of Maryland Baltimore, and Washington Seattle in United States of America, Manitoba and Toronto in Canada, and Oxford, and Imperial College London both in the United Kingdom, Ghent in Belgium, Helsinki in Finland and the International Aids Vaccine Initiative (IAVI) in the United States of America and Centre for Disease Control (CDC) located in Atlanta Georgia, United States of America.

Regionally, the VCs of the Universities of Rwanda in Rwanda, Dar es Salaam in Tanzania, Juba in South Sudan, Somalia in Somalia, Makerere in Uganda, Addis Ababa in Ethiopia, and Khartoum in Sudan, visited the University of Nairobi severally. Within the African continent, the University received visits from VCs of Universities of Cape Town, Kwa-Zulu Natal, Witwatersrand, Pretoria, Johannesburg, and Stellenbosch all in the Republic of South Africa; University of Botswana in the Republic of Botswana; Universities of Ibadan, Lagos, Ilorin, Jos, and Obafemi Awolowo all in the Federal Republic of Nigeria; Zambia in the Republic of Zambia; Namibia in the Republic of Namibia; Universities of Cape Coast, and Ghana in the Republic of Ghana; Zimbabwe in the Republic of Zimbabwe, and Yaoundé in the Republic of Cameroon.

On linkages, the University focused on internationalizing its brand and profile. Born out of these efforts were increased collaborations with leading international universities and organizations worldwide. As a result, the University increased its research and innovation portfolio, international visibility and increased staff and student exchange. In this regard, many universities from across the world firmed up their collaborative relations with the University of Nairobi. These efforts further brought increased collaborations and partnerships with other organizations such as the Office of the High Commission for Human Rights (OHCHR). This type of internationalization is exemplified by the 2013 visit by the president of the University of Maryland Global Programs to further strengthen existing collaborative research running into millions of USD.

During this period the Faculty of Veterinary Medicine undertook cutting edge research in Aflatoxins and Fumonicins contamination of maize and animal feeds. This particular research project was carried out by the University of Nairobi in collaboration with MTT Agrifood Research Finland and funded by the Finnish Ministry of Foreign Affairs.

The Association for Strengthening Agricultural Research in Eastern and Central Africa (ASARECA), for example funded the implementation of a research project on the diagnostic and control tools and strategies for Taenia Solium Cysticercosis, between the University of Nairobi, International Livestock Research Institute (ILRI) Nairobi Kenya, Makerere University, Uganda, and Sokoine University of Agriculture, Tanzania. Some of the other research projects undertaken by faculty were in physiological and ecological of the unique aquatic life in Lake Magadi Kenya, conservation genetics and forensics in Kenya, development of biopesticide for use against mosquitos from selected plants in Msambweni District Kenya, and animal welfare research and policy in Africa among others. The faculty has many rich external links including the Universities of Wyoming, Colorado State, and Minnesota, United States of America, University of Copenhagen in Denmark and Mac Master in Canada among many others. All these activities greatly enhanced our international research and innovation profile and visibility that propelled our institution to world class excellence.

In 2013, the Wangari Maathai Institute (WMI), hosted an International Round Table Discussion on "Impacts of Trade and Investment-Driven Biotechnological Innovations on Food Safety-Security in Africa". The meeting was convened by the United Nations University-Institute for Sustainability and Peace, Japan. In another forum, WMI, international scholar, Professor Peter Blaze Cochran was the lead discussant on the "Urgency of Sustainability in Higher Education: Promise of the Earth Charter". Peter Mburi of University of Nairobi Fab Lab, won the People's Choice Award at the National Aeronautics and Space Administration (NASA)

Space Applications Challenge for his 'Bit Harvester' invention made possible by 3D Technology. The Bit Harvester is an electronic device designed to monitor remotely using SMS, the wind turbines and solar installations to find out if they are operating normally and optimally or otherwise, and taking the necessary steps to correct the problems if any. These innovation activities by students of the Fab Lab of the University of Nairobi, and its link with the international network of Fab Labs, greatly enhanced the research and innovation profile of the University.

As VC, I took up the challenge to further enhance the internationalization of the University by serving in various international organizations. For instance, I represented the AAU, the umbrella body for all the 1,500 universities within the continent. I was elected to the Governing Board at its Annual General Meeting held at the University of Cape Town in February 2005, a position I still hold. I was elected and served as Vice President between 2009 and 2010. In 2011, I was elected President, a position I held till 2013. As the immediate past President, I was retained as board member for another four years untill 2017. The University's visibility and performance increased tremendously as a result of my continued exposure and interaction with top African university heads from universities of Cape Town, Pretoria, Stellenbosch, Witwatersrand, and Kwa-Zulu Natal, among others.

I was also appointed a member of the Governing Board of the African Network for Scientific and Technological Institutions (ANSTI) in 2005, and again elected Chairman of the Governing Board in 2010, a position I hold to date. ANSTI gets substantial funding from UNESCO and its ultimate goal is to strengthen the regions' capacity for training, research and innovation, and for establishing service intensive and purposeful utilization of science, engineering, and technology for development. Serving as ANSTI Chairman enabled many of our science, engineering and technological academic staff to engage in research resulting to enhancement of the University's research output.

I was elected Chairman of the East African Community Sectoral Committee on Health when Kenya's President, Uhuru Kenyatta headed the East African Heads of State Summit between 2013 and 2015. It was during this period that the East African Community (EAC) declared the College of Health Sciences of the University of Nairobi a Centre of Excellence for health training in East Africa. I was simultaneously elected President of the Association of Medical Councils of Africa (AMCOA) in 2013, a position I still hold to date. In this position, I was responsible for medical, dental and health regulations in the continent. These medical professional activities and responsibilities significantly enhanced the international visibility of the University.

I wish to acknowledge the approval of Council and the government for my travels. Indeed, internationalization of the University progressed during my tenure only through such support. Some of the institutions I visited include the US State Department for research, academic and governance. I also had meetings with presidents of four leading universities in the US, six universities in Japan, four leading universities and technikons in Israel, five leading Canadian universities, three leading universities in the UK, seven universities in China, five universities in South Africa, three universities in Germany, three universities in Nigeria, four universities in Australia and two universities in Belgium. I also visited Makerere in Uganda, Dar es Salaam in Tanzania, Addis Ababa in Ethiopia, Ghana and Cape Coast in Ghana, Universities of Zambia, Botswana, Zimbabwe, Rwanda, and Burundi, among others.

The University of Nairobi also hosted many important international conferences and meetings, one of which was the Association of Commonwealth Universities Centenary Celebrations in 2013. The end result of all these activities resulted in a significant increase in the number of external linkages at the University which rose from 125 in 2005 to 1,300 in 2015.

Rehabilitation and Development of Infrastructure

When I was appointed VC, the infrastructure was dilapidated, student indiscipline was alarming, and staff morale quite low. This state of affairs had persisted for a while and impacted negatively on the institution's objectives, making it difficult to achieve its goals. My job therefore, was to effectively and systematically confront these challenges. My strategy for rebuilding the institution, in all aspects was based on the Strategic Plan 2005–2010, 2008–2013 and 2013–2018.

Several problems compounded the rehabilitation and development of infrastructure. For instance, inadequate financial resources compounded the problem of reviving and completing several stalled building projects on the campuses of the University. The University management and the Council prioritized the projects and with prudent management and injection of funds generated from internally generated resources, we completed most of the stalled projects and also constructed new ones.

College of Education and External Studies

The physical infrastructure at the College of Education and External Studies (CEES) was in very bad shape with many stalled projects, some going as far back as 15 years. Students and staff grappled with inadequate teaching space, library facilities, accommodation, and transport. The old library at Kikuyu Campus was inadequate to meet the academic demands of the 12,500 students to and from the Jomo Kenyatta Memorial Library (JKML) at the Main Campus. All this changed in 2005 following the facelift and new constructions. The Kshs 250 million Library Hill Complex of a two storey library, with a sitting capacity of 1,200 and over 200,000 thousand books and reference materials was completed and handed to the college. The modern library was fully computerized with access to many e-books and e-journals. The teaching facilities for the CEES, included two large lecture theatres, tutorial rooms, office space for teaching and non-teaching staff, and communication and speech laboratories. The shortage of accommodation at Kikuyu Campus was addressed by the construction of the Pioneer Halls.

As a result, performance of the CEES improved tremendously upon completion of these buildings and led the other five colleges in the performance contract for several years. This translated into enhanced performance for the entire university.

At the Kenya Science Campus, a new large and smart lecture theatre with a seating capacity of 500 students was constructed. Further, three large ultra-modern fully equipped laboratories for Physics, Chemistry, and Biology were constructed at a total cost of Kshs 239 million. This enabled the university to admit more students in the Bahelor of Education Science.

In 2007, the University purchased the former British Council Library building in Kisumu, at a cost of Kshs 40 million. This acquisition, consolidated and improved the university's academic presence in western Kenya. The University now had an office space, classrooms, modern computerized library, computer laboratories and an amphitheatre. The Kisumu Campus housed the Schools of Law, Open and Distance Learning, Education, and Business, and the Faculty of Arts. A seven floor academic building is under construction. Once complete, it will house modern lecture theatres, tutorial rooms, offices for teaching and non-teaching staff, a well stocked and fully computerized library, and computer laboratories. This is the first phase of a planned 16-storey building at Kisumu Campus.

College of Biological and Physical Sciences

In order to accommodate the increasing number of students studying physical sciences at the University, two new large state of the art laboratories were constructed.

The School of Computing and Informatics had been a leading centre for training computer experts in the region, but was now challenged as it could no longer operate effectively with the existing facilities. The University therefore put up two modern and large computer laboratories at a cost of Kshs 28 million. One of these laboratories was specifically earmarked for postgraduate training, enabling the University to increase its capacity for training additional Masters and Doctorate degrees. Furthermore, another floor was constructed above the main School of Computing and Informatics building at a cost of Kshs 27 million. This further increased the urgently needed space for new servers and office space for teaching and technical staff. The School is currently enabled with computers for over 300 staff and students at a single sitting. Indeed, the laboratory which is open to all students of the University has been used by a cross section of students and is forming a big part of the University's heavy investment in ICT infrastructure.

A Computing for Development (C4D) laboratory was recently activated. The lab is focuses on technology incubation and prototype development. Already, the innovation laboratory is incubating 12 technology start-ups which are undergoing mentorship and training with the aim of nurturing them into sustainable companies in the near future. It also addresses some of the problems and challenges in creating employment opportunities in the society and has thus greatly enhanced the capacity in research, creativity and innovation.

The University extended by one floor, the facilities at the Information and Communication Technology Centre (ICTC). The Centre has a principal mandate of assisting the University to enhance the innovative use of ICT products and services to support teaching, learning, research administrative and other processes. Many additional servers were purchased and installed in order to improve the efficiency of the services offered at the Centre. The University purchased close to 9,000 computers and established a computer store at the Centre.

Furthermore, the University increased its bandwidth from 8Mbps in 2005 to 580Mbps in January 2015. The Centre is well staffed, with 135 fully qualified and proficient technical staff working across all the University's colleges and units. ICT remains the key driver to all University operations. The staff are efficient, dedicated, reliable and disciplined, and create a strong working team that has achieved many goals despite a few challenges. It is because of this dedication and cohesive teamwork that students and staff continued to enjoy stable and reliable ICT services. The colleges were connected to the University backbone through a Local Area Network (LAN). The latest of this LAN extension involved extra-mural centres in Nakuru, Nyeri, Kisii, Kakamega and Meru, and the library in Kisumu Campus. This enabled the University fraternity, in these extramural centres, to enjoy the same excellent ICT services offered in the main University network.

In partnership with the Kenya Education Network (KENET), which is the only National Research and Education Network in Kenya, wireless networks were established in all colleges, campuses and units of the University. Wireless networks were also set up to cover all open spaces, hostels, lecture rooms, libraries, laboratories, and staff offices within the University. The latest wireless access points were successfully installed in Parklands, Upper Kabete and Kikuyu campuses. The ICT Centre installed a reliable Kaspersky Antivirus in the University network in addition to the firewall upgrade, in response to advanced security needs of the network.

In 2007, the University established the Centre for Biotechnology and Bioinformatics (CEBIB). The Centre has been critical in facilitating, and strengthening research and development in these fields in the region and is contributing immensely to the University's, Kenya's and Africa's development agenda. The facilities have opened up space for a molecular biology laboratory, a transformation laboratory, a tissue culture laboratory, a bioinformatics unit, a genomics platform, microbiology and mycology laboratories, and office space for staff.

The University of Nairobi Library

The University of Nairobi Library system consists of the main library – Jomo Kenyatta Memorial Library (JKML), and 13 other college and campus branch libraries. This is the largest library system in the country. During my tenure as VC, the entire library infrastructure was refurbished and an additional four modern libraries constructed and equipped. The library system has over

700,000 books and journals, mainly acquired systematic purchasing and a few from donations. The library is also subscribed to over 45,000 peer reviewed full journals in all disciplines and over 54,000 electronic books.

The Library maintained collaborative, international and local external links with the International Network for the Availability of Scientific Publications (INASP), the International Federation of Library Associations and Institutions, Association of Commonwealth Universities (ACU), Electronic Information for Libraries (EIFL), Kenya Library and Information Services Consortium (KLISC), and the Kenya University Librarians Committee (KULC). These links greatly enhanced access to resources and strengthened the institution's capacity for resource management.

The Library utilizes a library information system called VUBIS smart with acquisitions, cataloguing, circulation, serials management, periodicals, and Online Public Access Catalog (OPAC) modules. The system offered access to electronic research articles to staff and students. The system has greatly enhanced learning and research activities in the University by providing the most current research articles in all fields. The system also fully computerized the process of borrowing and return of library resources making it more efficient and effective. The system was upgraded in 2014. The Library played a very prominent and critical role in the uploading of academic, research and administrative resources the staff and students, to the institutional e-repository.

The College of Health Sciences

The College of Health Sciences was declared the only Centre of Excellence in health training in East Africa by the East African Community, in 2013. In the last decade, demand for training in health-related courses has increased due to the high population and the opening up of more training opportunities to more qualified applicants who would otherwise not be absorbed in the Government sponsored programmes. This in turn led to the urgency to expand the existing facilities.

I led a delegation from the University to Toronto, Canada and successfully competed for a Kshs 289 million grant from the Canadian Foundation for Innovation. The funding was for the construction of a Level 3 biocontainment laboratory at the Institute of Tropical and Infectious Diseases (UNITID) at the Kenyatta National Hospital Campus. The four storey building has laboratories that handle highly contagious emerging pathogens such as Ebola, Rift Valley Fever, Marburg virus and other haemorrhagic diseases in Kenya, and the continent.

The laboratory was officially commissioned in 2007 by the Canadian Minister for Health, Tony Clement and his Kenyan counterpart, Charity Ngilu. It was the second one of its kind in sub-Saharan Africa with the only other one being in the Republic of South Africa. UNITID had many collaborative research links with the University of Manitoba in Canada, University of Copenhagen (DBL-Centre for Health Research and Development) in Denmark, Faculty of Life Sciences and the Department of Human Nutrition, Universities of Washington Seattle, West Virginia, SUNY upstate, and Centre for Disease Control and Prevention, Atlanta, Pfizer Laboratories of South Africa, and Kenya Medical Research Institute (KEMRI) among others.

At the School of Medicine, an extension block to the Department of Surgery was constructed and inaugurated in 2009 by the Chancellor, Dr. Wanjui, at a cost of Kshs 30 million. The extension contained tutorial rooms, a resource centre and offices for the teaching staff from the Departments of Surgery and Anaesthesia. It also enabled rationalization of adequate space for the Department of Orthopaedic Surgery from the previous shared premises. There was also the construction of an extension of the Department of Paediatrics and Child Health through donor funding to the tune of Kshs 20 million. This extension enabled enhanced postgraduate training in the speciality. The Kenya AIDS Vaccine Initiative (KAVI) constructed an additional floor above the

KAVI laboratories with funds from global research collaborators like the International AIDS Vaccine Initiative (IAVI). KAVI carries out numerous cutting-edge medical research.

A new state of the art funeral parlour was constructed at the preclinical section of the School of Medicine situated within the Chiromo Campus at a cost of Kshs 60 million with a capacity of 120 resting chambers, offices and a chapel. Surgical Skills Laboratories were also constructed and inaugurated at Chiromo. Construction of the Human Anatomy Annex was also completed at Chiromo Campus to address the increasing numbers of medical students at the University.

In late 2005, the University built a modern three storey block to house the School of Nursing Sciences at a cost of Kshs 31 million. It contained lecture theatres, tutorial rooms laboratories, demonstration rooms and offices for teaching and non-teaching staff. It has been a partner in collaborative research on adolescent reproductive health, substance abuse, health systems management and pica practice among pregnant women. The School of Nursing has strong collaborative research links with the Universities of Salford and Manchester in the UK, and the Boston College of Nursing in the US.

Plans for the construction of a Kshs 152 million modern School of Pharmacy building also commenced in 2005. The phased project is nearing completion. It will provide pharmaceutical research laboratories, lecture theatres, tutorial rooms, a library and offices for teaching and non-teaching staff. The School has a strong tradition of research and collaborative partners including: Kansas and Mercer Universities in the United States of America, Tianjin University of Traditional Chinese Medicine in China, Katholieke Universiteit Leuven, in Belgium, and University of Cape Town, South Africa. In addition, the School had strong links with industry players on drug analysis and manufacturing including Pfizer Laboratories, Reckitt Benckiser Limited, Bayer E.A Limited, Medox Pharmaceuticals, Intas Pharmaceuticals, GlaxoSmithKline Limited.

The School of Public Health was officially launched on 22 February, 2011. The School was the successor to the former Department of Public Health in the School of Medicine. It was refurbished and equipped to provide quality public health education and training, research and service delivery that embodies the aspirations of the Kenyan people and global community. It had a tradition of involvement in innovative research on typhoid fever, malaria, and health systems management at community level. The School maintained active collaborative research links with bodies such as the Centre for Global Public Health, USAID division of nutrition, Cornell University, John Hopkins School of Public Health Baltimore, Tufts University, University of Minnesota, and Centre for Disease Control (CDC) Atlanta, World Bank, Regional AIDS Training Network, University of Manitoba and Simon Fraser, University of Vancouver Canada. Regionally, the School had research collaborations with universities in East and Central Africa.

The Dental School, which is one of the only two dental schools in the country was refurbished and re-equipped by the University with modern dental chairs to replace the old dilapidated ones. This enable the University increase the intake of dental students enrolled at the University from 25 to 40, to meet the country's demand. Other essential equipment including phantom heads and dental consumables such as gold were also purchased. The University Dental Hospital was also adequately equipped and operationalized. The former Kenya School of Law premises on Valley Road was allocated to the Dental School, by the government. These facilities were renovated and provided the additional needed lecture theatres, tutorial rooms, computer laboratories, and offices for teaching and non-teaching staff.

College of Agriculture and Veterinary Sciences

The construction of the stalled 8-4-4 building at this College was completed in 2008 at a cost of Kshs 40 million.

In order to enhance the development of seeds, the University oversaw the construction of the Seed Enterprise Management

Institute (SEMI's) seed laboratories and processing facilities at a cost of Kshs 97 million. The Faculty of Agriculture recently handed over the 'White label breeders seed' of the Kenya Sugar Bean variety to the Kenya Seed Company. The Kenya Sugar Bean variety is an invention of the University of Nairobi, through the University of Nairobi's Seed Company (UNISEED), in collaboration with the SEMI's project. Through the Department of Plant Science and Crop protection, several high yielding bean varieties were released for seed production by farmers in Kenya. Six of these bean varieties are licensed to the Kenya Seed Company, which has entered into a memorandum of understanding with University of Nairobi, to commercialize the bean varieties.

The Faculty of Veterinary Medicine, one of the oldest faculties at the University, started training diploma students in animal health, in the 1940s, but later in 1962, became a full-fledged faculty offering degree courses. During my tenure, all infrastructure including buildings containing operating theatres, research and teaching laboratories, lecture theatres and tutorial rooms and computer laboratories were refurbished. This Faculty is renowned for training veterinarians in the region.

The Wangari Maathai Institute for Peace and Environmental Studies was established at Upper Kabete Campus as a Centre of Excellence in environmental governance and has linkages with peace and democracy. Currently, a state of the art green building is being constructed to permanently house the Institute through donor funding. This institute was established in close collaboration with the 2004 Nobel Peace Laureate Professor Wangari Maathai and will house her works and walks for posterity. The Institute aims to promote good environmental practices and to cultivate a culture of peace by shaping values, ethics, and attitudes through experiential learning, mentoring and transformational leadership. The US Department of State the MacArthur Foundation, has created a POWER Hub at the WMI, to build the evidence base on women, energy access, and climate solutions; and training of trainers workshops; facilitate African and Indian women entrepreneurs; and leadership exchanges to build a network of women climate change and build public awareness.

The University management and Council also carried out massive renovations of offices, laboratories, lecture theatres, and seminar rooms in other departments within the College. The University has also drilled several boreholes at Upper and Lower Kabete Campuses, Central Catering Unit (CCU), Main, Kikuyu, and Kenya Science Campuses at a cost of Kshs 55 million, in addition to purchasing two large water browsers in order to address the increasing water needs by the students and staff at the University. During my stewardship, the University management purchased 13 additional 65-seater buses, and two 33-seater mini buses to ease the transport of students and staff. Eleven 500 KVA generators were also purchased at a cost of over Kshs 100 million, and installed in all the campuses. There were also smaller capacity generators installed in specific sensitive sites like the ICT Centre, the Central Examination Centre, Chiromo Funeral Parlour, the Jomo Kenyatta Memorial Library, KAVI, and the Level 3 Biocontainment Laboratories.

The College of Humanities and Social Sciences

The infrastructure at the College of Humanities and Social Sciences has been a challenge given the substantial increase in student numbers, coupled with increased number of market driven academic programmes. The challenge therefore mainly related to inadequate physical facilities. At the Lower Kabete Campus, a tuition block consisting of four large lecture theatres, each with a seating capacity of 300 was constructed. Also constructed were office blocks, tutorial rooms, computer laboratories and a library. The library was constructed at a cost of Kshs 31 million and has a seating capacity of 600, computer laboratories and offices for staff. It was fully stocked with relevant books, and computerized and networked to access various electronic books and journals.

In order to alleviate the accommodation problem at Lower Kabete Campus, the University management spent Kshs 240 million, to partly complete a students' hostel, an earlier abandoned stalled project. This hostel reduced accommodation problems at the Campus for 224 more students. Biashara Hall was also given a complete facelift and brought to international standards.

At the School of Law, the Moot Court was constructed in order to enhance training of lawyers. So consistent have our law students performed in the International Moot Court competitions, that our Law School won the African Moot Court competition held in 2014. This competition was hosted by the University of Nairobi Law School, lead by Professor Patricia Kameri Mbote as the Dean. The School of Law has research links with the International Development Research Centre (IDRC) of Canada, the Ford Foundation, and the Norwegian Agency for International Development (NORAS), the Norwegian Research Council, and South and Eastern Africa Research Centre on Women's Law, University of Zimbabwe. It also runs a joint program with Widener University Law School in the US.

In 2008, the University of Nairobi expanded its fixed asset portfolio by acquiring the eight storey, Kenya Reinsurance Plaza, in Mombasa at a cost of Kshs 190 million and further renovated at a cost of Kshs 8.5 million. The University Plaza (Mombasa Campus)is currently being utilized as teaching space for Law and Business courses, as well as housing the Department of Extra-mural Studies, It also houses computer laboratories, offices for teaching and non-teaching staff, lecture theatres, tutorial rooms, a well-stocked and computerized library with access to electronic books and journals, a Moot Court, and a bookstore.

The University of Nairobi Towers
The feather in the cap of my tenure was the construction of the University of Nairobi Towers at the Main Campus. The idea behind the 22-storey, ultra-modern Towers was to increase facilities to cope with the rising demand for University education in Kenya. Undoubtedly, this is the most ambitious and expensive project ever to be undertaken by the University of Nairobi, since its inception

in 1970, and cost about Kshs 2.8 billion. The funds utilized for the construction were realized through firm and prudent financial management that resulted in substantial internal savings over the years. Two donors also contributed towards the construction. The Chandaria Foundation gave Kshs 50 million towards construction of the Chandaria Theatre for Performing Arts which is housed in the auditorium, and the Chinese Confucius Institute Headquarters in Beijing gave Kshs 150 million towards the construction of their offices in the Towers.

The ground-breaking ceremony was held in 2013, by the then Chancellor, Dr. Wanjui and by January 2015, the building was 85 per cent complete. The Towers draws from the strong architectural character of the Great Court. On completion, the Towers will not only provide the much needed teaching space for the College of Humanities and Social Sciences but also assert the position of the University of Nairobi as a leader in architectural thought and innovation. The Towers are an inspiring and attractive showcase of 'green' buildings, and have attained a signature status in all aspects of cutting-edge architecture. The facility is a place where users will be proud to undertake world class scholarly work, receive global leaders and scholars, the private sector, as well as other prominent guests.

The building consists of a Podium and the Tower. The Podium contains, lecture theatres, Senate Chamber and the Chandaria Arts Theatre. There are two 500-seater lecture theatres and four 300-seater lecture theatres. The Council Chamber is at the top most level of the Tower with a scenic view of Nairobi and beyond. The top level also contains executive offices of the VC and his four deputies, the public relations office and a business centre to serve the Senate and the Council. It also contains six lecture rooms, each with a seating capacity of 60, and ten tutorial rooms, each with a seating capacity of 50. The Tower will also house the Graduate School, Confucius Institute, Graduate School of Business, Centre for International Programmes and Links, and the Institute of Development Studies, among others. Additionally, the Tower

My Ten-Year Agenda as Vice-Chancellor

contains a helipad, and can simultaneously accommodate more than 3000 persons. It also has 82 parking spaces at the basement.

The building design is ecologically sustainable, with world class aesthetics, and environmental design considerations incorporating natural ventilation, day lighting, room acoustic design, and bio-gas electricity generation with bio-degradable waste from the building, being channelled to a suitable adjacent location within the precincts of the Main Campus. Furthermore, the building meets stringent criteria for carbon footprint achieving close to 100 per cent carbon neutrality. The Towers, creates harmony with Gandhi Memorial Library Building, the Education Building, the Norfolk Hotel, the Conservatoire of Music, and the National Theatre; and becomes a thoroughfare through which the Great Court shall be accessed.

Despite the successful completion of the Towers, it is worth noting that I went through considerable opposition in order to get this project on course.

I was very clear in my mind about the kind of building I wanted, and the architectural designs were sourced through design competition. The next step was to procure a reputable firm to construct the building round the clock and complete it on time, during or even after my tenure. Most importantly, I required a company with a previous track record of constructing highrise buildings.

The first major hurdle was the termination of the initial procurement process by the public procurement review board as a result of an appeal by one of the bidding companies that felt aggrieved. Consequently, we lost considerable time because the process had to be repeated.

The second major bottleneck was the delay in the actual commencement of the construction. The ground-breaking ceremony was delayed by several months because some of the contracted professionals delayed in providing us with a priced bill, and when they eventually did it, it was in excess of our budget brief by over Kshs 1 billion. The underground structural design was too expensive. I did not want a white elephant. I sought advice from construction professional bodies in the country and the

University management and was advised to terminate everything except the architect. After approval by management and Council, the concerned professionals were sent packing and paid for the value of work done. We consequently engaged others on the recommendation of various construction professional bodies. Some of the professionals accepted the termination and left while others proceeded to the High Court. This further delayed the construction. What actually saved us was the ruling by the Court authorizing the construction to proceed alongside the court processes.

The third barrier was with regards to the finishes on the building. As the building was nearing completion, I had just a few months left to the end of my tenure. When I inspected it, I found out that they were substandard for a twenty first century world class building. For example, there were terrazzo finishes instead of granite, internally, and external concrete finishes instead of granite and aluminium cuddling. I had to very firmly and against all odds insist that the materials used in the building be exactly as I had ordered. That is why that excellent building is standing today.

Reflection

From the foregoing, it is quite clear that my transformative leadership policies and style, which were adopted by management, Senate, staff and students worked very well and succeeded. This is despite the fact that few staff equated my leadership style to a form of benevolent dictatorship. However, the important and overriding fact is that I can now be objectively judged on the basis of the measurable and sustainable achievements of the University, during my ten year tenure as VC. I created sustainable systems and policies that propelled the University to world class excellence. These systems and policies, which are long-term and sustainable, are most unlikely to be affected by any subjective wrangling within the University in the near future. Furthermore, they are guided by other external quality assurance organizations such as the Commission for University Education (CUE), and the Kenya Bureau of Standards for the maintenance of ISO 9001 Standard Certification, among others.

The University has consistently remained within the top ten best performers in Africa. During my last two years in office, the University was ranked positions nine and seven, respectively, out of 1,500 Universities in Africa. Indeed, only a handful institution are still ahead of us, and the very firm strategy that I left behind at the University was to propel us to first position in Africa and among the top 100 globally. This is not only achievable but also sustainable. The last ranking of January 2016 witnessed an improvement to position six. In 2015, the University was in position 855, out of the 25,000 institutions. This position improved to 687, a year later. This is a sustainable and measurable development.

In terms of Public Service, the University under my stewardship, remains the only public institution to attain the grade Excellent, in Performance Contracting Process in the entire Public Service in Kenya. This was not by chance as it had in the past consistently performed well and led the State Corporation's Category by being among the top three performers. In the University Sector (both Public and Private), the University of Nairobi has commanded an undisputed leadership and became the Top Centre of Excellence in teaching and learning, research and innovation, consultancy and community service in the entire Republic of Kenya.

I therefore believe that I have left a sustainable legacy of, 'Excellent and Exemplary Transformative Leadership'.

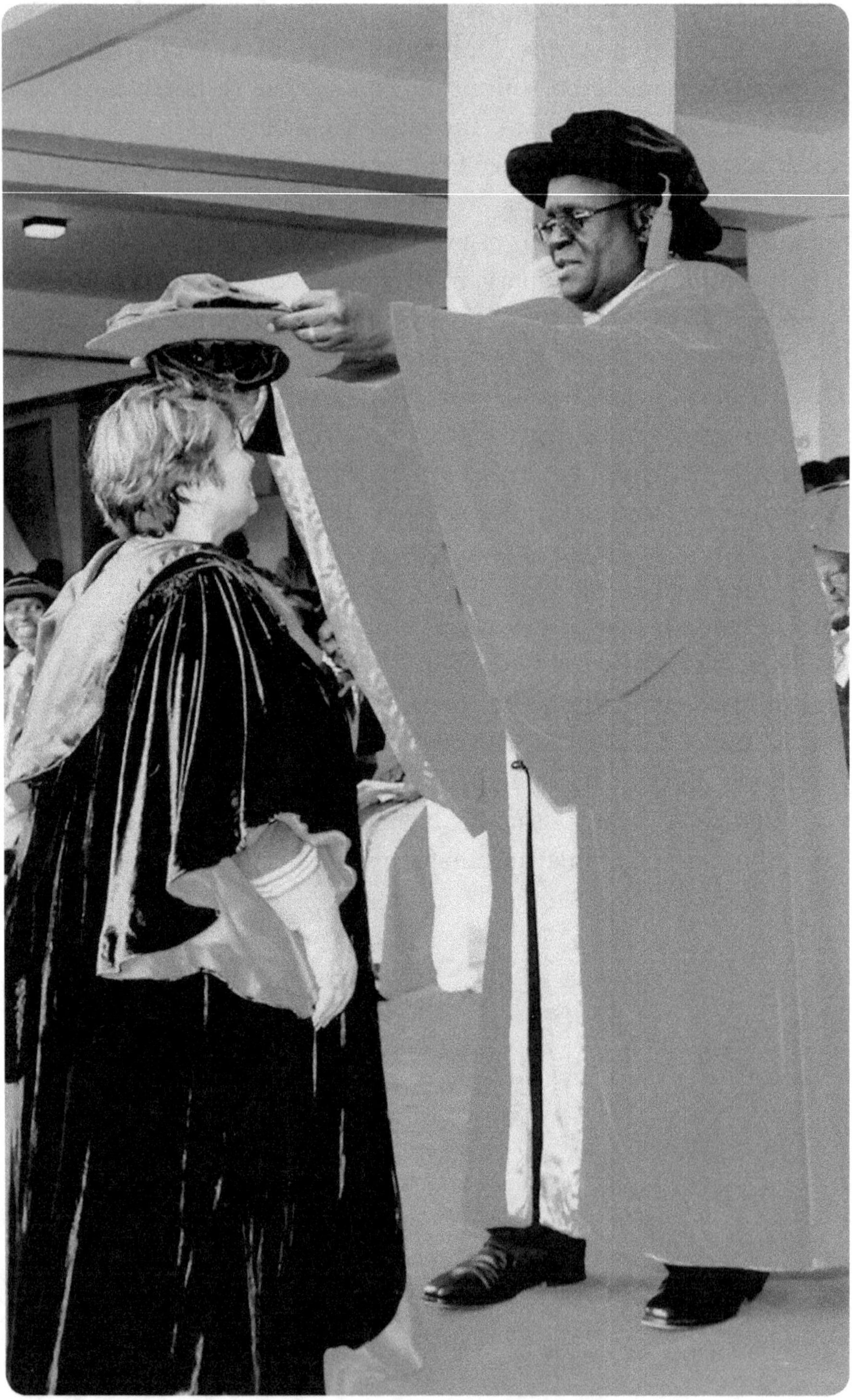

Appointment of the 6th Vice-Chancellor of the University of Nairobi by the Chancellor, Dr. Joseph Wanjui on the 6th January, 2005

Seated from right Prof. H. Mutoro, Principal CEES; Prof. J. Kaimenyi, DVC(AA); Prof. A. Mwang'ombe, Principal CAVS; Prof. L. Irungu, Principal CBPS; Myself; Prof. P. Mbithi DVC(A&F); Prof. I. Mbeche, Principal CHSS, Prof. B. Njoroge, Principal CAE, and Prof. I. Jumba, Deputy Principal CEES at a UMB Training Retreat, Lake Naivasha Simba Lodge, 2010

Seated from left Prof. P. K' Obonyo, Deputy Principal, CHSS; Prof. H. Mutoro, Principal CEES; Prof. I. Mbeche, Principal CHSS; Prof. L. Irungu, Principal CBPS; Myself carrying the Performance Contract Trophy; Prof. P. Mbithi DVC(A&F); Prof. A. Mwang'ombe, Principal CAVS; Prof. B. Njoroge, Principal CAE, and Prof. I. Kibwage, Deputy Principal CHS at a UMB Training Retreat, Merica Hotel Nakuru, 2010

Earlier in my tenure, UNES Board retreat seated from left Prof. Kameri Mbote, Dean School of Law; Prof. L. Irungu, Principal CBPS; Prof. P. Mbithi, DVC (A&F); Prof. J. Kimani, MD, UNES; Mr. J. Simba, Chairman of Council; myself; Prof. J. Kaimenyi DVC (AA) and Prof. I. Mbeche, Principal CHSS, 2005

Seated from left Mr. Yusuf Omar, Coorperate Director, BBK; Prof. J. Kaimenyi, DVC(AA); Prof. L. Irungu DVC(RPE), Prof. I. Mbeche, DVC(SA), Dr. J. Simba, Chairman of Council; myself; Prof. P. Mbithi DVC(A&F); Prof. J. Ogengo, MD, UNES; Prof. E. Njeru, Principal CHSS and Dr. S. Nzuve, Dean, School of Business at a Joint Strategic Planning Worshop of UNES Board of Directors and UMB at Nyali International Beach Hotel, 2012

Attending stakeholders retreat to discuss National Cohesion and Integration Commission (NCIC) on Ethic Diversity Audit in Public Universities in Kenya at Great Rift Valley Lodge Naivasha. Am seated centre with red cap, 2012

Induction of Trustees of the University of Nairobi Pension Scheme, seated front row, second from right, 2014

Receiving the ISO 9001:2008 certificate from the MD of KEBS, Engineer Kioko Mang'eli, 2008

Myself with Barack Obama, then Senator of Illinois, United States of America, 2006

With Barack Obama planting a tree during his visit at the University of Nairobi, 2006

From left to right Chairman of Council, Dr. John Simba, Minister of Higher Education Science and Technology, Dr. Sally Kosgei, American Secretary of State Hillary Clinton on her arrival at the University of Nairobi, Chancellor Dr. Joseph Wanjui and Prof. Chrispas Kiamba, Permanent Secretary Ministry of Higher Education Science and Technology, 2009

With Hon. Niccolò Rinaldi member of the European Parliament during a courtesy call to the Vice-Chancellor University of Nairobi after delivering a guest lecture at Faculty of Arts, 2012

Presenting a gift to H.E. Mr. Li Changchun, member of the Standing Committee of Political Bureau of the Central Committee of the Communist Party of the People's Republic of China (CPC) on official visit to the University, 2011

With the German Chancellor, Her Excellency Angela Merkel during her visit to the University of Nairobi, 2011

Accompanying Her Excellency Angela Merkel Germany Head of State on her visit to the University of Nairobi, 2011

South Korea's Prime Minister H.E. Kim Hwang-Sik shakes hands with me as VC, UoN after the signing of an MoU in the presence of the Prof. Crispus Kiamba, Permanent Secretary for Higher Education Science and Technology

Myself as the President of the Association of African Universities with the Prof. Naana Jane Opoku Agyeman, Ghanaian Minister for Education during the AAU (COREVIP) meeting in Stellenbosch, South Africa, 2013

Myself with the former UN Secretary General, H.E. Dr. Kofi Annan and looking on is Dr. Wanjui, 2008

Myself during the Launch of the Starehe Boys Centre Endowment Fund by H.E. President Daniel Arap Moi, 1999

Myself shaking hands with H.E. President Mwai Kibaki, during the award of Charter to the Technical University of Kenya, January 2013

Myself with H.E. Retired President Mwai Kibaki on his right is the CS for Sports, Culture and the Arts of Kenya, Hassan Wario and CS, Michael Kamau for Transport and Infrastructure after delivering a Public Lecture titled: Kenya@50: Of Hindsight, Insight and Foresight at the University of Nairobi, December, 2013

With H.E. President Uhuru Kenyatta at the University of Nairobi as Finance Minister, 2010

Prime Minister the Right Hon. Raila Odinga (centre) during his visit at the University of Nairobi with Dominique Strauss-Kahn, Managing Director of the IMF, left, 2010

With Dr. Mohamed Gharib Bilal, Vice President of the United Republic of Tanzania on the right during an International Universities Exhibition in Arusha, Tanzania, 2014

On the occasion of signing of the Collective Bargaining Agreement (CBA) with the University Academic Staff Union (UASU), on the left Prof. Fredrick Onyango, VC, Maseno University and on the right partly hidden, Prof. Ezra Martim, VC, Egerton University, 2005

With Prof. Crispus Kiamba, former VC, UON, on the right on the occasion of a public lecture by Prof. Wangari Maathai at the University of Nairobi, 2004

From left Christine Noe, Prof Thandabantu Nhlapo, Prof Martin West, Rafiki Yohana, Nan Warner, Prof George Magoha and Norbert Musekiwa at a braai to celebrate the success of USHEPiA at the University of Cape Town, 2009

With a Delegation from the Embassy of the People's Republic of China led by Mr. Zhao Shunguo, 2012

With the United States of America Ambassador to Kenya, His Excellency Robert Godec, 2014

With the German Ambassador to Kenya, Her Excellency Margit Hellwig-Boette, 2009

With the Indian High Commissioner to Kenya, His Excellency Yogenshwar Varma, 2014

With the Kenyan High Commissioner to Australia, His Excellency Isaya Kabira, on the right in Canberra Australia, 2014

From left to right Prof. John Ddumba Ssentamu, Vice-Chancellor Makerere University, Prof Thandabantu Nhlapo, Deputy Vice-Chancellor University of Cape Town, with Humphrey Webuye to my left during the USHEPiA consultative meeting at the Univeristy of Nairobi, 2012

With the World Bank Lead Economist, Apurva Sanghi, during a courtesy call to the Vice-Chancellor, University of Nairobi, 2014

KUSU Secretary General, Charles Mukwaya accompanied by his Colleagues, presents a cheque for the support of needy students at the University to the Vice-Chancellor, Prof. G.A.O. Magoha in the presence of his Deputy Vice-Chancellor, Prof. Lucy Irungu, Isaac Mbeche and Henry Mutoro, 2014

Unveiling Dr. Joseph Wanjui's Book entitled "The Native Son" during the launch at the University of Nairobi, 2014

My Self at the Centre together with KNH Director, Richard Lisiyampe accompanied by the University of Nairobi Management presenting donations to Sinai fire victims through the Kenya Red Cross, 2011

Myself with Prof. Wangari Maathai during a courtesy call to the Vice-Chancellor's office, 2011

Presenting a gift to the current Cabinet Secretary in the Ministry of Information & Communication Technology, Joseph Mucheru (centre) when he was Google sub-Saharan Africa Ambassador and Kenya Country Manager, 2012

Myself on the right receiving the Trophy of Excellence as number one (1) in Performance Contracting from H.E., President Mwai Kibaki and the Right Hon. Prime Minister Raila Odinga in the presence of Dr. John Simba, the Chairman of University of Nairobi Council 3rd from right and Prof. Peter Mbithi DVC, (A&F), 2nd right, 2012

Myself centre with Hon. Chief Justice Dr. Willy Mutunga, second from right during a visit to the University of Nairobi, on extreme right is Prof. Peter Mbithi, DVC (A&F) and Prof. Jacob Kaimenyi, DVC (AA) of the University of Nairobi, 2012

Dean, School of Law, Prof. Patricia Kameri-Mbote, fourth from left presenting the Moot Court Winners Trophy to the Vice-Chancellor, Prof. G.A.O. Magoha, 2014

The University top Management together with the Unit heads after signing Performance Contracts with the Vice-Chancellor, front centre, 2014

The University top Management being shown architectural model of the proposed School of Pharmacy building located at the KNH campus of the College of Health Sciences, 2012

At a Graduation Luncheon with Dr. Manu Chandaria on the right, 2009

With Dr. Joseph Wanjui, (2nd right) Chancellor University of Nairobi, Dr. John Simba (extreme right) the chairman of Council and former Vice-Chancellor, Prof. Francis Gichaga (extreme left), 2009

Myself 2nd left, with the President of Yokohama University, in the Centre at Yokohama University, Japan, 2011

Myself with the President of Tongji University Shanghai, China, 2015

Myself with the Prof. David Barnard, President of the University of Manitoba, Winnipeg, Canada, 2015

With Prof. David Barnard, President of the University of Manitoba in Canada with which we have had an active MOU for 40 years, 2013

Myself with the President of University of Maryland Baltmore, United State of America, Dr. Jay A. Perman, in his office, 2012

Myself, left with the Vice-Chancellor and Principal of the University of Edinburgh, Prof. Timothy O'shea in Urumqi, China attending a Confucius Institute Council Round Table Conference, 2015

Myself, with the Prof. Louis Antonio Paulino from Brazil (in cap) and Prof. Jaime Vatter, President, University of Santo Tomas, Santiago, Chile third from right in Kufundong, China attending a Confucius Institute Council Round Table Conference, 2015

Myself with Prof. Synn Ilhi, President, Keimyung University, Republic of South Korea, 2015

Myself with a visiting Chinese official, 2008

Myself with Rector Prof. Thomas Wilhelmsson of the University of Helsinki after signing a MoU with the University of Nairobi, 2011

Signing an MoU with Mr. Nam Jin Jeon for the Korean Foundation and myself (left) for the University of Nairobi, 2012

Myself with Ambassador (Eng.) Mahboub Maalim, Executive Secretary of the IGAD, 2011

Myself with Prof. Li Yuanyuan, President, Jilin University, China, 2016

With the Vice-Chancellor of the University of Somalia, Prof. Mohammed Yusuf, 2013

Signing an MoU with Vice-Chancellors of the University of Cape Coast, Ghana and Bonn-Rhein-Sieg University of Applied Sciences, German, 2013

Myself, with the Prof. Zhu Chongshi, President Xiamen University, China, 2016

Signing of an MoU with the President of the Colorado State University (CSU), Dr. Tony Frank, left. Looking on is Prof. Peter Mbithi, DVC (A&F) extreme right, and Ms. Rebecca Ngondo, University Chief Legal Officer, 3rd right, 2012

With Prof. Sidney A. McPhee, President of Middle Tennessee State University (MTSU), United States of America, 2013

With Prof. Chu Minwei, President of Shanghai Finance University during the exchange of an MoU, 2012

With Prof. Stephen Knapp, President of George Washington University, Washington DC, United States of America, 2016

Prof. Lillian Tibatemwa-Ekirikubinza DVC(AA), Makerere University (left) interacts with the Prof. Mukanadla Rwekaza, Vice-Chancellor, University of Dar es Salaam (center) and Prof. George Magoha, Vice-Chancellor of the University of Nairobi, during the UEA 50th Anniversary celebrations 29th June 2013, Makerere University, Kampala Uganda

Myself seated second from right with the President of Shiga University of Medical Science in Otsu, Japan seated centre on the front row, 2012

Myself seated 5th from left, Madam Liu Yandong, the Vice premier of the People's Republic of China, tenth from left and other world University presidents during the Confucius Institute Conference in Beijing China, 2009

Myself 7th from left, standing next to Madam Liu Yandong, the Vice premier of the People's Republic of China, on the front row during the Confucius Institute Conference in Beijing China, 2014

Congratulatory message from the University of Nairobi Alumni Association, 2012

Ground breaking ceremony at the School of Pharmacy at the College of Health Sciences, 2012

Myself with His Excellency Jacob Keidar the Israeli Ambassador to Kenya, 2011

With the Managing Director of Barclays Bank International during the endowment of Barclays Chair in the Department of Finance and Accounting in the School of Business, University of Nairobi, 2009

Myself with the Managing Director of Barclays Bank of Kenya, Mr. Jeremy Awori, 2014

With Ford Foundation President Luis Ubiñas at the University of Nairobi after delivering a Public Lecture, 2012

With visiting South Korean diplomat

With Prof. Marleen Temmerman of the University of Ghent, Belgium, 2012

Myself with the Speaker of the National Assembly, Hon. Justin Muturi and Deputy Speaker of Senate Hon. Kembi Gitura, 2013

Myself with members of staff at the Vice-Chancellor's office during my farewell party, December, 2014

With the Vice-Chancellor University of Juba on the right and Deputy Vice-Chancellor, Academic Affairs, University of Nairobi, Prof. Henry Mutoro, at Gazi University in Ankara, Turkey, 2014

Attending Confucius Council Round Table Conference at Qufundong, People's Republic of China standing centre next to the director general to my right Dr. Xu Lin, Director General of Hanban and CEO at the Confucius Institute Headquarters, Beijing, China, 2015

After chairing ANSTI Management Board Meeting at African Union Headquarters in Addis Ababa, Ethiopia. Myself standing at the back centre, 2015

Conferring a Higher Doctorate Degree to Dr. Vijoo Rattansi, the current Chancellor, University of Nairobi, 2014

Giving a Speech during a Graduation Ceremony at the University of Nairobi, 2013

In an academic gown, as the Vice-Chancellor, University of Nairobi, 2005

Giving a speech during a Graduation Luncheon, 2009

In a Graduation Ceremony with the Chancellor, Dr. Wanjui on my right, 2009

At a Graduation ceremony with Prof. Florida Karani, Chancellor Maseno University and Prof. Crispus Kiamba, Permanent Secretary, Ministry of Higher Education Science & Technology (MoEST) and my immediate predecessor as Vice-Chancellor, University of Nairobi, 2009

At a Graduation Luncheon with the Chairman of the University of Nairobi Council, Dr. John Simba on the left and member of Council, Dr. Manu Chandaria on the right, 2009

In my Office with the Excellency Trophy on Performance Contracting in the Public Service, 2012

With the Excellency Trophy on Performance Contracting in the Public Service, 2012

Myself with Prof. Olusola Oyewole (centre) President of Association of African Universities (AAU) and Prof. Silas Lwakabamba (right) Rwandan Minister for Education, during a Conference of Rectors, Vice-Chancellors & Presidents of African Universities (COREVIP) in Kigali, Rwanda, 2016

At the Conference of Rectors, Vice-Chancellors & Presidents of African Universities in Kigali, Rwanda. Seated 4th from right is Professor James McWha, Vice-Chancellor, University of Rwanda and Prof. Silas Lwakabamba, Rwandan Minister for Education, 5th from right, 2015

At the 6th Regional Conference of Vice-Chancellors Provosts and Deans of Science, Engineering and Technology (COVIDSET), at Enugu, Nigeria with me standing at the centre, 2015

Seated from right Charles Ringera, CEO, HELB, myself representing public universities, Prof. David Ndetei, Chair, KUCCPS, Prof. Noah Midamba, VC, KCA University representing private universities and Prof. Mabel Imbuga, VC, JKUAT, representing public universities attending strategic planning retreat, 2015

With the Prof. Simon Gicharu, Founder and Chairman of Board of Trustees, Mt. Kenya University (right), Prof. Stanley Waudo Mount Kenya University Vice-Chancellor and Prof. John Struthers, Director Centre for African Research on Enterprise and Economic Development, University of West Scotland (left), 2016

Cake cutting session with Prof. Simon Gicharu, Founder and Chairman of Board of Directors, Mt. Kenya University, left and Jane Nyutu, Co- Founder Board of Directors, Mt. Kenya University (centre) on the occasion of the 11th Graduation Ceremony, 2016

From left to right Prof. S. Lwakabamba, Rwanda Minister for Education, myself and Prof. J. McWha Vice-Chancellor University of Rwanda at a post-COREVIP Press Conference in Kigali, Rwanda, 2015

Confucius Institute Conference at the headquarters in Beijing, People's Republic of China, am on second row 5th from left, 2012

MOU signing ceremony between United Nations University (UNU) and partner African universities. From left: Prof. George Magoha, Vice-Chancellor, University of Nairobi; Prof. Olive Mugenda, Vice-Chancellor, Kenyatta University; Prof. Konrad Osterwalder, Rector, UNU; Prof. Ernest Aryeetey, Vic-Chancellor, University of Ghana; Prof. Steven Simukanga, Vice-Chancellor, University of Zambia

Myself, as Vice-Chancellor University of Nairobi welcoming lead auditor Prof. Tolly Mbwette, the Vice-Chancellor, Open University of Tanzania. Looking on from left: Prof. Jacob Kaimenyi DVC(AA), Prof. Isaac Mbeche DVC (SA) and Prof. Peter Mbithi DVC (A&F)

Stanford Executive Program 2009, at the Stanford University Graduate School of Business (in the middle, second row from the back)

My last photograph as VC with members of the UMB. Front row from right Prof. B. Njoroge, Principal CAE, Prof. E. Njeru, Principal CHSS, Prof. J. Ogengo, MD, UNES, Prof. H. Mutoro DVC (AA), Chairman of Council, Dr. Idle Farah, Dr. Betty Gikonyo, Vice Chairman of Council, Myself, incoming VC, Prof. Peter Mbithi, Prof. Isaac Mbeche, DVC (SA), Prof. Isaac Kibwage, Principal CHS, Prof. Lucy Irungu, DVC, RPE and Dr. D. Bulinda, Registrar, Administration, 2015

Handing over the University of Nairobi Mace to Prof. Peter Mbithi, the 7th Vice-Chancellor of the University of Nairobi at the Vice-Chancellor Committee Room on 5th January, 2015

Receiving a gift during my farewell luncheon from Morris McOloo of Ford Foundation (third left) witnessed by (right to left) Prof. L. Irungu DVC (RPE), myself, Chancellor Vidjoo Rattansi, Prof. A. Mwang'ombe, Principal CAVS 5th and Prof. I. Mbeche DVC (SA). In the background from right Dr. Joseph Wanjui and Dr. Mrs. Barbara Magoha, 2015

CHAPTER SEVEN

LESSONS LEARNT

One of the most important lessons that I learnt early in my training was that with hard work and determination, coupled with good time management and the grace of God, everything is possible. I was placed in a position of professional leadership and trainer quite early in my career as a surgeon. After my clinical examinations at the University of Ibadan's Teaching Hospital in May1981, I was appointed senior resident in charge of the urology unit of the department of surgery at the Lagos University Teaching Hospital. In this position, I found myself organizing, allocating duties and managing many other surgical residents, some of whom were senior to me. I therefore had to tread very carefully while at the same time training them professionally.

This experience later proved extremely valuable to me. I became VC at the age of 52 and was well aware of the fact that there were many other senior and older professors at the University, whom I had to manage while respecting their professionalism, wisdom and seniority.

The lessons I learned from my surgical training at various universities and colleges in Nigeria, Ghana, UK and the Republic of Ireland was that surgeons were professionally trained to be crystal clear and concise in their analogy, diagnosis, management and outcomes. The success of a surgeon would thus be measured by the number of successful operations among other things. When I applied these principles by replacing the 'patient' with the 'University', I found them quite useful in leading the change management at the University of Nairobi.

I also learned many important lessons from my mentors including Dr. Griffin and Mr. Shaw, David Sperling of Strathmore College

Nairobi, Professor Mungai and the Nigerian fraternity of Professors Mabayoje, Ransome-Kuti, Elebute, Akinkugbe and Amaku of the College of Medicine of the University of Lagos. I was particularly impressed by the humility and simplicity exhibited by the Vice-Chancellor of the University of Lagos, Professor Ade-Ajayi.

During my ten years as VC, I learned several important lessons. Although I was a top-grade surgeon and clinical researcher, I realized soon enough that leading the University of Nairobi was a different ballgame altogether. The location of the main Campus of the University, together with the halls of residence within the Nairobi Central Business District (CBD) became one of the many bottlenecks to the efficient and successful running of the University. This was because the National Government, the Judiciary, the National Assembly and the Senate were all located in the CBD. In addition, most of the businesses in Nairobi had their headquarters within the CBD.

A sizable number of diplomatic missions also had their offices located within the CBD. This meant that the smooth running of the city depended also on a similar smooth running of the University. The National Government had significant interest because any chaos at the University by students or staff would immediately overflow into the CBD. This would frequently result in confrontations with the police, looting and subsequent closures of businesses and disruption of government functions. Therefore, the first lesson I learned was to continually engage directly, not only the elected student leaders at the University, but also other popular opinion leaders among the students fraternity.

With regards to staff, I kept an open 24-hour direct communication channel with all the three different staff trade unions of the University: UASU, KUSU and KUDHEIHA. In addition, I developed and kept very special relations with the professors and other lecturers at the University, because as a very last resort, before any drastic action was taken against indisciplined students, it is these lecturers that provided counsel to students. A great majority of such students listened to advice from their professors and lecturers. On the government side, I ensured continued cordial and close contacts with police chiefs, and all other senior government officials involved in security, including the Director-General of the National Intelligence Service (NIS). This enabled me to discover a considerable number of problematic events at the planning level, empowering me to intervene before their execution.

I also learned that it was far much better to be forthright with students concerning their demands rather than making promises that would be impossible to implement. I also learned that I had to be very firm in dealing only with the elected student leaders who were also (SONU officials) instead of large groups of students. Therefore, during my ten years as VC I never went down, even once, to the Great Court of the University 'to address students'. I successfully dealt with their elected leaders, usually meeting them in small groups but occasionally meeting the whole SONU executive.

Previously, students would come directly to the VC even with trivial issues which would otherwise have been sorted out by other equally competent University managers. I was extremely firm that solutions to students problems should, in the first instance be sought from the offices of the chairmen of departments, deans or directors, dean of students, special students advisor, and respective college principals, before being escalated to DVC, and finally to the VC. We agreed on the *modus operandi* with student leaders, while leaving my doors open at all times to the Chairman and Secretary General of SONU for any emergencies. I wish to commend our student leaders, for observing their part of the agreement and never storming my office during the entire ten years I was the VC, but came on appointment or during genuine emergencies such as when a student was knocked down by a vehicle and required specialized treatment in a private hospital. The Chairman and Secretary General of SONU had my personal phone numbers and could therefore reach me at any time, something that they appreciated very much.

The greatest lesson I learned from the above was that when a manager was firm, fair and reasonable, the students took him seriously, greatly reducing the level of truancy. The other positive act that contributed immensely to the students leaders understanding was their involvement in many of the management structures at the University. They for example belonged to faculty, school, and institute boards, the Senate and Council. They participated and contributed freely without undue hindrance in all the management organs of the University, except during extremely sensitive and confidential matters. This empowerment of the students leaders enabled them to contribute constructively on matters touching on student affairs. This greatly reduced the potential areas of conflict between students and management. The management on its part, swiftly implemented the agreed requests such as purchasing additional buses to facilitate transport, and facilitating the travel of a few students leaders abroad for exposure. The students were further exposed through participation in inter university games within Africa.

This international exposure of the selected student leaders, every year, to learn about best practices from students in other international universities, undoubtedly broadened their thinking and understanding. On their return, they shared their experiences with the rest of the leaders, and eventually with the general student population. The University management also benefited tremendously from these experiences. In addition, the University provided SONU with a healthy annual budget line. The students were empowered to make their own budget, depending on their priorities and needs, without undue interference from the University. The money however had to be spent according to the set financial regulations. One permanent feature of the budget was the annual SONU elections. Otherwise, the only other management input was that of oversight to ensure that the budget was spread through the year and that all Colleges benefited and excluded the sharing of cash among themselves.

There are quite a number of instances during my leadership that student leaders were either unable or unwilling to control the anger of the larger student population. For example, when a "comrade" was killed by a hit and run motor vehicle, students would pour out into the streets to vent their anger against the general public and usually destroyed property. They would sometimes loot from businesses within the CBD and light bonfires blocking major roads including Uhuru Highway, State House Road and University Way. This was spontaneous and legitimate anger by the students mourning their fallen colleague. The only challenge was that it was directed at the wrong targets. Therefore, in order to control the situation and minimize destruction and loss of property, the police would be called in to persuade the students to return to the University precincts and if that failed, they would disperse the students using minimal force, to avoid other casualties. In this regard, the police mainly used tear gas, water cannons and only in some rare extreme instances, used rubber bullets.

However, at nightfall they would cool down and by the following day the management would engage them in a more constructive and fruitful discussions thereby avoiding closure of the University. One of the key demands conceded by the VC in such challenging situations was the authorization of the use of one University bus, to take some students, including their leaders to a funeral service of the student. The students together with their leaders greatly appreciated such simple gestures, unlike in the past when they would demand many buses, and if denied, would proceed to commandeer University and public transport buses.

Overseeing annual SONU elections was the greatest lesson, nightmare, and challenge of my stewardship at the University. The challenges arose from the fact that the location of the University within the CBD made it very attractive for politicians who wanted to quickly mobilize students for their own gain. The students would then disrupt normal activities within Nairobi's CBD. It is for this reason that political parties and politicians always wanted friendly student leaders that they could easily manipulate and control.

As a policy the University did not condone students' direct participation in national partisan politics, and therefore these activities did not take place openly as that would lead to automatic disqualification of the candidate from the election process. Nevertheless, some campaigns were very high profile, involving expensive vehicles and posters that cost way beyond the financial capabilities of the candidates.

The University management largely survived by being extremely interactive, firm and most significantly, neutral. For the avoidance of doubt, there was no time ever, that the University management supported a student contestant financially during my leadership. This act of neutrality strengthened our position in dealing with the issues at hand. At a personal level, my policy was to work with any student leadership, provided that they were legitimately elected.

There was also an elaborate appeal mechanism in place against any electoral malpractice, which was presided over by an independent advocate of the High Court. The advocate was agreed upon in advance by all contestants and Senate before commencement of the elections. The elaborate appeal process gave the aggrieved parties the opportunity to prove their allegations by providing evidence and witnesses.

It was further agreed that the results of the SONU election appeals panel would be final and binding to all contestants. This process had to be completed within strictly stipulated timelines, before the legitimately elected student leaders were sworn into office. It had always been the practice that the swearing in ceremony was held at the Chancellor's Court led by the University Chief Legal Officer, in the presence of the VC and management. This historical arrangement changed during one ceremony when the students became unruly, indisciplined and uncontrollable and threatening my physical safety and that of the University Management Board members. I left the Chancellor's Court with my management team, without performing the swearing in ceremony. The following day, an elaborate arrangement was made by the management to swear in the newly elected student leaders in the VC's Committee Room, one at a time and without any ceremony. This was the last time that the VC was involved in the swearing in ceremonies of elected students leaders, during my tenure as CEO. Consequently, the ceremony was delegated to the DVC, Academic Affairs, and later, DVC, Student Affairs who performed this function competently and successfully on behalf of the VC.

The University management oversaw ten SONU elections. Nine of these were successful while one was nullified due to destruction of election materials by two SONU officials and some hired goons. The students responsible were disciplined as per the University statutes. Since it was not possible to verify the genuinely elected student leaders, the results were nullified and a SONU Caretaker Committee, appointed by the Senate to run the affairs of SONU for one year, until the following year when another proper election was carried out.

At the same time, the SONU Constitution was overhauled and reviewed to be in tandem with the Kenya Constitution 2010. The SONU Constitution Review Panel, which was chaired by Professor Muriuki had a majority of student membership but also included the University's Chief Legal Officer, Rebecca Ngondo, the Dean School of Law, Professor Kameri Mbote, and Professor Bernard Sihanya, in addition to the Dean of students, Dr. Fr. Dominic Wamugunda.

The firm and elaborate establishment of structured systems of direct communication and immediate engagement at different administrative levels, entrenched objective dialogue as the preferred method of engagement with student leaders against the usual subjective, open, chaotic and mostly violent confrontations of the past. As a result, this became a routine rather than an exception, and the students leaders started to enjoy taking active part in University management as part of a larger transformative team. They were assigned a specific procurement officer to ensure that they got value for money as they independently carried out their normal business. Whenever a conflict arose, it was swiftly resolved.

These systems were further strengthened by the appointment of a DVC whose specific duties were student affairs.

The lesson I learned from this was that students were a great intellectual human resource which upon constructive engagement and harnessing, would definitely positively contribute to the University's achievement of its vision, mission, strategies, and goals. I can still vividly remember when the government declared famine a national disaster as a result of severe drought due to rain and subsequent crop failure. The University as part of its Corporate Social Responsibility, appealed to the entire University community including staff and students, to contribute voluntarily to this national initiative by donating foodstuff which would in turn be distributed affected areas. Staff contributed very generously to this initiative. However, what touched me most was the generosity of our students in this significant philanthropic effort. A large number of them responded by contributing foodstuff which when pooled together became very significant. Furthermore, some of them decided to skip several meals and donated money to the initiative. It became very clear to me that one did not have to be necessarily able but only willing to contribute freely and willingly. But perhaps the most pleasant surprise was when some student leaders and other students volunteered not only to assist us package the foodstuff but also to accompany the University management to distribute the donations in Kajiado and Mwingi districts.

From this act the general public could see our students and their leaders performing very positive roles in the society. Our students could once again secure industrial attachments as a result of their good behaviour. This drastic transformation was a welcome relief to the University management and the general public, and marked the beginning of rebuilding the students' public image and they once again became the graduates of choice for the industry. Due to the direct dialogue and engagement, the University management had succeeded in transforming the students through their leaders and getting the best out of them.

Students at the College of Health Sciences organized many medical and dental camps during my leadership as VC. These camps were a joint effort between pharmaceutical companies, the College, and the University management. The initiative originated from the student leaders who together with their clinical teachers solicited for drug and other donations from various companies in Kenya and the East African region. The University management provided logistical support including transport to the various destinations. This teamwork further enhanced the leaders confidence in dealing effectively and fruitfully with University management. Initially, the camps targeted the slum areas within Nairobi such as Kibera, Korogocho, Mathare, Kawangware, Uthiru, Sinai, Mlango Kubwa, Mukuru Kwa Njenga, Huruma, and Dagoreti. However, they were later extended to different parts of the country including Nyeri, Homa Bay, Kajiado, Narok, Machakos, Meru, Siaya, Kiambu and Murang'a.

The medical camps involved free diagnosis and treatment for common ailments such as diabetes, hypertension, malaria, anaemia, urinary tract infection and common stool parasites. Patients were also taught simple public health tips such as human and other waste disposal, hand washing and proper sanitation.

Students from the College of Biological and Physical Sciences at Chiromo Campus led by their Principal, Professor Lucy Irungu, contributed clothes, foodstuff, a 5,000 litre water tank, and books towards the Kajiado Children's Home. It is such humanitarian actions that quickly endeared our students once more, to the general public, and restored the public respect and confidence in the University of Nairobi which had hitherto been eroded.

SONU also takes credit for organizing clean-up exercises in different campuses of the University as well as donating blood during national tragedies. Such tragedies include the Sinai slums fire tragedy in Nairobi in which tens of people were killed and dozens others hospitalized with severe burns. SONU mobilized its members and within a very short notice, donated many litres of blood to save the lives of patients admitted at the Kenyatta

National Hospital, and other hospitals. Our students once again proved that they were caring and the previous indiscipline was a thing of the past.

Of more significance however, was the public noticing the empathetic and humanitarian side of the students with appreciation and great satisfaction. The student community went further to donate foodstuff and clothes to the same fire victims, and other survivors displaced by the tragedy.

The generosity of our staff was demonstrated when they contributed Kshs 1 million to the Kenyatta National Hospital to offset emergency medical bills accruing from many of the patients admitted at the institution. The money was utilized to purchase some of the urgently needed medical consumables essential for the treatment of serious burns.

In addition, our staff went a step further and donated blood for survivors of the Sinai Slums fire disaster. The staff once again gave foodstuff, water and clothing items, and handed them over to the Kenya Red Cross for onward transmission to the victims of the disaster.

These noble acts greatly assisted in positively changing the mind-sets of the general public towards the University of Nairobi. The University, as a corporate entity, on the other hand, acquired greater visibility as a result of the multiple, orderly and philanthropic behaviour of our students. It may now become very clear to all, that the University of Nairobi would not have successfully achieved the status of world class excellence without the full and active participation of our gallant students and their leaders who are a bigger part of the stakeholders of the University.

SONU also commenced a programme of fostering cordial relations with the neighbours and surrounding. For example, they successfully organized a visit to Christ Chapel Children's Home located in Huruma slums in Nairobi for orphans and vulnerable children between the ages of 2 and 15 years. Our students took time to thoroughly clean the Home and share stories with the children, in addition to actively participating in various sports activities with them. They finally donated foodstuff, clothes, shoes and money. This humanitarian and philanthropic act was quite encouraging and was part of the University's Corporate Social Responsibility which strengthened our brand and enhanced local visibility and standing.

Students from the School of Law who are also members of the Students Association for Legal Aid and Research (SALAR) conducted free legal aid clinics and public awareness campaigns in other slum areas within Nairobi, such as Kibera and Mathare. During these clinics they provided legal advice on a variety of issues including labour, criminal, land and human rights targeting those in the community who have legal problems but cannot afford the services of a lawyer. They also held public barazas which were sit down forums with youth groups and members of the public to discuss the constitution and the legal issues affecting young people in general, and residents of the affected slums in particular. The students also carried out research, on the challenges and hindrances facing people as they try to access justice within the area. A major focus in the legal aid clinic was to advise minors on their rights under the Children's Act and international conventions. The Legal Aid desks also offered additional free legal advice to many clients with issues ranging from family disputes, especially related to custody and maintenance.

The University of Nairobi Women Students Welfare Association (WOSWA) is an umbrella organization for all female students. Of the over 35 professional student organization. WOSWA prominently stood out as one of the most efficient and visible in championing the rights and welfare of our female students. They were mature and professional in the manner in which they carried out their businesses and worked very well with the University management and SONU, whose activities they complemented. They organized several events to sensitize the public on the plight and rights of the girl child in Kenya and also supported women through various activities. This was best exemplified by WOSWA's visit to Marigat where they donated sanitary pads and toilet papers to needy girls. They also mentored female students in high schools, and donated foodstuff and clothes to the less fortunate in the society. They specifically distributed foodstuff and clothes to victims of Post-Election Violence of 2008, and organized an anti-jigger campaign in Kandara Division, Murang'a County. WOSWA also held a cervical cancer awareness week in addition to organizing blood donations on various occasions to save lives of needy patients in various hospitals. Most of these activities augmented the Corporate Social Responsibility of the University.

The lesson I learned from this was that all our student leaders and specifically WOSWA played extremely significant roles in our change management process at the University. My role was to ensure a conducive environment that enabled and empowered members of the University community to produce their very best towards the realization of our strategies and goals.

In order to ensure that students from underprivileged families do not drop out of the University due to lack of fees, the University management set up a Central Needy Students Fund worth Kshs 5 million. The kitty was administered by the special students advisor, Professor Muriuki who always performed thorough due diligence before disbursement of funds to ensure that only the genuinely needy students are supported. This effort was further cascaded to the six colleges of the University, with each College contributing Kshs 1 million toward this noble and worthy cause.

Further, SONU set up a scholarship fund worth Kshs 3 million for the same purpose. The University of Nairobi Alumni Association on its part also set up an additional scholarship fund worth Kshs 5 million to further assist needy students of the University.

One can imagine the extent to which the University management, students leaders and the Alumni were sensitive to the plight of the needy students. These practices are some of the unique qualities that distinguished the University of Nairobi from the rest and placed it ahead of the pack.

To successfully have led the University for ten years, and to steer it through a transformative change process to world class excellence, I had to continually lead my team from the front.

As the accounting and CEO of the University, I had to sign all the procurement contracts for the supply of goods and services. The lesson I learned quite early in my leadership was that excellent procurement processes, accompanied with good paperwork, did not always translate to getting good value for money for the University. I therefore got used to performing 'due diligence' before signing some of the tender contracts. My principal concern was to be absolutely sure that the entities that were awarded the contracts had the capacity to execute the said contracts in a timely manner, and that the University would get value for money. This was made more challenging because accounting officers are not members of the tender or procurement committees, and therefore do not benefit from the debates that transpire during these committees meetings. For the record, I trusted my tender committee members, but I still performed due diligence anyway. Initially, there was a very high turnover of procurement officers presumably because the University management insisted on their thorough and professional performance of duties.

The results of the due diligence that I performed greatly benefited the University. I found out that businesses can go to great lengths to falsify their documents in order to comply with the tender requirements. For example, a company falsified its audited accounts by inflating the value tenfold in order to reach the threshold required in the tender advert. At face value, the accounts looked absolutely genuine. I approached the audit firm in order to get the genuine audited accounts whose value was only a tenth of the ones presented. In another instance, the winning bid for a construction company had listed many completed buildings in various parts of the country. A quick due diligence with these entities, which included government departments revealed that the had abandoned most of the projects uncompleted. So I signed the contract with the second lowest evaluated bidder, after the award by the tender committee.

In yet another situation, substandard pavement blocks were being supplied for road repairs and when I challenged the procurement manager to take me to the physical address of the supplying company that he had confirmed inspecting, he was quite hesitant. He insisted that it was very late – past six o'clock in the evening. When I persisted and finally went to the indicated company address, it turned out to be an open field in Kawangware, without any buildings or materials in sight. You can guess what happened to that officer after that incident. There were also a few instances where camouflage by bidding entities was so perfected that even due diligence failed to unmask the deficiencies. As a result, the University management only realized the truth, after the contracts had been executed.

At the beginning we had many challenges with the procurement of computers, which we urgently needed in large numbers of between 500 and 1,000 per year, to effectively manage the change management process at the University. Our challenge was that we awarded these tenders to local companies. Some of the companies were unable to supply the computers sometimes for up to one year. As a result, the University management and Council decided to float an international tender with computer manufacturers, which ended up being much more efficient and cheaper. Branded computers were purchased annually in bulk and stored at the University, so that user departments could purchase them within one day; according to their needs. At the completion of my tenure, there were over 9,000 computers at the University.

One of the most important lessons I learned from staff was that they needed to be appreciated, empowered and firmly encouraged to perform their duties which frequently resulted in enhanced outputs far beyond the set performance targets. This is best illustrated by teaching staff, and the manner in which they carried out their research. When I was appointed VC, the University research fund stood at Kshs 350 million. The then management mainstreamed research, and appointed a DVC to be specifically in charge of Research, Production and Extension. We then developed a strategy to systematically train more staff in research and grant proposal writing. This was effected through various well-funded workshops where participants were also encouraged to join the networks of international researchers from other countries, and to participate in interdisciplinary research as one way of enriching and enhancing their research. This was against the background that research had been identified as the missing link in Africa's development needs, with UNESCO statistics indicating that Africa was home to only a paltry 2.3 per cent of the world's researchers. A sizable number of academic staff was progressively trained across the entire university, resulting in the formation of a critical mass of active researchers able to write internationally competitive research and grant proposals, and therefore continually competing for research funds in the global arena.

The great increase in successful research and grant proposals written by the University staff in collaboration with international researchers from our many global collaborating institutions was part of the University's strategy of increasing research grant funding to at least 25–30 per cent of the entire University budget. These activities resulted in numerous positive and measurable outcomes. To begin with, the annual research fund value had increased tremendously more than tenfold to a whooping Kshs 4.5 billion, from the previous Kshs 350 million at the end of my tenure. This enabled the University to carry out more relevant research in many critical areas. For example, in August of 2010, the University of Nairobi's College of Health Sciences competitively won a five-year, 12.5 million USD grant from the National Institutes of Health (NIH) as part of the Medical Education Partnership Program Initiative (MEPI) targeting medical education institutions in sub-Saharan Africa. The programme dubbed Partnership for Innovative Medical Education for Kenya (PRIME-K) has the mission of improving health outcomes in Kenya through training and research. It was implemented in collaboration with the Universities of Washington, and Maryland at Baltimore. This programme has focused on the improvement of the quality of medical education, extending the reach of medical training, increasing the retention of University of Nairobi faculty by providing opportunities for clinical or applied research, and supporting research and administration oversight.

The College of Health Sciences also received an additional research grant focused on Neonatal, Child and Maternal Health. In collaboration with the University of Washington it established a Collaborative Centre of Excellence in Maternal, Newborn, and Child Health at the University. This undoubtedly increased our capacity in addition to providing outstanding training in implementation of science, applied research, health metrics and evaluation.

The other prominent international research grant competitively won by the University researchers was the Partnership for Advanced Clinical Education (PACE), which is a President's Emergency Plan Fund for AIDS Relief (PEPFAR). This was a Centre for Disease Control (CDC) funded by University of Maryland Baltimore and the Kenya National AIDS and STI Control Program (NASCOP) to strengthen pre-service and in service HIV education and training in Kenya. Our researchers in this project interacted with prominent international scholars among them Professor Robert Gallo, from the University of Maryland Baltimore, renowned for his prominent role in the discovery of the Human Immunodeficiency Virus (HIV), the infectious agent responsible for AIDS.

The University of Nairobi was among six leading African universities alongside: Stellenbosch in South Africa, Mekelle in Ethiopia, Nigeria Nsukka in Nigeria, Dar es Salaam in Tanzania, and University of Ghana in Ghana that were selected to train 72 postgraduate doctoral and masters students within Africa. The research grant value was Euros 2.3 million for the Trans-disciplinary Training for Resource Efficiency and Climate Change Adaptation in Africa (TRECC Africa). The training would provide Africa with the next generation of academics and professionals able to address an interlocking set of real challenges for Africa's future development with regard to climate change and natural resource depletion.

Africa's position in this complex required unique trans-disciplinary skills and competencies to enable the graduates to generate policy-relevant research work. Such a network would incorporate the various research environments from the six participating Universities into a sustainable partnership for climate change and resource efficiency by sharing the research human resource capacity, among partners. This was against the background of the fact that Africa is a continent dominated by poverty, contributes relatively little to total greenhouse gases, and in recent years has become the focus of the new global scramble for primary natural resources with the entry of new players like China. It is generally accepted that Africa might well experience the most severe impacts of climate change, while it remains the least prepared to handle these impacts, hence the significance, timeliness, and relevance of this research. To be truly sustainable, Africa will need to ensure that it uses its rich natural resource endowment responsibly to fund investments in human resource capacity and knowledge infrastructure that will sustain development after the primary natural resources have been depleted. This in turn, will establish the kind of funding base needed to finance adaptations to climate change.

The University of Nairobi was also one of the 24 universities selected to participate in the Development of Research Uptake in Sub-Saharan Africa (DRUSSA) programme. This important programme sought to assist participating universities to ensure that their research and other relevant work directly impacts on policy and practice in their countries by supporting and strengthening their in-house expertise. The DRUSSA programme was led by three international collaborating partners, including the Association of Commonwealth Universities (ACU), Centre for Research Evaluation, Science and Technology (CREST), and the Organizations Systems Design (OSD), and is funded by the United Kingdom Department for International Development (DFID).

The benefits accruing to the University included at least ten scholarships to participate in a specialist programme of continuing professional development in research uptake management, access to a bursary program to support staff participate in an M.Phil programme in research evidence and impact, and support to externally-facilitated events on research uptake management for up to twenty four key staff members. The DRUSSA programme also supported emergent research managers in universities across the East, West and Southern Africa and had four key programme areas. These included: capacity strengthening via research management and update molecular training; organizational and institutional strengthening; evaluating the impact of research uptake within specific research projects at selected Universities; and the development of an online community for the twenty four universities and a network for others who may be interested in the field of research management and uptake. The programme came at an opportune time when the University had embarked on building the management of research for a bigger impact on University policy making and on the Kenyan society.

All these interdisciplinary, inter-university, and international collaborative research activities by our excellent academic staff meant that the university management had succeeded in completely mainstreaming research at the University. These activities resulted in increased measurable outputs at the University in terms of peer reviewed journal publications, and enhanced numbers of postgraduates trained to completion of Masters and Doctorate levels. The enhanced research kitty also enabled many of our researchers to travel to various international collaborators' institutions, which undoubtedly assisted with the enhanced internationalization of the University through increased international visibility. I acknowledge and appreciate the fact that our researchers formed one of the most critical pillars that unconditionally supported the transformative change management process at the University.

I believe firmly, that through my activities, I have not only left suitable legacy of a very cohesive and transformed staff, but also that our actions have collectively secured and entrenched our University into a world class entity. In my life, I have tried to live by example so that I reach out and help others spiritually, intellectually, physically, financially, and relationally. I have tried to be an example of what an exceptional leadership should be. I have let others argue and express themselves, and I have been careful, too careful with the futures of others. I believe that leaving a legacy is like planting a tree. As that seed grows into a tree, it will provide seeds, so that future generations can then plant their own.

CHAPTER EIGHT

WITH THE BENEFIT OF HINDSIGHT

I must admit that I was extremely privileged to serve my country as the Vice-Chancellor of the University of Nairobi for two terms totalling ten years. Despite numerous challenges I am specifically grateful because I was able to serve the entire period without any major incidences or interference with the academic calendar of the University.

As I reflect over the ten years, I am trying to consider whether there are certain tasks and functions that I could have performed differently. Despite having been in the University administration for 6 years: as Chairman of the Department of Surgery; Dean of the Faculty of Medicine; Principal of the College of Health Sciences; and Deputy Vice-Chancellor in charge of Administration and Finance, I must candidly admit that none of these positions prepared me in any significant manner for the work that I was to find in the Vice-Chancellor's office.

However, my grounding from Starehe dictated that if one accepted a job, he had to perform it to the best of his ability, with measurable outputs, and give time for the less fortunate in society. This was irrespective of whether the task was cleaning a toilet or presiding over a graduation ceremony. Therefore, after being appointed VC I had a duty to complete the task. I found myself in a catch-22 situation because failure was not an option. The first thing I would have done differently, with the benefit of hindsight, was to try and understand in much greater detail what the day-to-day duties of a VC entailed. These would have included an understanding of the numerous intrigues, politics and controversies associated with the office. Despite these hurdles, I did take up the challenge and as a matter of fact thoroughly enjoyed my work.

I am glad that one of the first tasks I accomplished was spearheading the realization of the first Corporate Strategic Plan for the University of Nairobi. Even with the strategic plan in place, and its implementation commenced, I still encountered numerous resistance. For example, it took me quite a while to holistically grasp the core strategic challenges facing the University resulting in a rather slow start of the implementation of the plan. With the benefit of hindsight, I realize that perhaps I should have been much firmer at the beginning, in the manner in which I dealt with staff and students during the formation of the transformative and change management team.

This would have invariably resulted in significantly faster turnaround times with greater and enhanced measurable outputs and achievement of world class status in academic excellence for our institution. However, this was quite tricky because an extremely firm hand would have been interpreted as some form of dictatorship, which was detested by both staff and students. This would have also invariably resulted in disastrous consequences. The bottomline is that academic staff needed reasonable intellectual discourse and factual persuasion, coupled with reasonable and factual firmness to come on board and embrace the new change and transformative strategy in the management of the University affairs.

However, there are times that I took certain risks which I was not quite sure would work. At the University, there was and still persists a great need to continually further train the academic staff to higher professional, doctoral and post-doctoral levels in line with international academic standards and best practices. The greatest challenge I had to deal with as a VC regarding these staff training programmes was the perception by some scholars that life abroad, including academic was much better, satisfying and preferable to what was available locally. Be that as it may, the main goal of sending academic staff to advanced academic and professional institutions elsewhere in the developed countries for higher studies was precisely to acquire and transfer the academic knowledge and wisdom to their local university and country.

The risk of not returning on completion of studies was higher with those in the US, Canada, Australia, UK and the Republic of South Africa. Over 80 per cent of academic staff seconded to these countries failed to return to the University. Scholars trained in Germany, Eastern Europe, Russia, Ukraine, India, and Asia including China and Japan usually came back on completion of their higher studies due to strict national and bilateral policies in those countries. In some instances, staff would, upon completion of the study leave, request for extensions one to two years after which they would disappear without a trace. Where the University was able to trace them, repatriation was still not possible due to the uncooperativeness of the host countries that cited the professionals' personal choice, human, and democratic rights. It is quite unfortunate that in some instances, the scholars were discouraged by the host institutions from coming back. For the University this has been substantial loss owing to the investments in training and temporarily hiring their replacements, only for them to abscond and opt for 'greener pastures'.

I have restated this because it is one area where I felt I did not succeed to my expectations. I had taken the risk of granting academic staff external study leave for training abroad with the hopes that they would return. I took it upon myself to personally interview and counsel them and they assured me of their total commitment to return. Towards the end of my first five-year term, I decided to bite the bullet by being more selective, having lost over 30 well educated professionals including doctors, dentists, biochemists, nuclear scientists engineers, computer scientists, lawyers, experts in finance and insurance and many others to the Western countries and South Africa – within a span of four years.

I remember vividly, a very critical training position which I declined to approve, despite the fact that the University would have benefitted tremendously from it. The request came only a few months after we had lost four professionals to the US within a year. The staff wanted to study for a doctorate degree in one of the life science professional courses in the US. I rejected the application because I felt that he would not return on completion of his studies despite his assurances. This was because the previous eight out of ten scholars trained in the US had declined to return despite considerable and sustained pursuit. They also refused to refund monies spent on their training and salaries earned during the training period. Surely, there is an urgent need for Kenyan academics training abroad at the cost of the local universities to be more patriotic.

In order to partially deal with the perennial staff poaching problem I went on an international recruitment drive. Incidentally, this turned out to be not only cheaper but more effective in that we were able to recruit fully qualified professors, senior lecturers and lecturers without the heavy financial investment in their training. We hired a reasonable number from Western Europe, India, Australia and South Africa. However, the numbers lost still exceeded those recruited by about 70 per cent.

I also came to realize much later that research is an extremely significant component of world class academic excellence. I therefore should have mainstreamed research with more energy much earlier than I did. I should have created the office of the DVC in charge of Research, Production and Extension much earlier during my first term as VC commenced training academic staff on research and grant proposal writing earlier than 2011. These would have enabled them to write many more research and grant proposals thus enabling them compete for more research grants internationally.

It took the establishment of the office of the DVC, Research, Production and Extension to effectively organize and train majority of the academic staff from other colleges of the University in research and proposal writing and prepare them for global competitiveness.

I must emphasize here that my main goal as a transformative leader was to carry the majority of my management team along. Therefore, even though the strategy for the establishment of the office of the DVC was in place from the beginning, it took quite a while to be actualized. This was because I believed in consensus, rather than majority decisions. With the benefit of hindsight, I perhaps would have acted much faster and better with the majority rather than waiting for consensus in key areas such as this one.

The statute for the establishment of the office of the DVC, Student Affairs was approved in 2005 but it took another five years to fill the position because I was waiting for some form of total consensus at University management level. I believed that I needed a cohesive transformative team within the management given the history of negative energies within the University.

During this period, the managing of student affairs rested squarely on my shoulders and this tedious and a heavy burden for me. Indeed, the direct handling of student affairs consumed quite a significant amount of my time, that would otherwise have been utilized more effectively in implementing the strategic plan. It was however extremely important at the time to have the entire management, Senate, Council and Chancellor on board so that, would own the recruitment process.

Now, with the benefit of hindsight perhaps I should have advised that the University Council proceeds to fill the position with the majority within the UMB, rather than wait for the entire management consensus. This would have tremendously reduced my workload and greatly improved managing of the students affairs, much earlier in my tenure.

The strategy of providing adequate and better equipped teaching facilities for students was one of my most important priorities. This was because the available facilities were not only inadequate but also lacking for holistic teaching. My original strategy was to purchase a building within the Nairobi CBD to accommodate the increasing number of students.

Accordingly, after identifying the building we requested the government for a loan to enable us purchase it. Unfortunately, the loan was not approved. However, this would later turn out to be a blessing in disguise. The building was eventually purchased by the Kenya Methodist University and converted into their

Nairobi Campus. We therefore went back to the drawing board and developed a new strategy to construct our building leading to the 22-storey, University of Nairobi Towers. As detailed earlier, the Towers has addressed most of the original space and academic challenges at the University and within the College of Humanities and Social Sciences.

With the benefit of hindsight however, I should have planned for the construction of the Towers much earlier in my tenure. This would have greatly enhanced the University's growth.

At the completion of my ten year tenure, the University of Nairobi had acquired world class status in excellence. This was a very significant milestone that the entire University community comprising of the Chancellor, the Council, the Senate, management, staff and students have remained extremely proud of.

Nonetheless, I am now of the opinion that this world class status in academic excellence could have been attained much earlier, had I been able to selectively deal with only core strategic and policy issues leaving operational and other mundane issues and processes to other management team members.

The issue of student unrest has always been a perennial challenge at the University. Violent student protests were more rampant prior to the beginning of my tenure as VC. It should however be noted that these acts of indiscipline reduced drastically during my ten year stewardship.

Nevertheless, looking back and with the benefit of hindsight, this reduction would perhaps have been enhanced further, with better measurable results if I had been brave enough to reduce the mandatory contribution of the SONU membership fee. This move would most definitely have been strongly and perhaps violently resisted by the students, and would in turn have resulted in the disruption of the University academic calendar.

I believe that the increase in the SONU membership fees before my appointment resulted in the availability of a substantial amount of money to the students. This funding, in excess of Ksh 30 million annually must have, partly encouraged student hooliganism and indiscipline. This is what informed my caution when dealing with this matter.

One of the most significant determinants of strategy implementation is organizational culture. The collective culture of the University community, including that of students, academic, administrative and other support staff has only changed minimally over the years despite the tremendous and sustained efforts by management and Council to effect significant and measurable changes. In my opinion, and in general terms, this change is not significant enough to measurably reverse positively the negative effects of culture on strategic management at the University. In order to improve and sustain gains already achieved at the institution through our strategic management style over the past ten years, a new leader would have to think very carefully and weigh all the options before radically changing the implementation of the strategy.

From my point of view therefore, my general strategy and management plan would not change significantly if I was to be Vice-Chancellor all over again. I still would carefully weigh the strategic gains of a very radical strategic action, against the expected negative holistic consequences. I would still adopt a midline position, mitigating all the factors. This method resulted in sustained improvement of the University, in all aspects over the past ten years.

CHAPTER NINE

My Professional Work as a Medical Regulator

I will not have done justice to myself, my profession, the medical fraternity and the general public if I ignored my very modest though significant contribution to the regulation of medical and dental practice in Kenya through the Kenya Medical Practitioners and Dentists Board (KMPDB); within the other East African Community; in the rest of Africa through the Association of Medical Councils of Africa (AMCOA) and globally through the International Association of Medical Regulatory Authorities (IAMRA). By 2016, approximately 10,500 medical doctors and 1,200 dentists had been registered in Kenya. For a national population of about 42 million, the doctor to patient ratio is significantly low, a far cry from the World Health Organization (WHO) recommended ratio of one doctor to 600 patients. This situation is further worsened by the fact that a significant number of doctors and dentists have left the country for the perceived 'greener pastures'. But what I can state without fear of contradiction, having travelled extensively all over the globe, is that there are actually no greener pastures out there and that the doctors who remain to serve our people perform much better than those in the diaspora.

The KMPDB was established in 1978 under the Medical Practitioners and Dentists Act Cap 253 of the Laws of Kenya. In summary, the Board has statutory authority to ensure the provision of quality and ethical healthcare through appropriate regulation of the training, registration, licensing, inspection and professional practice of doctors and dentists. In detail, it is responsible for among other things: the approval of training institutions for medical and dental practitioners; renewal of the annual licences of training institutions for medical and dental practitioners; approval of curriculum and training facilities for undergraduate and postgraduate training in medicine and dentistry approval and accreditation of the continuous professional development of health providers the supervision of medical and dental education and regulation and the supervision of internship training. The Board is also responsible for the indexing of medical and dental students upon their admission to a University and the registration of eligible private, community and faith based medical and dental institutions.

With regard to licensing, the Board is responsible for the issuance of internship licenses, annual private practice for specialist and general practice, annual licenses to private, community and faith based health care institutions and locum licenses. The Board also conducts internship qualifying and pre-registration examinations for foreign-trained doctors and dentists, assessment for foreign-trained specialists and monitoring university examinations for medical and dental students.

In addition, the Board provides regular advice to the Cabinet Secretary for Health on matters related to healthcare and training, medical and dental training institutions, research regarding human subjects and institutions that provide health care. Further, the Board performs a disciplinary function through the conduct of preliminary inquiries unprofessional conduct and medical practice, professional conduct committees and full board tribunals and conducts inquiries into the health and fitness of medical and dental practitioners. The Board collaborates with many bodies with similar mandates. At the international level, it collaborates with IAMRA, and AMCOA within the African continent.

At the regional level, the collaboration is with the East African Community Boards or Councils, and locally with the Nursing Council of Kenya, the Pharmacy and Poisons Board, the Clinical Officers Council, the Kenya Medical Laboratory Technicians and Technologists Board, the Nutrition Council of Kenya, and other relevant health regulatory authorities.

Dr. Malaki Wilson Warambo became the first Chairman of KMPDB in 1987. He was the first African Kenyan to be trained as a specialist general surgeon. He was trained at Makerere University and the Royal College of Surgeons in the United Kingdom and is the most senior surgeon in Kenya today. During his time as Chairman, the Board operated from the Ministry of Health at Afya House, Nairobi. He served as Chairman until 1994 and was succeeded by Dr. Richard Baraza, another eminent and senior surgeon trained at Makerere University, the University of Nairobi and the Royal College of Surgeons in the UK.

Dr. Baraza served one term of five years ending in 1999 and was succeded by Professor Kyambi, an eminent scholar and the first African Kenyan paediatric surgeon, who served for the maximum allowed two terms of until 2009. During his tenure, the Board improved not only in its management style and service delivery but also relocated from Afya House to its own premises on Woodlands Road.

I was first elected a Board member in 1999. At the time I was already serving as Chairman of the Department of Surgery at the University of Nairobi and therefore was already known by many doctors, most of whom I had trained. Furthermore, I had been teaching surgery for 11 years. This placed me in good stead with many young doctors who appreciated me not only because of my availability but also the firmness with which I had dealt with them during their clinical training in surgery. I was also actually quite fortunate because another senior member of our department, Professor Kyambi was appointed Chairman of the Board at the same time. I worked very well with Professor Kyambi who incidentally was Chairman of the Department of Surgery at the University of Nairobi when I was recruited. After the successful completion of my five-year term, I was re-elected to the Board again in 2004 and 2009. The significance of the 2009 election was that I was elected with a very strong majority.

Then the most unexpected thing happened; I was pleasantly surprised when I was appointed Chairman of the Board by the then Minister for Medical Services in November 2009, without lobbying. I have always strongly believed that one should be seen and recognized based purely on their ability to perform and provide measurable results. I therefore do not believe in lobbying. After the successful completion of my first-five year term, I was re-appointed by the Cabinet Secretary for Health in November 2014. Again I did not lobby. The lesson to be learnt here is that performance still counts in some institutions in this country.

Therefore, as one can easily deduce, I have represented and served the doctors of this country faithfully and diligently, as their preferred representative at the board for a total of 17 years, to date; ten of them as a member and the rest as Chairman. I must honestly confess that this trust, bestowed on me by fellow professional colleagues impacted on me tremendously. Their encouragement added my zest in the discharge of my regulatory duties at the Board.

I can vividly recollect that as a Board member, and chairman of its private practice committee, I initiated critical and relevant reforms and good corporate governance. The reforms enabled the Board to initiate systematic and countrywide inspections of all private and faith-based medical and dental facilities, institutions and outpatients clinics in Kenya. At the beginning, government medical and dental facilities, institutions and clinics were excluded. However, this changed. There was now a more comprehensive approach to medical regulation as far as the mandate of the Board with regard to inspections was concerned. The composition of the current inspection teams from the Board was further excluded to include professionals from other health regulatory authorities in Kenya including the Nursing Council of Kenya, the Clinical Officers Council, the Pharmacy and Poisons Board, the Radiation Protection Board and the Kenya Medical Laboratory Technologists and Technicians Board.

During my tenure as Chairman – from 1999 to 2016, the Board received 896 complaints from patients and other entities, related to malpractice and negligence. To date, the Board has competently determined 840 of them at Preliminary Inquiry Committee (PIC) level, 14 at Professional Conduct Committee (PCC) level, and 15 at full board tribunals. Currently, the number of complaints against medical practitioners, dentists and institutions, still pending before the Board are only 27, making it one of the most efficient Boards in the country.

Nonetheless, this is a clear indication that the Kenyan patient has become increasingly aware of his rights as outlined in the 'Patients Rights Charter' which was launched by the Board in 2013 and which is currently guaranteed by The Kenya Constitution 2010.

As the Chairman, I dealt with some very disturbing and near scandalous cases. One such case comes to mind against medical officer on emergency call, in one of the public district hospitals in the country attended to a pregnant woman. In order to attend to the patient he had first to be traced and transported by an ambulance from a bar at night. Medical practitioners on emergency call are professionally barred from consuming alcohol and should actually be on stand by either in the hospital premises or at home. The medical officer correctly made a diagnosis of obstructed labour and prepared the patient for an emergency Caesarean Section. In the middle of the operation, he abandoned the patient and rushed back to the bar. By the time he returned to the theatre to complete the operation the patient had died from excessive bleeding as there was no other medical doctor within quick reach at the hospital. During the tribunal proceedings, the doctor denied these charges. They were however proved beyond reasonable doubt by nursing and technological staff, and other witnesses. The full Board Medical Tribunal under my chairmanship found him guilty of medical negligence and he was subsequently removed from the medical register among other penalties imposed. This information was shared with the regulatory bodies within the East African Community as per the East African Community Protocol.

In another similar case, a consultant performed an elective Caesarean Section (not an emergency) and carelessly forgot to write the mandatory operation notes. He then travelled to another medical work station in another town, some 300 kilometres away without handing over the post-operative management of the patient to another competent medical practitioner. By the time the medical practitioner returned to review the patient the following day the patient had died. Only then did the practitioner realize that the post-operative notes had not been written. It was quite obvious that the practitioner was in a hurry, and was therefore not professionally diligent. This particular practitioner is being retrained. The lesson to be learned here is that, a medical practitioner should always ensure he or she is available to competently and professionally manage the patient in the post-operative period and especially during the first six to 24 hours. This is the most critical period and should not be neglected or delegated. If however for any unavoidable circumstances such as a medical emergency, one cannot review the patient post operatively as required, another competent medical practitioner must review the patient routinely every six hours after the operation without fail.

In yet another case of preventable medical negligence, a consultant in a private hospital performed an elective Caesarean Section on a healthy patient. According to the medical practitioner, the operation was successful and therefore he went to another private hospital to perform yet another elective operation. The practitioner did not return to review the patient post operatively as is required, until the next day. Another specialist was also not requested either by the medical practitioner or the concerned private hospital to come and review patient. The nurses on the other hand had contacted the doctor several times on the deteriorating condition of the patient but did not convince the doctor to review the patient. When the doctor returned the following morning the patient had unfortunately died from excessive but preventable blood loss. This is one of the cases pending before the full Board Medical Tribunal because one of the parties in the case rushed to the High Court and obtained a court order restraining the Tribunal from proceeding on with its determination despite very clear medical facts.

Therefore, my most significant frustration as the Chairman of KMPDB is with the several cases of medical negligence and malpractice pending before the full Board Medical Tribunal. This is occasioned by one of the parties, either the accused medical practitioners or the health institution filing a case in the High Court and obtaining a court injunction preventing the Tribunal from determining the case. The Board is obliged to first obey the court order in compliance with the law and in the process, invariably delays the final professional determination of such cases. Several such cases have been pending before the full Board Medical Tribunal for a number of years. This in my opinion has delayed the dispensation of justice to the patient, medical practitioner, and the concerned medical institution. The ideal situation would have been to allow the full Board Medical Tribunal to professionally determine such cases to conclusion, then appeal the Tribunal's judgement.

With regard to the joint sponsored inspections of medical training institutions within the East African Community partner states there is one particular memorable incident involving a private university that comes to mind. In this case, I was leading the Kenyan delegation and was the overall team leader in my capacity as the Chairman of the Board. Other members of my team were Chairman of Uganda Medical and Dental Council Professor Joel Okullo, Vice Chairman of Tanganyika Medical Council Professor David Ngassapa, chairman of Rwanda Medical and Dental Council Dr. Emmanuel Rudakemwa, and representatives from Burundi Medical and Dental Council, Medical and Dental Council of Zanzibar, and the East African Community Headquarters in Arusha, Tanzania.

The main purpose of the inspection was to ensure that all medical and dental schools within the East African Community partner states possessed the requisite facilities and the prescribed number of lecturers per subject necessary for the adequate professional training of the medical and dental personnel. In the case of this particular private medical school, we found abnormally large numbers of medical students, inadequate physical facilities, teaching equipment, and lack of patients in an excellent teaching hospital whose inpatient bed occupancy levels at best was below 30 per cent, probably because of high consultation and treatment costs. There was also severe shortage of lecturers in all subjects both pre-clinical and clinical. The inspection team stopped further student admissions into the school and prescribed what had to be effected before further admissions could be allowed within a specified period.

On a subsequent re-inspection several months later, all the conditions had been met and surpassed. There was massive infrastructural development in place, many more lecturers and professors had been employed, the main teaching hospital bed occupancy rate had increased to above 80 per cent, and there were many other satellite teaching hospitals with newly appointed clinical lecturers adequately teaching the clinical medical students. In some cases, the satellite teaching hospitals had been greatly improved to acceptable East African Community medical and dental training standards. The university was subsequently given a clean bill of health and allowed to re-admit students as an excellent training institution. At a personal level I felt very satisfied that my inspection team had made a measurable difference in the standards of medical and dental training within the East African Community partner states.

As I served the Board during my first term, I was concurrently serving as the VC of the University of Nairobi. Therefore, brought into the Board very significant and wide institutional management experience. I was elected the President of the Association of Medical Councils of Africa headquartered in Johannesburg, South Africa in 2013, a position that I still hold. AMCOA is responsible for the regulation of medical and dental health practice within Africa. As President of AMCOA, I have organized successful annual conferences attended by many international stakeholders from the medical and dental fields. We have also continued to strongly benchmark with the General Medical Council of UK and the International Association of Medical Regulatory Authorities.

Within the East African region, we have developed regional guidelines for joint inspection and accreditation of medical and dental schools in Kenya, Uganda, Tanzania, Rwanda and Burundi. We have continued to work very closely with health regulatory bodies within the EAC partner states which include the Medical Council of Tanganyika, Uganda Medical Council, Medical Council of Zanzibar, Rwanda Medical Council, Medical Council of Burundi, and more recently the Medical Council of South Sudan. As a result of this collaboration, a total of 33 medical and dental schools have been jointly inspected in all the EAC partner states, since November 2015.

Perhaps my singular, most significant achievement so far as Chairman of the of the KMPDB is the institutionalization and implementation of very strict financial discipline that led to the realization of budgetary savings, enabling us within five years to construct an ultra-modern, four-storey office block with adequate underground parking. These offices have provided a serene environment with adequate office space for all the Board members, management, the secretariat, doctors, clients and stakeholders. There are also adequate facilities for full board tribunal hearings, preliminary inquiry sessions and professional conduct committee hearings.

Previously, the Board's offices were located in an old and dilapidated three bedroom house thoroughly inadequate and lacking even the very basic facilities necessary for the Board to successfully carry out its core functions and responsibilities. As a matter of fact, in order for the Board to satisfactorily perform its statutory functions in the past, all the large committees and full board tribunal meetings were held exclusively, in the University of Nairobi's College of Health Sciences Boardroom, situated at Kenyatta National Hospital Campus.

The strategy for the construction of a new building for the Board offices was developed in 2009, when I was first appointed Chairman. The ground breaking ceremony for the construction of the new offices was held in April 2014 and the building was completed and occupied in 18 months. The actual total cost of the construction of the building including landscaping and professional fees was about Kshs 300 million.

I am extremely proud and privileged to have been associated with this development, which I sincerely hope will serve the medical and dental practitioners of our beloved country for years to come.

I am currently still serving as Chairman of the Board until November 2019 when my second term will come to an end. By then, I shall have completed 20 successful years of service.

As a student leader of International Students Association of the University of Lagos, 1974

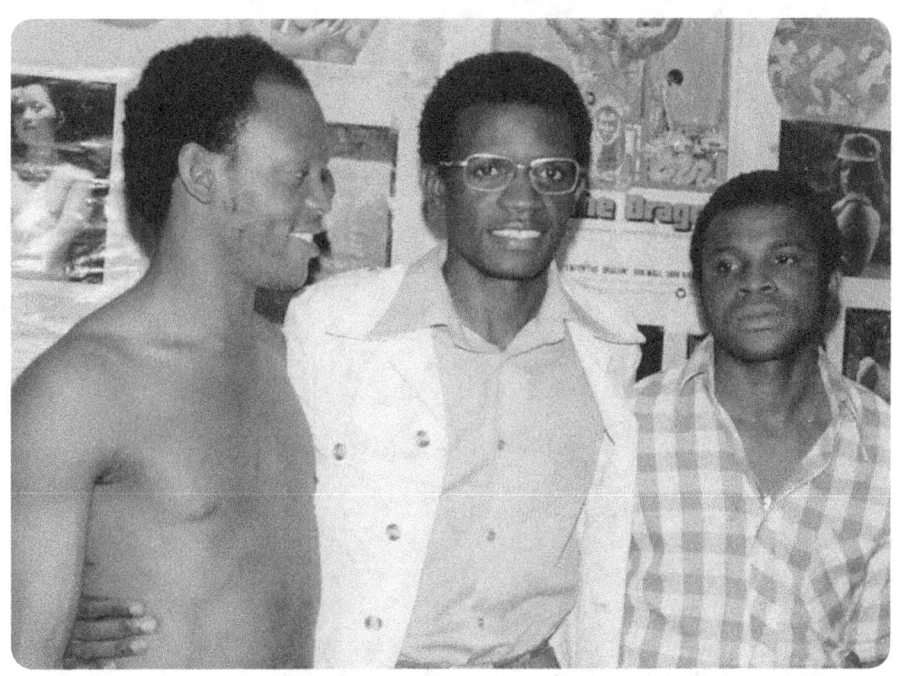

With classmates (centre) at the College of Medicine University of Lagos, 1977

As a medical student at the College of Medicine of the University of Lagos, 1977

With a friend as a medical student at the Lagos University Teaching Hospital, Lagos, Nigeria, 1977

With a Tanzanian Diplomat as a medical student at the University of Lagos, 1977

With Prof. E.O. Odunjo of the College of Medicine University of Lagos, 1985

As a young doctor in Lagos, Nigeria with Kenya High Commissioner to Nigeria H.E. Alfred Machayo, 1979

As Dean Faculty of Medicine, 2nd left on the occasion of the laying of the foundation stone for the Office of the Dean, School of Medicine, with funds personally sourced from colleagues in South Korea. On the extreme right is Prof. Francis Gichaga, Vice-Chancellor, 2000

Prof. Vak Yong Yoo (donor) opens the newly constructed offices of the Principal and Dean Faculty of Medicine, College Boardroom and Registry at the College of Health Sciences, KNH Campus, 2001

Prof. Vak Yong Yoo (donor) in the presence of the VC Prof. Francis Gichaga (front row left) Prof. David Wasawo, Chairman of Council, Ag. Dean Prof. Ndinya Achola, faculty of medice and my selft extreme right during opening of the newly constructed Principal's and Dean's offices at College of Heath Sciences, UON, 2001

Myself extreme right with Prof. Joseph Oliech and on the extreme left Dr. Said Samnakay next to Dr. Alex Danso at Urology Conference, 1995

Standing 3rd from left with members of the Erectile Dysfunction Advisory Council in Dubai, 1998

Myself (second right) attending a Urology Conference in Dakar, Senegal. Extreme right is Prof. Baye Assane Diagne President of the Pan African Urological Surgeons Association (PAUSA), 1999

At the Water Front in Cape Town, South Africa with the Table Mountains at the back with a group of researcher assembled by Pfizer Laboratories to discuss the research and launching of sildenafil (Viagra). Am in the back row extreme right, 1997

As Principal of the College of Health Sciences (CHS), 2nd right on the occasion of the launch of the Kenya Aids Vaccine Initiative (KAVI) laboratories, in the presence of Bill Gates Senior, on the extreme left and President Jimmy Carter, second left, 2001

Standing back from left Prof. O. Anzala explaining a point; Prof. J. Bwayo; Prof. S. Ongeri, Minister for Health, myself and Bill Gates senior (right), during an inspection visit to KAVI offices at KNH, 2001

With Dr. Emòke Szathmáry, President and Vice-Chancellor, University of Manitoba, Canada (standing) on the occasion of ground breaking ceremony for the UNITID building at the College of Health Sciences, Kenyatta Hospital Campus, 2005

Myself as DVC (A&F) (centre) during the occasion of the delivery of my inaugural lecture "Urological Footprints in Kenya "That Water May Flow": A Story About Male Genital Cancer and Dysfunction", October 9, 2003, with Prof. Crispus Kiamba, VC UON (left) and Prof. Florida Karani DVC (AA) (right)

Canadian Minister for Health, Dr. Tony Frank, third from left, accompanied by the Kenyan Minister for Health, Hon. Charity Ngilu on the occasion of the opening of the UNITID building at the College of Health Sciences, 2007

On my Inauguration as the Chairman of the Kenya Medical Practitioners and Dentists Board (KMPDB), 2012

Myself right with the Minister for Medical Services Prof. Anyang' Nyongo (centre) and Hon. Attorney General Prof. Githu Muigai, extreme left during the launch of the 6th edition Code of Professional Conduct and Discipline for doctors at Hotel Inter-Continental, Nairobi, 2012

From left Dr. Elly Nyaim Opot, member, KMPDB, Daniel Yumbya, CEO, KMPDB, Dr. Emmanuel Rudakemwa, Registrar, Rwanda Medical and Dental Council, myself incoming AMCOA President and Dr. Eugene Ngoga, outgoing AMCOA President, in Kigali Rwanda, 2013

Receiving a certificate of long and meritorious service at the Medical Practitioners and Dentists Board from the Minister for Medical Services Prof. Anyang' Nyongo, left, looking on is Ms. Rose Wafukho, personal assistance to the CEO, KMPDB, 2009

On the occasion of HIV Symposium with Prof. Lucy Irungu, DVC, Research Production and Extension extreme left, Prof. J. Kaimenyi, DVC, Academic Affairs, my self fourth, Prof. Robert Gallo, Director, Institute of Human Virology at the University of Maryland Baltimore, School of Medicine, 2012

H.E. First Lady, Margaret Kenyatta, on the occasion of the laying of the foundation stone for the construction of the new offices for the KMPDB. Accompanied by Cabinet Secretary for Health, James Macharia, Director of Medical Services Dr. Nicholas Muraguri and CEO of the Board, Daniel Yumbya extreme left, 2014

H.E. the First Lady, Margaret Kenyatta, receiving a gift from the Chairman of the KMPDB, Prof. G.A.O. Magoha. Looking on are: the Cabinet Secretary in the Ministry of Health, James Macharia (left), Dr. Betty Gikonyo, Daniel Yumbya and Prof. Julius Kyambi (right), 2014

On the occasion of the contribution of Ksh. 5 million by the University of Nairobi to H.E. First Lady, Margaret Kenyatta for the Beyond Zero Health Campaign, 2014

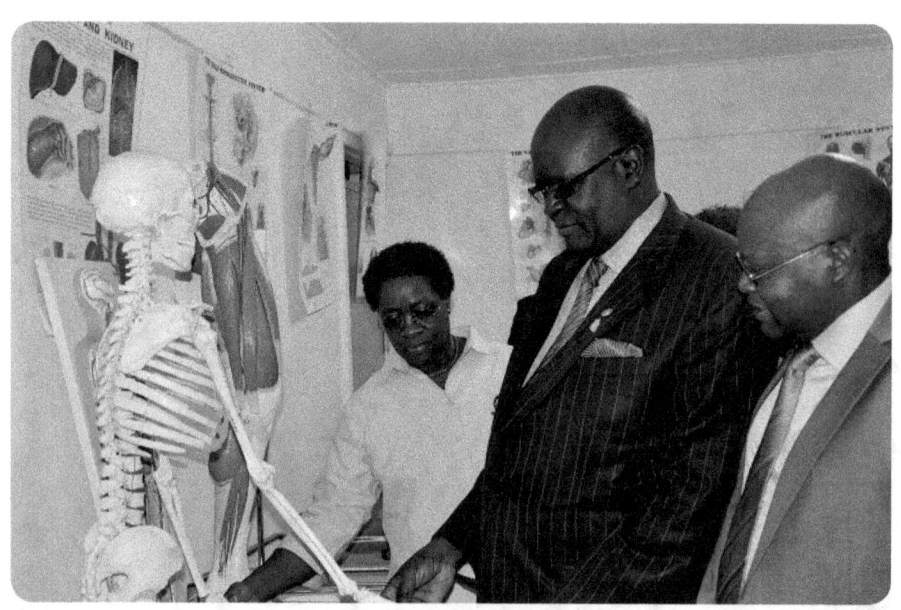

Prof. G. Magoha, Chairman, KMPDB (centre) in the Human Anatomy laboratory during the inspection of the Jomo Kenyatta University of Agriculture and Technology (JKUAT), Medical School. On his left is Prof. M. Imbuga, VC, JKUAT and Mr. D. Yumbya, CEO, KMPDB, 2014

Dr. S. Kaggia (right) explains a point to the board chair, Prof. D. Ngassapa, Vice Chairman, Tanganyika Medical and Dental Council (third left). Looking on (from left) is Dr. R. Thuo, Prof. G. Magoha and Prof. M. Imbuga during a Joint EAC Medical Practitioners and Dentists Boards and Councils inspection of Jomo Kenyatta University of Agriculture and Technology medical school, 19 January, 2016

KMPDB Chairman, Prof. G. Magoha (left), hands over a Certificate of Authority for Practicing Human Anatomy to Mount Kenya University (MKU) VC, Prof. S. Waudo as the Dean, School of Medicine Prof. K. Kigatiira (centre) looks on at MKU in Thika, 2013

Seated second right with members of staff of the KMPDB on the occasion of being declared the best performing Medical Regulatory Board in Kenya, 2015

With the CEO of the KMPDB, Daniel Yumbya, left on the occasion of being declared the best performing Medical Regulatory Board in Kenya, 2015

Explaining a point to Dr. Nicholas Muraguri PS for Health (right) during the inspection tour of the KMPDB Office Complex building. Looking on is the Health Cabinet Secretary, Dr. Cleopa Mailu (left) and the KMPDB CEO Mr. Daniel Yumbya, 2016

Myself extreme right and Daniel Yumbya the CEO, KMPDB, left, with Health Cabinet Secretary Dr. Cleopa Mailu (second left) and Ms. Sarah Were (seated) on the occasion of inspection of the Newly Completed Office Complex Building, 2016

With the Vice-Chancellor of Mount Kenya University Prof. Francis Waudo, left, on the occasion of inspection of Mount Kenya University Medical School by the KMPDB, 2013

H.E. the First Lady Margaret Kenyatta plants a commemorative tree during the official opening of the KMPDB Offices accompanied by Dr. Cleopa Mailu, CS for Health, myself and Mr. Daniel Yumbya, CEO, KMPDB, 2016

Dr. Loice Mutahi Consultant Paediatrician, left, consults with prof. Peter Ndaguatha, Chairman of Academic Department of Surgery (centre) and myself at Kenyatta National Hospital, 2016

H.E. the First Lady Margaret Kenyatta on her way to opening and inspecting the new board offices building, 2016

H.E. First Lady, Margaret Kenyatta cutting the tape during the official opening of the new KMPDB offices building, 2016

Seated fourth from right H.E. the First Lady Margaret Kenyatta with Staff at the newly opened KMPDB office complex, 2016

Giving a speech on the occasion of the official opening of the new building for the KMPDB, 2016

Seated centre H.E. the First Lady Margaret Kenyatta with from left to right Dr. E. Njenga, CS for Health Dr. Cleopa Mailu, myself, MPDB CEO Mr. Daniel Yumbya and Prof. A. Mutungi. Standing right from left Dr. F. Were, Dr. C. Muyodi, Dr. S. Wanjala, Prof. L. Atwoli, Dr. F. Kairithia, Dr. S. Sharma, Dr. D. Kiima, Dr. N. Bosire, Dr. E. Nyaim, Dr. T. Ochola, and Dr. M. Akama (Board Members) at the newly opened KMPDB offices, 2016

The newly completed building housing the offices of KMPDB, 2016

With the Chairman of the East African Community Medical Council, Prof. David Ngassapa, Chairman of the Joint East African Medical and Dental Practitioners Boards and Councils from Tanzania on the extreme left and Prof. Joel Okullo, Chairman, Uganda Medical and Dental Practitioners Council during the Medical Councils of East African Community partner States inspection of all Medical Schools in Uganda, 2015

Myself with the Chairman of the Uganda Medical and Dental Practitioners Council, Prof. Joel Okullo, 2013

As President of the Association of Medical Councils of Africa (AMCOA) together with the Chairman of Uganda Medical and Dental Practitioners Council on the left and Rwanda Medical and Dental Council on the right, 2013

Myself at the top extreme right, attending Société Internationaled Urologie (SIU) Conference in Montreal, Canada with Dr. Alex Danso from Zimbabwe to my left, Prof. J.M.K Quartey of Ghana, top left and Prof. Dominic Nwankwo Osegbe of Nigeria (bottom right), 1998

Myself with Mr. Gordon Williams consultant urologist, attending British Association of Urological Surgeons Conference in Bournemouth, United Kingdom, 1995

With James Macharia, Cabinent Secretary of Health (right) and Nial Dickson, (left) CEO of the General Medical Council of UK and Chairman of IAMRA Management Board during the 19th AMCOA Annual Conference, Sarova Whitesands Beach Hotel in Mombasa, 2015

On the occasion of the official opening of the Kenya Medical Association Headquarters by H.E. President Mwai Kibaki. I am standing behind the President, 2013

With Prof. John Chisi (left) during the 20th AMCOA Annual Conference in Mangochi, Malawi, 2016

As AMCOA President receiving a gift from Dr. Mary Zulu, Registrar, Health Professions Council of Zambia during the 20th AMCOA Annual Conference in Mangochi, Malawi, 2016

At the IAMRA 12th International Conference on Medical Regulation in Melbourne, Australia, September 2016

Attending IAMRA Conference in Melbourne, Australia, September, 2016

In Pretoria South Africa with the president Dr Kgosi Letlape left and registrar advocate Khumalo centre of the Health Professions Council of South Africa at HPCSA headquarters, 2016

Front row from left Dr. Khadija Shikely, Mombasa County Director of Health, Myself, Binti Omar, Mombasa County Health Executive, Daniel Yumbya, CEO, KMPDB during the Joint KMPDB, NHIF and Council of Governors Induction for Re-categorization of Health Facilities in Coast Region at Pride Inn Paradise Resort – Shanzu, Mombasa county, 2017

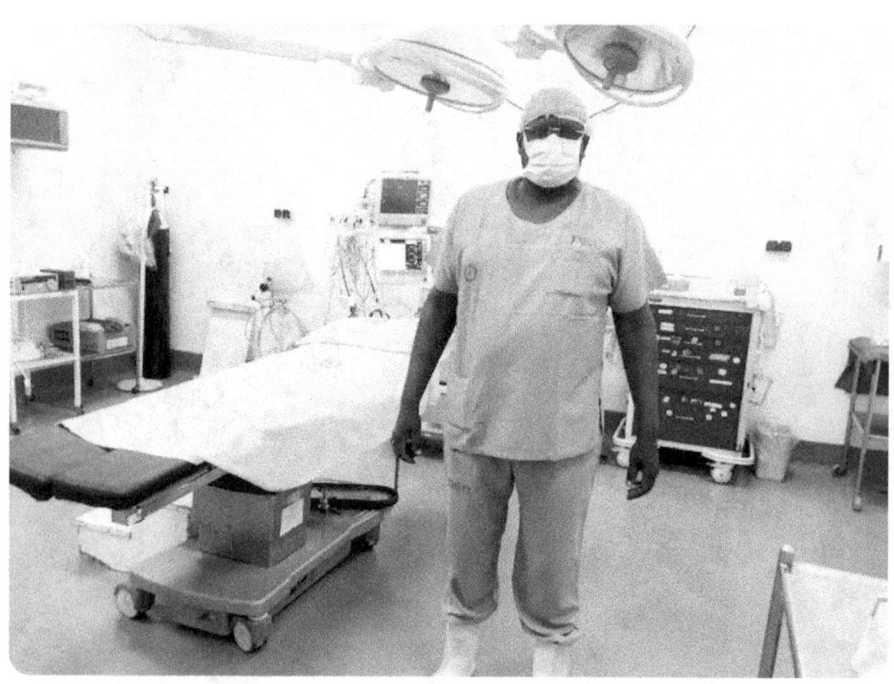

In a theatre, 2017

Seated from right to left Prof. Joel Okullo, Chairman Uganda Medical and Dental Council; Prof. Humayun Chaudhry, President and CEO, Federal of State Medical Boards, in the US; Lesotho delegate; John Chisi, Chairman, Malawi Medical Council, Dr. Emmanuel Rudakemwa, Chairman Rwanda Medical and Dental Council; Malawi Minister for Health; myself. Standing from right Mr. Eley Atikpui, Registrar Ghana Medical Council; Dr. Kgosi Letlape, President of Medical and Dental Council of South Africa and Health Professions Council of South Africa and Daniel Yumbya, CEO, KMPDB during the 20th AMCOA Annual Conference, Mangochi, Malawi, 2016

CHAPTER TEN

REFLECTIONS

It is now over 52 years since I transferred from Jina Primary School in rural Gem, Siaya County to the relatively modern and cosmopolitan Dr. David Livingstone Primary School in Jerusalem, Nairobi County in 1964. The main reason for my transfer which was at my parent's request and insistence was that I suffered from severe bronchial asthma and therefore needed better and constant medical care and regular follow ups. The assumption was that I would have quick and continued access to better medical facilities and services from qualified medical doctors who were presumably readily available in Nairobi, compared to Gem at that time. This actually turned out to be the case as I ended up being treated not just by a medical doctor, but a chest specialist.

In Nairobi, I was hosted by my elder brother, John Obare and his wife, Agatha Christine. I was soon to find out that primary school education in Nairobi's metropolis was far much better and of superior quality than that in Gem. There were also many more well trained teachers, together with adequate essential materials including the relevant text books needed for effective teaching at primary school level. Furthermore, all the teaching was done in the English language except for the Kiswahili lessons, unlike at Jina where some of the teaching was still conducted in vernacular.

When I reflect on this period in my life, I cannot but imagine what would have happened to me if I had not relocated to Nairobi for treatment and subsequent education. Maybe the asthma could not have been properly controlled, leading to more severe medical complications or even death. With poor health, maybe I would also not have focused on my education in a good school like Dr. David Livingstone. In brief, the story of my life would have been quite different from the one told in this book, except for the fact that I was given an enabling opportunity.

I therefore wish to convey my sincerest gratitude specifically to my elder brother and his wife for their very kind gesture of hosting me during my early formative years in primary and high school education despite all my teenage truances and faults. I would also wish to thank my parents for requesting my sibling to host me. Of course, I must not forget to thank Dr. Angawa who was responsible for competently managing my medical condition resulting in my continued good health and uninterrupted school attendance.

My second reflection refers to 1967 when I left Dr. David Livingstone Primary School to join Starehe Boys Centre. At this time and because of extreme peer pressure, I was already an active member of a local band lead by Kabbasselleh Ochieng, playing bass guitar for the then L'Ochestre Lunna Success De La Capital in Nairobi. As mentioned previously in this book, I was initially attracted to Starehe because of their excellent school band and had a soft spot for music and musical instruments, especially the drums and bass guitar. I was also fascinated by the large drum within the band and their bright uniform. Although I was shortlisted for the interview to join Starehe for my high school education I nearly missed the chance because my brother had suggested to my parents that his good friend John Sabwa, an education officer in Western province would find me a 'better School'. However, as destiny would have it, my mother would hear none of it. She insisted that I go to Starehe, which I enrolled in January 1967.

It was at Starehe that academic, social and emotional discipline was instilled in me. This was however not a very smooth process at the beginning because of my very spirited, though misguided rebellion. At Starehe, it was further ensured that I left Ochieng Kabbasselleh's band and had no time to sneak out of school. It was also at Starehe that I first discovered totally to my surprise that, I was a bit talented and intelligent as I came top of my class in my second year. This feat was something that I least expected at the time.

I became more serious with my studies and soon developed a strong liking for History subject in which I remained top of the class throughout my stay at Starehe. This can be attested to by my History teacher Mr. Wanjohi, who was equally amazed at my capacity to grasp the subject. It therefore, comes as a complete surprise to many that I actually ended up becoming a medical doctor, a surgeon and urologist all of which did not require prowess in History.

I sometimes wonder and shiver at what would have happened to my life if for whatever reason, I had not joined Starehe. I would probably have continued playing with the band and either failed my examinations, or dropped out of school altogether to concentrate on the band as was the case with the band leader, Ochieng Kabbasselleh. I would probably also be dead by now. For the record, all the other members of the band have since passed on.

Starehe therefore played one of the most pivotal roles in defining my formative years, and in shaping my future academic, professional and social life. I shall always be grateful to the Centre, its leaders and its ethos.

After completion of my four years in high school, I proceeded to Strathmore College for my A Levels. I did not want to go to Strathmore College because I did not think I was smart enough to make the necessary grades required to join the top academic institution. Starehe was relatively new, and its previous form 4 classes had not produced any graduates with a first division. I was therefore not sure that I would make those grades to enable me to join Strathmore. The second reason was that Strathmore College at that time only offered A Level in science subjects while personally I preferred a combination that included my favourite subject of history. It took the gentle but firm persuasion of Dr. Griffin and my father to convince me to apply to Strathmore. My hopes were strengthened by the fact that I was successful in the interview conducted by Strathmore's Vice Principal, Mr. McDermott. So it came to pass that I performed well in the form four examinations, attaining a division one with excellent grades and therefore joined Strathmore in 1971.

Sometimes I stop for a moment and reflect at what would have happened if I had not made the grades for Strathmore. This is because it was at Strathmore that I was trained to organize my thoughts as an intellectual, scientist and scholar and as a young adult. I discovered myself and my abilities all over again but entirely under different circumstances. At Strathmore one was allowed to think and interact with teachers who advised on a variety of careers, their progression and their consequences. It was at this institution that I learned to voluntarily make intellectual and informed choices on my own.

I had a stint at student leadership at Strathmore where I was elected chairman of the debating society and vice chairman of the Strathmore Students Association. I passed my A level examinations with three good principals in Physics, Chemistry and Biology, qualifying for admission to the University of Nairobi's medicine programme. However, this did not happen. Apparently, since I had performed relatively well, I was awarded an AAU INTERAF scholarship to study medicine at the University of Zambia's medical school in Lusaka.

However, I never made it to Zambia; my slot was switched with the daughter of the then Kenyan High Commissioner to Zambia, Mr. Leo Odero who had originally been selected to join the College of Medicine of the University of Lagos, Nigeria.

I don't know what would have happened if I had and joined the University of Zambia's Medical School rather than the College of Medicine of the University of Lagos. My life would most definitely have been very different. This is because it is at the University of Lagos that I met and married my loving wife, Barbara who gave us a son, Michael. After the Almighty God and Jesus Christ my personal savior, these two individuals form the nucleus of my family and the centre of my life. My love for them is immeasurable. I can only be most grateful to God who I know and believe planned and executed my switch from Lusaka, Zambia to Lagos, Nigeria. His glory is always sufficient for us as He is in control of our lives.

While studying Medicine at the College of Medicine of the University of Lagos, I discovered plenty of opportunities in Nigeria. These opportunities enabled me to support my three younger siblings through high school education and universities in the United States of America, India and Nigeria. This was the period of oil boom in Nigeria and the Naira was quite valuable. It was actually much stronger than the USD and even the British Sterling Pound in 1974. I was on a very good scholarship of about 6,000 USD annual upkeep. While many African beneficiaries of the scholarship opted for expensive holidays in Canada, United Kingdom and the US, I opted to use my scholarship money to assist my father who had by this time retired. The savings also enabled me to support my three younger siblings successfully through high school and university. I also further saved quite a substantial sum of money and by 1979, only a year after my graduation, I was ready to consider purchasing a house in Nairobi through a mortgage, a feat that I accomplished two years later.

For no particular reason, after the completion of my studies, I decided to undertake my medical internship training in Nigeria at the Lagos University Teaching Hospital. I experienced a very short period of indecisiveness because I did not have a convincing reason to remain in Nigeria as all other graduates returned to Kenya on completion of their undergraduate studies. During this period, I was simultaneously engaged as a part-time demonstrator in gross anatomy at the department of anatomy. It is in this department that I would meet my wife, while she was a second year medical student.

Now, as I reflect on my short stint as a demonstrator in the anatomy laboratories, I can't help but wonder what would have become of me if I had not been offered the position. Perhaps, I would never have met my wife. Perhaps I would have completed my internship and returned to Kenya. My life would therefore definitely have been very different. Perhaps I may never even have become a surgeon at an early age as was the case. I strongly believe that my extended family responsibilities would definitely have slowed down the pace of my surgical and urological specialist training and consequently my surgical and urological academic career progression. The good news is that I was able to specialize rapidly, ending up as a urologist and a transplant surgeon in record time. This enabled me to pay back to the society at large and particularly the less fortunate.

When I reflect back on my life, particularly about London, while training and working as a renal transplant and urological surgeon, I quickly conclude that I probably have had the very best that life can offer in terms of surgical and urological professional training. At the renal transplant and urology units of the Hammersmith Hospital London, I had the opportunity to carry out cutting-edge, prospective research, on renal transplant allograft rejection, and male infertility. I also had the very unique but pleasant privilege of harvesting kidneys from brain-dead, card-carrying kidney donors, most of who had died from traffic related accidents. I have fondly recollected these operations mainly because I thoroughly and professionally enjoyed my being part of a very successful surgical renal transplant team actively involved in saving lives on a twenty four hour basis. I also enjoyed being paged, even in the middle of the night and informed that a potential card carrying kidney donor was available, and that I should proceed to harvest the kidneys. It was usually a good harvest as one donor provided two healthy kidneys which we used to save two lives. There is nothing more satisfying for a urologist than to see the newly transplanted kidney starting to make clear and healthy urine. At this point, good urinary flow usually signals a very successful kidney transplant operation.

I have had several excellent offers of opportunities for professional jobs outside our country which I turned down over undivided loyalty to my country. The first such opportunity was in London, within the British National Health Service (NHS) system after my training as a renal transplant surgeon at the Hammersmith Hospital in the early eighties. I was offered a well-paying and training position which if I had taken up, would most certainly have completely changed the direction of my professional career and social future.

The offer was quite tempting because it would have ensured 'better' living conditions in a developed Western world where life was much more comfortable and secure as compared to the life in a nascent African nation such as Nigeria or Kenya. It is important to note that at this time there were already very many African doctors working and living in different parts of the UK. I was determined to return to the Lagos University Teaching Hospital, in return for their financial support while I was training in England. My return to Nigeria would be only temporary as I planned to return to my motherland on completion of the course. I was also scheduled to complete my on-going research and thesis on cancer of prostate on Nigerians.

So when I reflect back, it is quite difficult for me to imagine whether I would have followed a clear surgical and urological academic career path which provided me distinct and chequered opportunities to serve my country. This was of course in many academic and administrative capacities including professor of urological surgery, Chairman of the Department of Surgery, Dean of the Faculty of Medicine, Principal of the College of Health Sciences, Deputy Vice-Chancellor in charge of Administration and Finance and finally the Vice-Chancellor for two terms of five years, all at the University of Nairobi. Perhaps I would have followed a surgical career where I would most probably serve in hospitals throughout the UK but within the NHS and if I was lucky, probably progressed to the level of consultant surgeon within that system. Consultant surgical places within the NHS have always been limited and therefore the worst case scenario would have been for me to progress to senior registrar position or just spend all my working life performing different surgical jobs in different hospitals within the NHS on contracts lasting between six and 18 months. For the avoidance of doubt these jobs would have been available in all hospitals throughout the UK but truth of the matter is that all these would have had absolutely no impact on my people and my country. I therefore know that I made the right decision because my activities have resulted in tangible and measurable impact. It is always noble to provide service above self considerations.

The second opportunity presented itself much later, after I had completed the Executive Training Program at the Stanford University Graduate School of Business in California, United States of America in late 2009. In our class, I happened to be one of least paid CEOs on the Program. Some of my classmates owned companies and earned as much as a million USD a month. On the completion of our training, I was approached by a millionaire classmate and offered a management job in one of his companies in the US. He told me that he had observed my very active and objective participation in class and was therefore satisfied and convinced that I had a lot to offer his companies, at management level.

Frankly speaking, I felt absolutely belittled and offended by this offer. This was because as an intellectual and scholar, I imagined that we were equal irrespective of how small, or poor our institutions and countries were. Secondly, my University and my country had invested heavily in my training and were eagerly waiting for me to return and implement the results. The salary offered was about 15 times the VC's salary in Kenya at that time but I flatly rejected it. He couldn't understand why a 'poor African Vice-Chancellor' could reject such a lucrative offer and he actually got very offended because he felt that he was doing me a huge favour. I politely informed him that both my country and the University of Nairobi needed me, and that I was not poor at all. I considered myself wealthy enough and that all my wealth was domiciled in my heart and brain, the rest was just vanity. I had been VC for four and half years and as far as I was concerned I had another five and half years to complete the two terms. As I relate this particular incident, I am keenly aware that if I had accepted the offer, my reputation would have been tainted at the expense of my own shallow, personal and temporary financial gain. The very strong lesson to be learned here is to always remember service before or above self.

On my clinical research life to date, I have published a total of 62 urological and general surgical clinical articles in peer reviewed medical, surgical and urological journals locally and internationally. I am basically a urological consultant and professor who has carried out extensive clinical research on male genital cancer including cancers of the prostate, testis and penis. I have carried out extensive clinical research on these three cancers since 1982. My flagship clinical urological research subject is prostate cancer where I have carried out extensive original clinical research both in Nigeria and in Kenya resulting in the publication of some 11 academic peer reviewed journal articles on the subject. I have also carried out clinical research on testicular cancer in Nigerians and Kenyans resulting in the publication of three academic peer reviewed journal articles, and on cancer of the penis where I published some two academic peer reviewed journal articles. My inaugural lecture entitled 'urological footprints in Kenya that water may flow: a story about male genital cancer and dysfunction' was delivered at the University of Nairobi in 2003.

In addition to genital cancer, I have carried out extensive original prospective clinical research on testicular torsion in Nigeria and Kenya which resulted in the publication of five peer reviewed journal articles, on benign prostatic hyperplasia resulting in the publication of four peer reviewed clinical journal articles, on chronic prostatitis and the publication of one peer reviewed journal article. I also carried out extensive clinical research on Fournier's Gangrene (Fournier's disease) and published three academic peer reviewed journal articles; male infertility where I have published two academic peer reviewed journal articles, in addition to my clinical research on Haemospermia; and priapism which resulted in the publication of one academic peer reviewed clinical journal article in each.

My original research on male circumcision carried out in Nigeria and Kenya resulted in the publication of two peer reviewed journal articles. Specifically, research on male circumcision carried out in Kisumu with researchers from Universities of Washington Seattle and Illinois in the US, and University of Manitoba in

Canada, in relation to HIV and AIDS has resulted in the practice being embraced by the Luo community who previously did not circumcise due to cultural reasons. As a result of this research it was established that circumcision reduced the risk of infection with HIV. I also carried out research on Female Genital Mutilation (female circumcision) which unfortunately is still rampant in some communities in Kenya, and published an academic peer reviewed journal article.

My extensive research on male erectile dysfunction resulted in publication of two academic peer reviewed journal articles. As a matter of fact, I was a member of the international Erectile Dysfunction Advisory Council (EDAC), and launched both Viagra and Cialis for the treatment of this sexual dysfunction in Kenya, Uganda, Tanzania, and Ghana. I have also carried out original clinical research on urolithiasis and nosocomial infection resulting in publication of peer reviewed journal articles. My original clinical research on renal transplantation carried out at Hammersmith Hospital, London and Nairobi, Kenya resulted in the publication of two peer reviewed academic journal articles, in addition to my publication on autologous blood transfusion in surgical practice in Kenya which resulted in publication of one peer reviewed journal article; and my research on the effect of aging on androgen levels in elderly males which resulted in the publication of one peer reviewed journal article. My original clinical research in general surgery has been restricted to appendicitis and breast cancer which has resulted in the publication of two and one academic peer reviewed journal articles respectively.

I look back with pride to see that I have trained many general surgeons and urologists for our country and Africa since joining the Department of Surgery of the University of Nairobi in January 1988. Some of the surgeons I have trained are from the East African Community partner states, while others came from as far as Liberia and Cameroon. When I reflect closely, I realize that I have supervised to completion some 40 Master of Medicine in Surgery dissertations in General Surgery and Urology. The surgeons I trained performed their original clinical research on various individual clinical surgical or urological topics including on cancers of the prostate, testis, penis, pancreas, gall bladder, breast, and a surgical audit of all urological malignant tumours. Others carried out original clinical research on testicular torsion, priapism, benign prostatic hyperplasia, erectile dysfunction, external hernias, urodynamics, surgical blood transfusion, and HIV seroprevalence among patients admitted for elective surgery, among others. The clinical research carried out by postgraduate students under my supervision was carried out at Kenyatta National Hospital which acts as University of Nairobi Teaching Hospital. The latest surgeon supervised to completion, Dr. Bernard Oburu Oreke graduated in 2015. Currently, I am supervising another four postgraduate surgical residents in the clinical fields of urology and general surgery.

At times when I reflect deeply on my life, I really and truly wonder what the world, mankind and humanity will remember me for after I am gone. What I know for sure is that if after the end of one's life, there is absolutely nothing tangible and measurable left behind for the continued benefit of mankind, humanity and charity then that life can be considered as relatively meaningless and perhaps just another mere human statistic.

My surgical training took me to many cities of the world including Lagos, Ibadan, Accra, London, Dublin, Edinburgh, Stockholm and Manchester. Is it possible that I will be remembered for my leadership qualities: as the Dean of the Faculty of Medicine of the University of Nairobi who within one year in office had mobilized adequate funds from Korean medical colleagues and built the current ultra-modern dean's and principal's offices at the College of Health Sciences? These offices were constructed solidly with natural stone and mortar and will probably last for hundreds of years. Or perhaps I will be remembered for my role in fundraising from the Canadian government for the construction of the UNITID building in the same college. Or shall I be remembered for my transformative leadership qualities as the VC of the University for ten years; a period that propelled the University to world class academic excellence? Or perhaps I could even be remembered for the construction of the imposing 22-storey University of Nairobi Towers. Or perhaps I will be remotely remembered for my very firm and strict administrative qualities which some people considered as some form of benevolent dictatorship or bullying. The list is long.

I however strongly believe that I most probably will be remembered for my published academic work as an eminent urological scholar and researcher in genital cancer. I believe that I will also be remembered for my research in erectile dysfunction, testicular torsion, circumcision and HIV, benign prostatic diseases, urolithiasis, Fournier's Gangrene, renal transplant, and appendicitis, among others. These published works are perhaps my very modest contribution to surgery, urology, humanity and mankind and will definitely outlive me for the greater benefit of future generations.

I believe that it is far much better to be remembered for good humanitarian and professional deeds that benefit mankind and humanity than being remembered for massive, accumulated personal wealth, that does not benefit or support the larger humanity in any way. Yet, at this point it is actually the history of your actions and deeds when alive, whether good or bad that shall be used to judge you long after you are gone. You have absolutely no opinion on this matter because history has a way of finding and finally documenting only the truth for the future and posterity.

What about you? Would you like to be remembered, at all, after you are gone to the great-beyond? If yes, what would you like to be remembered for? Will you have made any tangible difference, for example to the lives of the less fortunate in the society during your lifetime? Will you have made this planet a better place than you found it?

At this point in my life, I am actually completely unable to know or even predict whether or not, I qualify to be remembered by any entity or anybody for any actions or deeds whether good or bad. It is of course one of those things that mostly happen when one has already departed. Therefore, I can only hope that my footprints which includes my memoirs as outlined in this book, will help future generations to make some form of a balanced, fair and informed judgement about my person and my life.

CHAPTER ELEVEN

KNEC: Return To Credibility

On 05 January, 2015, on completion of my second and final term as Vice-Chancellor of the University of Nairobi, I opted for a low-keyed handing over ceremony. Those in attendance included Chairman of University of Nairobi Council Dr. Idle Farah, the incoming VC Professor Mbithi, my three other deputies: Professors Lucy Irungu in charge of Research, Production and Extension, Mbeche in charge of Student Affairs and Henry Mutoro in charge of Academic Affairs. Others were the Principals of the six colleges of the University, two Deputy Principals, the Chief Legal Officer, the Chief Finance Officer, the Chief Internal Auditor, the Academic Registrar, and the Administration Registrar.

The main handing over ceremony, which took place in the VC's committee room was quite brief, lasting approximately half an hour. It involved my frank, down to earth and very well intended farewell speech to my team. I recognized each team member's invaluable support during my ten-year tenure without which would not have succeeded.

I implored them to extend the same level of support and commitment to the incoming VC and other management organs. To the incoming VC, my advice was very specific; that he continues with the transformative leadership. After all, he had been my very loyal principal assistant for ten years and together we had succeeded in bringing the University to its current status. In any case, one does not usually dismantle a performing and very successful team like the one that I was leaving him in charge of. In that way he was bound to further empower his transformative team members and as a result achieve even much higher measurable outputs.

My parting shot to him was to employ Solomonic wisdom when discharging his duties and to seek God for guidance. I reminded him that he will get plenty of unsolicited advice (from 'friends'), and therefore should exercise his discretion – after all, these 'advisors' would definitely not have been VCs previously. My intellectual take is that you cannot be an expert advisor on what you don't know. I further emphasized that only the holder of the VC's office would be aware of the intricacies and intrigues associated with that office. The many advisors do so from a point of view of information that is not backed with any actual facts or experience, and from my personal information and experience, mostly for their own personal aggrandizement. They never understand the holistic picture, and either deliberately ignore or are unaware of the consequences of their advice.

I then proceeded to hand over the instruments of the VC's office, which included: the University Mace, the University Standard, the University Seal, the Universities Act number 42 of 2012, the University Charter and Statutes, and my complete handing over notes. The Chairman of Council, Dr. Farah thanked me for my selfless and exemplary service to the University. His remarks were followed by those of the incoming Vice Chancellor, who also heaped praises on my transformative leadership style. I then handed over the office to him and proceeded home to my family and to my department, the Department of Surgery.

I did not know that an elaborate inauguration ceremony had been planned for the incoming VC about two weeks later, until I was invited to attend the same. In the invitation card, it was clearly stated that a farewell ceremony would be held simultaneously for me, the outgoing VC. During my appointment as VC in January 2005, I had opted for no ceremony. My inauguration was very simple involving a press conference during which the Chancellor, Dr. Wanjui, and the Chairman of the Council, Professor Wasawo announced my appointment as VC to the general public. The press conference was held in the Council Chamber, and on the following day, I assumed duty.

The inauguration ceremony for Professor Mbithi, was however grand, attended by the Cabinet Secretary for Education Science and Technology, Principal Secretaries, the Chancellor and many other chancellors of public universities, the Chairman of Council and many other chairmen of councils of public universities, VCs of other public and private universities, other distinguished guests, stakeholders and the entire university community. There was an academic procession and graduation style marching around the Great Court before settling down in Taifa Hall. There was entertainment by the University of Nairobi choir, followed by speeches including one from the University Chancellor, Dr. Vijoo Rattansi, and Council Chairman, Dr. Farah.

Listening to their speeches, I felt absolutely humbled and thanked God that I had decided to return home to serve my people; especially when they emphatically stated that I had made a very significant, visible, and measurable difference at the University as VC. A tribute was read by Professor Olive Mugenda, the then VC of Kenyatta University, on behalf of all other Vice Chancellors of public and private universities in Kenya. I was deeply touched by her words. I did not know that other VCs, herself included regarded me as an astute and competent transformational manager and eminent international urological scholar, until that day.

Suffice to say that I felt very accomplished and satisfied with myself and my life, and to God be the glory. I now know for sure that many people including my peers, colleagues and other stakeholders had noticed the sacrifices we undertook in order to transform the University. By the time I was given an opportunity to give my 'farewell speech' I was completely overwhelmed with emotions. It was a feeling that no earthly material riches can provide. I did not expect so many pleasant things to be said about me and my management style which in my view was very firm. I therefore got another opportunity to say a proper thank you and goodbye to a community that had become a part of my life. I took the opportunity to ask the entire University community and other stakeholders, to accord Professor Mbithi, all the support in the same manner that they had given me. Professor Mbithi was then installed as the seventh VC of the University of Nairobi by the Chancellor, Dr. Rattansi.

The inaugural speech of the VC was incisive and detailed. It provided a bird's eye view of the policies and practices that he intended to pursue during his tenure. He also heaped praises on my leadership style and tangible achievements during my tenure and further emphasized how well we had worked together as a transformative team, over the ten year period. At the completion of the speeches, all were invited to a four course luncheon at the Great Court. But it is what followed the luncheon that was a complete surprise to me.

Some form of informal speeches continued during the luncheon, but towards the end I was called forward accompanied by my dear wife, Barbara. Remember that I had already left the University leadership and returned to my department of surgery as a professor of urology. I had seven and a half more years left to serve the University before retirement, contrary to the widely held view that I had already left service. I had actually only retired as VC but not as a professor. Standing beside my wife before the entire University community and other stakeholders, I was offered gifts by the Chancellor followed by the Council Chairman. This was followed by assorted gifts from the Senate, the staff unions, colleges, the University of Nairobi Alumni Association and many other stakeholders and individuals. To this day, I am completely amazed and grateful for the totally unexpected kind gestures. The gifts from the College of Health Sciences were particularly poignant, as a gauge on how staff felt about me. I was welcomed back to the Department of Surgery and to the college with open arms.

I had been offered a visiting professor position by one of our long term collaborating institutions, the University of Washington Seattle, but I turned it down. I wanted to understand what was happening at my department after the 15 years of absence while serving as Dean, Principal, DVC and VC. I returned to my department on 8 January, 2015. I had previously worked with about 80 per cent of the teaching staff in the department and therefore did not find it difficult to settle back in. The department was lucky to still have on its staff list three of the most senior members: Professors Kyambi, Peter Odhiambo and Joseph Oliech. Since majority of our departmental staff was growing old, it became extremely important to engage a number of tutorial fellows, and train them to take over as lecturers and consultants in a few years time when we eventually retire.

Currently, I am supervising four postgraduate students, training in urology and general surgery. I also take part in other departmental duties such as undergraduate and postgraduate examinations, surgical journal club, grand rounds, lectures and tutorials, in addition to other clinical duties that may be assigned by the chairman of the department.

I was handled quite satisfactorily because this was the second time for the college, school and departmental administration to handle a former VC and rehabilitate him back to an academic department. On my part, I did not intend to make the process difficult or challenging. The first Vice-Chancellor to be appointed from the College of Health Sciences, Professor Mungai was from the academic department of human anatomy, a preclinical department located in Chiromo Campus. I was therefore the first, medical clinician and by extension, the first surgeon to be appointed VC of the University of Nairobi.

The next big shocker that awaited me was when I was informed that the academic staff of the University had nominated me for the position of trustee of the University of Nairobi Pension Scheme. I was very surprised because as far as I was concerned, I had done my bit and therefore it was time for others to serve. In order for me to run for the slot, I had to accept the nomination. At first I did not accept it, and only did so after consulting widely. My nuclear family, and specifically my wife reminded me that she had never known me to retreat from any challenges. It is true that I have always faced my challenges squarely without fear. She therefore wished to know why I wanted to retreat from this particular one, thereby possibly betraying the confidence and respect the academic staff had bestowed on me through the nomination. I consulted further with some professionals and colleagues and eventually accepted the nomination. The term of one of the trustees had expired, after the mandatory two terms of three years each and had to be replaced through a competitive process.

I was elected by a landslide majority, receiving over sixty two per cent of the votes cast. I am therefore currently serving as a trustee representing academic staff in the Scheme, with effect from December 2015. It is a challenging task but given the fact that I had served previously as a trustee representing the Council between 2002 and 2014, I believe I possess the requisite experience necessary to contribute objectively to the running of the Scheme, for the benefit of the members.

Although I have retired as the VC, I continue to be extremely busy professionally in the medical front, as one of the most senior urological and transplant surgeons and an experienced surgical consultant, still practicing in the country. This is largely because, I was re-appointed chairman of KMPDB in November 2014, for the second and final five year term. Since then, I have continued to successfully and diligently discharge my professional duties.

In this capacity, I have led a professional team of excellent doctors that is responsible for the provision of quality medical and dental practice in Kenya and the East African Community partner states. I was first elected the President of the Association of Medical Councils of Africa at the 17th Annual Conference held in Kigali, Rwanda in 2013. I was also re-elected the President of AMCOA for a second term, at its annual international conference held in Mombasa, Kenya in August 2015. I have been responsible for the regulation of health care practice in the African continent. I organized the AMCOA international general conference held at Lilongwe, Malawi in August, 2016, having just chaired the AMCOA Management Committee meeting in Johannesburg South Africa.

In September, 2016 I travelled to Melbourne, Australia to attend the 12th International Conference on Medical Regulation, organized by the International Association of Medical Regulatory Authorities. This conference was hosted by the Medical Board of Australia and the Australian Health Practitioners Regulation Agency (AHPRA). The biennial conference has become an international, thought-provoking forum where international medical practitioners, policy makers and academics share ideas, best practices in international medical regulation, experiences and learn from each other. In this conference, I represented both KMPDB and AMCOA. One can therefore see that I remain busy on the medical professional front, despite having retired as VC.

I was first appointed to the Global Confucius Institute Council in 2007 in my capacity as the VC of the University of Nairobi to represent the African continent. The Confucius Institute at the University of Nairobi was the first to be established in Africa. I continue to serve as a member of the Council, representing the African continent. In that capacity, I have interacted with many different ministers of education and even the Vice Premier of the People's Republic of China, Madam Liu Yandong, who incidentally chairs the Confucius Institute Council at the headquarters in Beijing, China. I have also interacted with very many eminent scholars, VC and presidents of various universities across the globe.

Indeed, in 2015, after my retirement as VC, I attended a Round Table Conference of the global Confucius Institute Council held in Qufundong, China and the global Confucius Institute Conference, held in Shanghai, representing the African continent on both occasions. I strongly believe that it is because of the confidence that the Chinese Government has in me, coupled with the high level of intellectual discourse and objective contributions which I have continued to provide within the Council that has ensured my continued membership. For example, in mid-2016 I attended another Round Table Conference in Urumqi, China. This was the ninth Conference that I have attended and the second one after my retirement as VC.

Furthermore, I remain an active and the longest serving member of the Association of African Universities Governing Board, in my capacity as a former President and will serve in that position until 2017. Since my retirement as VC, I have actively participated in the 18th Conference of Rectors, VCs, and Presidents of African Universities (COREVIP), held in Kigali Rwanda in June 2015. The theme of the conference, 'Internationalization of Higher Education in Africa' was quite relevant and extensively discussed, under five significant sub themes: the harmonization and quality of higher education; mobility and transferability of credits; curriculum relevance and employability; new methods of teaching and the emerging centres of excellence in the African continent.

In June, 2016 I attended yet another AAU Governing Board meeting, in Accra, Ghana. This meeting discussed among other things the preparation for the 40th General Conference of the Association and the planned 50th Anniversary Celebrations to be held sometime in 2017. We also discussed extensively, the impact that the Association has had on the development of higher education in Africa and beyond, since its inception half a century ago. I have also been a member of the African Network for Scientific and Technological Institutions (ANSTI) Governing Board, having been first appointed in 2005. ANSTI was established in 1980 by the United Nations Educational Scientific and Cultural Organization (UNESCO), with funding from the United Nations Development Program (UNPD) and the German Government. The network was conceived in response to the resolution of the Conference of African Ministers of Science and Technology, held in Dakar, Senegal in 1974. UNESCO has continued to provide financial, technical and logistical support to ANSTI and its Governing Board, following its assigned responsibility to coordinate its activities. The ultimate goal of ANSTI has been to strengthen the African regional capacity for training and research, and for establishing services for intensive and purposeful utilization of science, engineering and technology for development. Additionally, the Network has also played a leading role in scientific innovations in Africa, and in matters related to the negative impacts of climate change and youth bulge within the African continent. I was appointed Chairman of the ANSTI Governing Board in 2010, a position I hold to date.

I have therefore been very active on the ANSTI professional front with the most recent major successful activity being organizing the African Regional Conference of VCs, Provosts, Deans of Science, Engineering and Technology (COVIDSET) Conference held in Enugu, Nigeria in August 2015. The main objective of the conference was to provide a platform for university leaders responsible for science, engineering, technology and innovation education, the private sector and development partners in Africa and the diaspora to deliberate on strategic issues affecting such educationist Africa. The theme of the Enugu conference, 'University Education and Training in Science, Engineering and Technology in Africa-Post 2015' was quite relevant to the solution on some of the current problems facing the African continent. The theme was discussed under four sub themes including: the state of science, engineering, technology, and innovation education in Africa; challenges and opportunities in post 2015 Africa; the role of universities and research institutions in climate change and sustainable development in Africa; making science, engineering, technology, and innovation education relevant to youth employability in post 2015 Africa; and the role of commercializing research in higher education financing in Africa.

CUE

In early January 2016, I was appointed a member of the Special Universities Advisory Committee, by the Cabinet Secretary for Education Science and Technology, Dr. Fred Matiang'i. The Committee, chaired by Professor Crispus Kiamba, also had a third member, a very distinguished and eminent legal scholar, Professor Kameri Mbote, Dean of the University of Nairobi's School of Law. The Committee had the mandate to assist Kisii, Laikipia and Kabarak Universities to put together corrective mechanisms to address the shortcomings of their campuses, identified for closure by the Commission for University Education (CUE). The Committee was to advise the Cabinet Secretary, and by extension the government on the provision of quality university education in the country.

Kisii University had ten of its campuses facing closure for not complying with CUE guidelines in establishing of new university campuses. These campuses had weak governance systems, lacked academic infrastructure and had inadequate number of qualified staff. Some of them were also located in environments that were not conducive for learning. The Committee is currently actively engaged in the process of rationalizing operations at the Kisii University by closing, merging and strengthening some of its campuses.

The committee visited all the ten campuses of Kisii University affected by the CUE closure notice. These included Main, Edoret, Kapenguria, Eldama Ravine, Kabarnet, Kehancha, Isebania, Migori, Ogembo, Keroka and Nyamira campuses. The committee engaged the University Council, the Senate, staff, students and other stakeholders as well as CUE. The goal was to place the University on a sustainable roadmap to reducing the ten campuses originally earmarked for closure. During the visits we discovered that the greatest challenges were related to: environment; inadequate physical infrastructure including lecture theatres, electronic libraries, laboratories and relevant equipment, academic staff offices; lack of students' recreation centre and facilities; and acute shortage of academic staff leading to unacceptable student staff ratios.

Together, we worked with the Council, management, and the Senate towards the rationalization and right-sizing of the campuses – from ten to four. The Eldoret Campus which was originally located in two different buildings about two kilometres apart, within the town centre was relocated to Kapsoya, and in conformity with CUE standards and guidelines. Furthermore, student numbers had been right-sized from over 5,000 in the previous campus to about 2,500 in the new campus. Additional and qualified academic staff was also recruited. The campuses closed included: Kehancha and Isebania whose students transferred to Migori Campus, in compliance with the CUE standards and guidelines; Eldama Ravine students were transferred to Kabarnet Campus; while Ogembo, Nyamira and Keroka campuses were scheduled for closure with students being transferred to the Main Campus. This activity was scheduled to be complete by mid-February 2016, the period which the mandate of the committee was due to expire.

However, this process has slowed down due to court orders against CUE, and therefore the campuses continue to operate outside the CUE standards and guidelines. Kapenguria Campus on the other hand was expanded and refurbished to meet the standards. As a result, the Campus remained open.

With regards to Kabarak University, its Nairobi campus was identified for closure primarily because it was located in two different buildings which did not conform with CUE guidelines for the establishment of new university campuses. The Committee engaged the Kabarak University Council, VC, Senate and management on several occasions and discussed the best way to conform to the CUE requirements. As a result, the University administration has successfully relocated the campus to a new single premises that is suitable for university education. They were also further advised to establish an office for quality assurance and compliance at the campus, a process that is ongoing.

The Nyahururu Campus of Laikipia University was also scheduled for closure due to its location in an inappropriate environment, lack of adequate numbers of academic staff, and inadequate library facilities. The Committee has met the Chancellor, Chairman of Council, some members of University Senate, management and the CUE officials on two occasions, and exhaustively discussed and agreed on an acceptable roadmap towards the compliance of the CUE requirements. Following the advisory, the campus relocated to new premises conducive for university education and in conformity with CUE requirements. The Laikipia University is also in the process of establishing an adequate and suitable library facility for the Nyahururu Campus in addition to employing relevant and qualified academic staff to effect teaching at the Campus.

KUCCPS

In 2014, I was appointed to represent public universities at the Kenya Universities and Colleges Central Placement Service (KUCCPS) board. KUCCPS was created through the Universities Act 42 of 2012, to competitively place government sponsored students into both public and private universities; Technical, Vocational and Educational Training (TVET) institutions; and middle level colleges after successfully completing their KCSE. This had hitherto been the responsibility of the Joint Admissions Board (JAB) of public universities. The JAB mandate was however restricted to admissions to public universities only. The mandate of KUCCPS was therefore broader and included disseminating information on available programs, their costs and areas of study as prioritized by the government. The Service is also in charge of developing career programmes for students as well as collecting and retaining data relating to college and university placement. KUCCPS is also tasked with advising the government on matters relating to university and college student placement. It promotes every student's rights to education through fair and effective placement to respective universities and colleges.

The KNEC Experience

As Napoleon Bonaparte observed, "A leader is a dealer in hope". This, it seems was my baptism of fire when I was appointed VC, and it seems that it has stuck on me, such because in March 2016, President Uhuru Kenyatta appointed me to serve as the Chairman of the Kenya National Examinations Council (KNEC). Truth be told, it was not a normal appointment, because the previous Council had been bundled out of office unceremoniously before the expiry of their term. There had been systematic and massive leakage of primary and secondary school examinations in 2015, which was partly due to the chronic failure of both internal and external management control systems at KNEC.

To start with, there was no pool of already set and moderated examination papers in every examinable subject from where a confidential examination would be selected as is the standard practice in many other examination syndicates. As surprising as it may sound, only a single examination paper for every subject was set yearly and labelled accordingly. Therefore, one was able to know in advance the examination which was for a particular year, in what can only be described as a fatal compromise of an already flawed examinations process. Further, two examination papers were also set and labelled for the consecutive years. For example, at any one time at KNEC, there would only be available three examination papers for every subject, labelled 2015, 2016, and 2017.

One can therefore see that it was relatively simple for any examination paper in any subject to fall into the wrong hands, at any time long before it was even printed and sat for. Secondly, in most cases the examination was set by only one subject specialist at KNEC, and later moderated by other external specialists identified solely by KNEC. This process was also fatally flawed as the labelled examination paper was revealed to the external specialists over whom the KNEC management had no authority and control whatsoever. The ideal situation would have been for the KNEC subject specialists to set a large pool of about 15 unlabelled examination papers, per subject, per year. These would then be moderated by external specialists, who at this stage would be unable to know which paper would be examined and in which year. One paper per subject would later be selected at random for printing and sitting for a particular year.

Thirdly, there also seemed to be everything wrong with packing, transporting and administration which invariably led to examination leakages. Coupled with the recent advances in modern telecommunications technology including the mobile phone and social media platforms, it had become relatively easy to leak an examination paper by just taking a picture of it, posting it online and thereafter spreading it widely. As a result, some schools posted very unrealistic results which defied all normal curves as currently known in the academic sector. For example, in 2015 several schools posted results with abnormally high pass-rates averaging about 96.6 per cent of the total marks for classes of more than 200 students, and where the examination was not multiple choice. Such results remain highly unrealistic and baffling, if not obnoxious. I can state this definitely, without any fear of contradiction whatsoever having taught surgery and anatomy to some of the most brilliant students during their study for medicine at the university level, since 1979.

My appointment as Chairman of KNEC therefore came at a time when the Council brand was at its lowest. Everybody expected the newly reconstituted Council to reorganize and put management systems in place in order to stem immediately, the perennial examinations leakage and restore the public confidence. After the reconstitution of the new Council all the senior management were removed from office in public interest. I therefore had a very challenging task of immediately forming a workable, transitional and transformative management team that would ensure the smooth continuity of the core functions of KNEC as the intended reforms were taking place concurrently.

To begin with, the government enabled us to co-opt two additional members into the Council. I opted for a chartered accountant, and another member with a security training, background and experience. I had identified these as the key gaps within the newly reconstituted Council. This was followed by the quick engagement of an acting CEO and the competitive appointment of acting senior management staff. The Council has recently carried out suitability interviews for all the current staff, a process which is nearing conclusion. The Council and management concurrently cancelled the examinations originally set for 2016, and set new ones in replacement. This drastic step was taken because of the strong belief that the said examinations were already compromised beyond salvage, with some subject questions even being taught in some schools.

The greatest challenge that faced the Council and management in 2016 was the swift provision of a workable policy framework for the logistics of packing, transportation, storage, actual sitting for, marking and finally releasing the examination results. In this regard, we provided adequate policy framework at strategic, tactical and process levels. In addition, we completely set new and large pools of examinations questions for both KCPE and KCSE in all the examinable subjects. The examination questions were set offline to avoid electronic leakage. The new examination pools were set by five people only, including myself. Only one of these people was a KNEC employee.

To ensure integrity and curb leakage, the 2016 examinations were printed and proofread in a safe place abroad. Only five people had contact with the examinations at this stage including the Principal Secretary (PS) in charge of primary and secondary education. Additional security features were incorporated in all the examination scripts to enhance integrity and ensure that tampering and cheating was made more difficult, if not impossible. Packing of the examination scripts was further reinforced by shrink-rapping of the individual cartons in addition to two other securely sealed polythene bags – before one could reach the examination scripts. Transportation was efficient, confidential and controlled, and the examination scripts were accompanied in each of the five flight trips from UK, by one of the five people who were involved in its setting and processing.

On arrival in Nairobi, the scripts were transported in eight 40-feet trailers under very tight security, and escorted by the mobile unit of the elite General Service Unit (GSU), officers of the Directorate of Criminal Investigation (DCI), and the National Intelligence Service (NIS), to two safe warehouses near the Jomo Kenyatta International Airport – equipped with CCTV cameras linked to a KNEC smart Command and Control Centre located at Mitihani House, Nairobi. It is from here that they would be monitored on a 24-hour basis by our staff and security experts.

The examination scripts were delivered in five jumbo jets over three weeks. On hand to receive and escort them to the smart warehouses were all members of KNEC Council, including myself. The pallets containing cartons of the scripts were transported whole into the warehouses from where they were dismantled into individual cartons which were fully labelled with their examination subjects and schools according to their sub-county destinations. Furthermore, the smart warehouses were guarded on a 24-hour basis by the elite GSU officers who permanently camped within the precincts.

With regard to storage of the examination scripts in the sub-counties, 346 twenty-foot long metallic containers were purchased and strategically placed at each sub-county headquarters country wide. The security of the containers was entrusted to the individual sub-county commissioners who promptly deployed 24-hour armed police guards, in addition to other government security agencies. Further, each container was locked with two different special locks manufactured in Israel, according to KNEC and management security specifications. The key to one of the locks was retained by the sub-county commissioner while the key to the other lock was kept by the sub-county director of education. In order for the container to be opened or closed at any one time, the two senior officials of government had to be present. This was to be done in the presence of the police and other security officers, county and national education officials, KNEC officials, and primary school head teachers, and secondary school principals who either came to collect or return the scripts.

The scripts were transported under tight security escort from the smart warehouses in Nairobi to metallic containers located in all the sub-county headquarters. On arrival, the deputy county commissioners and sub-county directors of education were on hand to receive store and lock them awaiting the dates for the actual sitting according to the examination timetable. Risk of examination over-exposure was reduced further by transporting the examinations scripts from Nairobi to the sub-county containers twice a week compared to once a week, as was done previously. This ensured that the scripts stored in the containers did not exceed a maximum duration of three examination days at any time, compared to five days in the past. In the past years, the examination scripts were stored in various police armoires in the country. We discontinued this practice in order to enhance the security and maintain the integrity of the examinations to the highest international standards.

On the morning of each examination day, the deputy county commissioner and the sub-county director of education opened the containers; originally at 5 a.m. for the first ten days, and at 6 a.m. for the remaining three weeks duration of the examination. The time was reduced from 5 a.m. to 6 a.m. in order to further safeguard and maintain the integrity of the examinations. This was because some of the monitoring teams had discovered attempts by a few unscrupulous handlers of the examination scripts to compromise the integrity of the examination process by unsuccessfully attempting to access the examination scripts long before the official time of 8 a.m. Such attempts were thwarted by continuous surveillance by our gallant security, KNEC, and the Ministry of Education agents. Moreover, the containers were opened every morning, Monday to Friday in the presence of the head teachers of primary schools and principals of secondary schools as the case may be. Also present were other senior government officials whom sometimes included the Cabinet Secretary for education Dr. Fred Matiang'i, Principal Secretaries in the Ministry of Education Drs Belio Kipsang, Dinah Mwinzi and Professor Colette Suda, Chairman, CEO and members of KNEC, directors of education and many armed security officers and officers from other government security agencies, all intended to escort the examination scripts to various primary and secondary schools.

The principals and head teachers collected the examination scripts in person and were responsible for their safety. The scripts were escorted by armed security officers to their various schools within the sub-counties from where they surrendered them to the examination supervisors who conducted the examinations. During the examination there were many examination-monitoring teams lead by the Cabinet Secretary which covered the whole country. These teams ensured, among other things that nothing untoward happened during the examination process that would compromise its integrity. Many of these teams witnessed the opening of the containers, monitored the examination administration processes in various schools, and also escorted the completed examination scripts back to the containers.

At the end of each examination, the integrity of the examinations was ensured and the scripts were publicly counted, packed and sealed in secure envelopes, a process which was witnessed by some pupils, the supervisor and the principal or the head teacher. The sealed examination scripts were transported back to the containers by the head teachers or principals under tight security and securely stored and locked independently by the deputy county commissioner and sub-county director of education. The answered examination scripts were later transported by KNEC officials and other government security agencies from the sub-counties back to Nairobi. The handling, transportation, and storage of all the examination materials for both the KCPE and the KCSE was closely monitored and managed at the secure KNEC smart Command and Control Centre manned by examination experts and armed security personnel on a 24-hour basis. All activities at the smart warehouses were directly linked to the Centre through CCTV cameras.

All KCPE subjects were marked using computerized Machine Optic Mark Reader (OMR) system except for English composition and Kiswahili *insha* which were manually marked by different vetted subject examiners. The OMR marking of the multiple choice examination questions in various subjects was effected at the Command and Control Centre. This was done by a select group of carefully vetted staff from KNEC and other government educational agencies such as Kenya Institute of Curriculum Development (KICD) in the presence of the KNEC officers and officers from various government security agencies. There was therefore no opportunity left for anyone to compromise the integrity of the examination at this stage. Special attention was paid to the scripts of the children with special needs.

The carrying of boxes containing examination materials was done by the NYS officers. The *insha* and composition were marked in 13 carefully selected school marking centres each within 50 kilometres from Nairobi City. This was to ensure effective and very close monitoring of the examination marking process in order to strengthen and maintain the integrity of the examination. This was unlike in the past when the marking centres were scattered all over the country making it challenging to closely monitor effectively. At the end of every marking day, the marks were forwarded from the marking centres to the Command and Control Centre. They were then fed into the computer through the OMR system.

The marking of the KCPE was completed and processed in a record four weeks and the results released to the general public immediately thereafter. The results were of course poorer than the previous year due to the fact that all opportunities for cheating were successfully blocked from the setting to the marking and release of the results. But the whole country was happy and satisfied because everyone knew that the examinations were for the first time in a long time done fairly and free of leakage. Furthermore, feedback from the public indicated that considerably more poor rural children were allocated places in top performing national public schools purely on merit unlike in the past when only a few could manage. All students transiting to secondary schools received their calling letters before Christmas of 2016, to report to their new schools on 09 January, 2017 unlike in the past when they reported much later. We also noticed that a sizable number of students were unable to even write their index numbers and names correctly, indicating that they had not been adequately taught because such skills and competencies should have been satisfactorily covered during the first three years of primary school.

It is common knowledge that there has been rampant cheating in both KCPE and KCSE examinations in the past. What is most shocking however is the fact that there's a significant possibility that some teachers are not teaching at all, hence some of the children cannot even write their names and index numbers properly. I personally am of the opinion that the government should urgently review the policy of posting primary school teachers to their sub-counties or rural areas. I strongly believe that this policy has contributed to some teachers not being dedicated to their duty and hence the deplorable state of some student's skills and competencies necessary for progression to secondary schools.

Secondly, whereas the said teachers could be engaging in business at the expense of their teaching, the fault is not entirely theirs. Part of the blame must go to the inspectorate division of the Ministry of Education who are expected to ensure that teachers perform their duties diligently and according to their terms of engagement. Failure to do so should be swiftly dealt with according to the law. For the avoidance of doubt, there are many other teachers who perform their teaching duties diligently and according to their terms of service. Such teachers should be commended in equal measure. Going forward, the greatest challenge for the government is how to sustain this very noble process of ensuring that the integrity of the examination remain sacrosanct.

The marking of the KCSE scripts was effected in 25 different secondary school marking centres located within 50 kilometre radius from Nairobi City. The majority of the marking centres which were carefully selected and vetted were located within Nairobi metropolis. This was to enable and facilitate effective monitoring during the marking process and avoid any form of cheating.

Furthermore, each of the marking centres was fitted with CCTV cameras in all the examination script storage rooms and data capturing rooms, which were all linked directly to the Centre for surveillance. In addition, there were many examination-monitoring teams headed by the Cabinet Secretary and Principal Secretary in the Ministry of Education, and included the entire KNEC members, and the CEO, and officers from various government security agencies.

Marking of the examination scripts was effected using a conveyer belt system. At the completion, all the marks for the day were keyed into the computers, immediately encrypted, transmitted and secured at the Centre. Access to the secure computer system with the encrypted marks was strategically restricted to only three key and senior ICT personnel unlike in the past when many other KNEC staff from various departments had passwords and could therefore gain access to the computer system and adjust marks even without appropriate authorization.

We continued to monitor the marking process at all the marking centres on daily basis. On completion, the chief examiner for each examinable subject submitted detailed, comprehensive and signed reports of the specific examination that they were responsible for. It is significant to note that all chief examiners gave their individual examinable subjects a clean bill of health. For example, they stated that questions were all within the syllabus and were appropriate and suitable. None of them recommended upward or downward moderation of the marks as there was no reason to do so. This was very professional of the chief examiners because, as a matter of fact the majority of the questions in the 2016 KCSE examinations originated from past examination scripts of the previous ten years. At this juncture I wish to commend and celebrate the professionalism, dedication and passion which the chief examiners and all the other examiners worked with. They worked tirelessly as a team to complete marking of the examinations in record time. My discussions and other engagements with them was always cordial and professional, only firm occasionally with a few of them. I therefore salute all of them for a job well done, for our children and our country.

At the completion of the exercise, individual subjects grade boundaries award meeting was held chaired by the acting CEO, Mercy Karogo. It is important to note that the KCSE 2016 grade boundaries were determined using the examination reports from the chief examiners, with input from quality assurance experts from the Ministry of Education, experts from KICD, KNEC and other relevant stakeholders. The grade boundaries were determined using the International Gold Standard, unlike in the past when sometimes the lowest pass mark was reduced to between 20 and 23 per cent in some subjects.

We discovered to our utmost surprise that the marks for many of the students in all subjects were very low. This was a confirmation that the 2016 KCSE examinations had neither leaked nor been compromised in any way compared to the previous years. In the pattern of the marks scored by individual students, we found a few very intelligent students with undisputed genuine 'A' grade scores. At the completion of the marking exercise, there were only 141 such candidates. This was in direct contrast to the several thousands of such students reported in the previous year. Furthermore, the individual scores of many candidates in many examinable subjects were very low, below 30 per cent. What actually shocked me most was the fact that on personally taking time to read through samples of marked examination scripts in the subjects of English, Mathematics, Kiswahili, Chemistry, Biology, Physics, History, Geography and even Christian Religious Education I discovered that majority of the 33,000 students who scored an 'E' grade actually had nothing to write – scoring only between one and 12 per cent which was the highest score in this group. I still cannot understand how students could be in school for 12 years and fail to learn anything. This strongly indicated that such students were most likely never professionally taught, and were probably waiting for leaked examinations as has been the practice in the past. The marking of all the examination scripts was completed in all examination centres by Christmas Day of December 2016.

For the avoidance of doubt, there were no schools this time round with 'super scores' where nearly everybody scored an 'A' grade with a ridiculous average performance of 96.6 per cent in all examinable subjects in a class of about 300 students – as was the case in the 2015 KCSE examinations. In 2015 several schools had scored over 200 'A' grades as compared to 2016 where the leading school with very consistent performance over the years scored 25 'A' grades. The schools which had scored between 50 and over 200 'A' grades all drastically dropped to a range of 0-14 'A' grades. The 2015 results failed the credibility test in 2016, as they could neither be reproduced nor sustained when due diligence was put in place. It is quite obvious that such results were not a true reflection of most individual student's academic ability.

This phenomenon has further been proven over the years at the various universities countrywide. For example, at the University of Nairobi where I am still a faculty member, a reasonable number of students who were admitted to study for professional degrees of medicine or engineering on a competitive basis with 'A' grades were completely unable to cope with the academic pressure and intensity of such disciplines, and therefore were discontinued on academic grounds. This shows that their grades were not genuine but obtained either through examination leakage or cheating. The undisputed return to the normal distribution of results in the KCSE 2016 can only be attributed to a battery of security, coordination and supervisory measures that were initiated and strictly implemented by the new KNEC Council, and the government through the Ministry of Education.

The 2016 KCSE results were released on 30 December, and were received very well by the general public as most credible in a long time. This was in a record time, in that it was only 29 days after the completion of the last paper, compared to the past when the release was effected in late February or early March of the following year. It is significant to note that this is the first time in 27 years that KCSE results have been released in the same year that they were sat. The important lesson for teachers, KNEC and the Ministry of Education officials to learn from this is that time is the most important constant in this exercise. When it takes too long to mark the examination scripts, followed by another unnecessary long delay before releasing the results, it poses very serious challenges to the integrity of the examination because this is the time many actors corrupt it for financial or material gain, in order to award 'A' grades to undeserving students.

It is now time of reckoning for our education system and every teacher should truthfully search his or her conscience to determine whether there is the need to urgently seek atonement or not. If as the majority of the teachers have done, you have given your very best in teaching your students and have achieved consistent results such as Kenya High or Alliance Girls High School, and many others then all I can say is well done. Keep up the good work of moulding our children into responsible young Kenyans with the necessary skills and competencies essential in furthering their future lives responsibly. If however, you are one of those who used to collect money from our children or their parents in order to encourage them to cheat, you must acknowledge that you have destroyed the future of many of them.

I personally charge you to stop and learn from your mistakes going forward. Just go back to class and teach our children according to your terms of engagement and complete the prescribed syllabus. Our children will forgive and respect you, but you must earn their respect as the teacher who imparts knowledge on them. They will never respect you for cheating or leaking any examination to them. They are definitely innocent and deserve knowledge and protection from both parents and teachers. Let us all seek atonement and start afresh. It can be done. It definitely shall be done for the sake of the future of our children and our country. After all, before this 'A' grade craze became institutionalised, in the late eighties and early nineties, reasonable and credible KCPE and KCSE results used to be posted regularly.

This important national assignment has been undoubtedly one of the most challenging in my life, and I proudly accepted it patriotically in honour of the Kenyan children and my country. I strongly believe that I have performed it to the best of my ability, and without prejudice, fear or favour. There is actually a lot of pride, honour and satisfaction in serving our children. I am fully satisfied with the measurable leakage-free results we have achieved, which was according to our goals at strategic, tactical and operational levels.

I believe that the credible results achieved during the 2016 KCPE and KCSE examinations will provide a very strong basis upon which the government can successfully reform the education sector for the benefit of future generations. At a personal level, I consider it a very significant national honour to have been recognized by His Excellency President Uhuru Kenyatta, as a competent transformative leader, and to be professionally identified to contribute to the solution of the perennial national problem of examination leakage. It is therefore extremely significant for readers and the public to fully appreciate that after all, there is a very active academic and professional life out there, even after one has served as Vice-Chancellor for ten years. All one needs to do is find it and engage.

Standing 4th from left with the Chancellor, University of Nairobi Dr. Joseph Wanjui, Chairman of Council Dr. Idle Farah, Dr. Manu Chandaria, Mrs. Manu Chandaria with the officials of the Construction Company of on occasion of ground-breaking ceremony, 2013

The Chancellor Dr. Vijoo Rattansi (centre) is being shown the building plans by architect Waweru Gathecha (second left). I am on the extreme right, 2013

With H.E. President Uhuru Kenyatta, accompanied by the H.E. the First Lady Margaret Kenyatta and H.E. the Vice President William Ruto and extreme left is Senator Kipchumba Murkomen on the occasion of laying of the foundation stone of the University of Nairobi Towers building, 2014

On the occasion of laying of the Foundation Stone of the University of Nairobi Towers by H.E. President Uhuru Kenyatta, 2014

University of Nairobi Towers, view from the Great Court showing the fountain of knowledge to the right, 2016

The University of Nairobi Main Campus showing the Great Court and Magnificent 22 storey University of Nairobi Towers Building on the left corner next to Education Building, Jomo Kenyatta Memorial Library (JKML), and Hyslop Building of the left, Gandhi Memorial Library, Gandhi Wing and Fountain of the knowledge on the right, and the School of Engineering in the background, 2016

One of the lecture theatres with a capacity of 300 pax, 2016

A larger lecture theatre, with a capacity of 500 pax within the Tower building, 2016

Staircase to the Arts auditorium, 2016

The Arts auditorium, 2016

The Arts auditorium, 2016

Ground floor entrance lobby, 2016

Officials from the Ministry of Education, Teachers Service Commission (TSC) and the Kenya National Examinations Council (KNEC) led by Cabinet Secretary Dr. Fred Matiang'i brief H.E. President Uhuru Kenyatta moments before the release of KCPE results on 02 December, 2016

With H.E. President Uhuru Kenyatta (third from right) standing next to Cabinet Secretary Dr. Fred Matiang'i, Ms. Mercy Karogo, Ag. CEO, KNEC, Prof. George Magoha, Chairman, KNEC (third from left), Ms. Nancy Macharia, CEO, TSC and Dr. Belio Kipsang, Principal Secretary Ministry of Education, at State House Nairobi, 2016

Shaking hands with H.E. President Uhuru Kenyatta at State House Nairobi. Looking on Cabinet Secretary Dr. Fred Matiang'i, Ms. Mercy Karogo, Ag. CEO, KNEC, Ms. Nancy Macharia, CEO, TSC and Dr. Belio Kipsang, PS, Ministry of Education, 2016

From left: Cabinet Secretaries Joseph Mucheru (ICT), Dr. Fred Matiang'i (Education) and Joseph Nkaissery (Interior) and I, Chairman, KNEC, during the release of the 2016 KCPE examination results in Nairobi

Receiving the 2016 Kenya Cerficate of Secondary School Examination at the Jomo Kenyatta International Airport together with Mercy Karogo, acting CEO, KNEC and other state officials

At Kisumu Girls High School in Kisumu County during the Physics practical of the 2016 KCSE

Addressing and encouraging Kisumu Boys students just before the Physics 2016 KCSE

Encouraging students at Kisumu Boys during the Physics practical in the 2016 KCPE

Encouraging a candidate during the 2016 KCSE at Moi High School Kabarak at Kampi ya Moto, Nakuru County

Inspecting the 2016 KCPE Examination scripts at the Star of the Sea Primary School in Mombasa, Mombasa County. Looking on is the examination supervisor

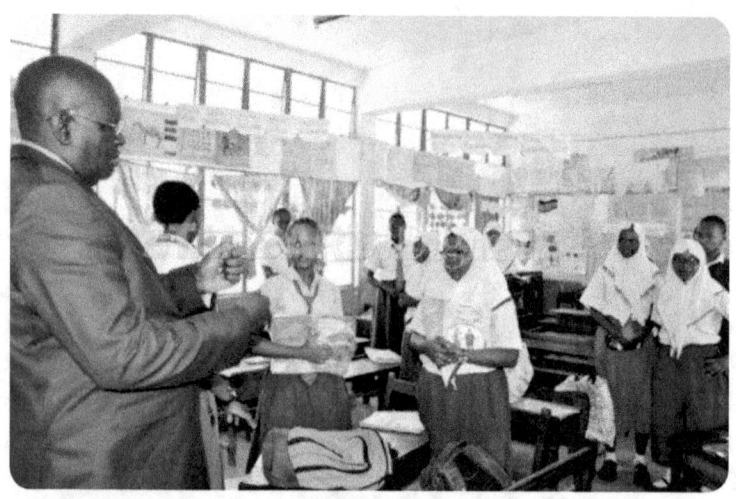

Charting and encouraging Star of the Sea Primary School 2016 KCPE candidates in Mombasa before the start of examinations

Encouraging candidates at Moi High School Kabarak in Kampi ya Moto, in Nakuru County, shortly before the commencement of KCSE 2016. Looking on to my left is the Principal of Moi High School Kabarak, Mrs Elisheba Cheruiyot

Shortly after opening one of the containers securing the examination scripts (in the background) in the presence of the County Commissioner of Kisumu Maalim Mohammed (extreme right with glasses) and the Kisumu Central Deputy County Commissioner Josephine Ouko (in uniform), 2016

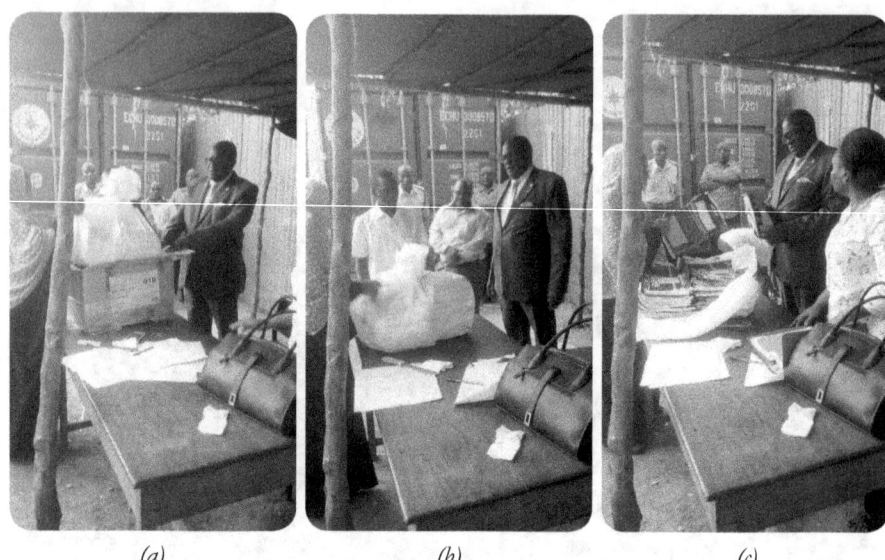

(a) *(b)* *(c)*
Ensuring the integrity of the 2016 KCSE examination scripts at the Changamwe sub-county in Mombasa County before the commencement of the examination

Talking to and encouraging students before the History examination in one of the secondary schools in Kenya, 2016

Seated 5th from left with Ag. CEO, KNEC, Ms. Mercy Karogo on my right and TSC, CEO, Ms. Nancy Macharia left during the KNEC Policies and Structures Review Retreat at Enashipai Resort Naivasha, 2017

Myself at the back with the Cabinent Secretary, Dr. Fred Mating'i presenting the results of the 2016 KCSE to H.E. President Uhuru Kenyatta at the State House, Mombasa accompanied by Principal Secretary Bellio Kipsang, Ag. CEO, KNEC, Ms. Mercy Karogo and TSC, CEO, Ms. Nancy Macharia

INDEX

Index of country names

A
Angola, 22, 87
Australia, 149-150, 154, 186, 247-248, 290-291, 313

B
Bahamas, 22, 27
Belgium, 151, 154, 161, 210
Benin, 27
Botswana, 67, 151, 154
Britain, 10, 156, 187, 298-299; see also United Kingdom
Burundi, 154, 258, 260

C
Cameroon, 22, 27, 151, 303
Canada, 27, 85, 115, 150-152, 154, 160, 162, 165, 272, 195, 247, 271, 281, 298, 303-304
China, 34, 150, 154, 161, 177, 184, 194, 196-197, 200-201, 205-206, 212, 221, 242, 247, 313

D
Denmark, 10, 12, 152, 160

E
Ethiopia, 20, 151, 154, 212, 241

F
Finland, 150-152
France, 27

G
Germany, 27, 150, 154, 177-178, 185, 201, 247, 314
Ghana, 19, 22, 27, 32, 36, 87, 151, 154, 179, 201, 222, 226, 241, 286, 293, 303, 314
Guyana, 22, 27

I
India, 5, 27, 67, 92, 150, 163, 186, 247-248, 298
Ireland, 32, 36, 55, 226
Israel, 154, 207, 322

J
Japan, 150, 152, 154, 204, 247

L
Lesotho, 22, 293
Liberia, 150, 303

M
Malawi, 4, 289, 293, 312
Mauritius, 87

N
Namibia, 151
Nigeria, 5, 19-20, 23-24, 31-33, 35-37, 46, 50, 55-56, 67, 87, 121, 151, 154, 218, 226-227, 241, 264-265, 286, 297-298, 300, 302, 315

P
Pakistan, 25, 27
Prince Edward Island, 150

R
Russia, 247
Rwanda, 87, 151, 154, 217-218, 220, 258, 260, 273, 286, 293, 312, 314

S
Somalia, 151, 200
South Africa, 22, 57, 67, 148, 151, 154, 160-161, 179, 241, 247-248, 259, 269, 291, 293, 312
South Korea, 60-61, 150, 178, 197, 209, 266

South Sudan, 151, 260
Sudan, 151
Sweden, 150
Switzerland, 120

T
Tanzania, 22, 24, 58, 87, 151-154, 182, 222, 241, 258, 260, 265, 285, 303
Togo, 27, 38
Trinidad and Tobago, 22, 27

U
Uganda, 2, 4, 22, 41, 58, 84, 87, 151-152, 154, 204, 258, 260, 285-286, 293, 303

Ukraine, 247
United Kingdom (UK), 10, 12, 18, 22, 27, 34, 55, 67, 109, 11, 150-151, 154, 161, 163, 165, 242, 247-248, 254, 287, 293, 298, 301-302
United States of America (USA), 5, 12, 22, 27, 89, 93, 150-152, 161, 175, 185, 202-203, 298, 301

Z
Zambia, 19, 87, 91, 151, 154, 222, 289, 297
Zanzibar, 258, 260
Zimbabwe, 22, 151, 154, 165, 286

Index of names of institutions

A
Academic Staff Association, 66
Ace Communications, 14
African Network for Scientific and Technological Institutions (ANSTI), 153, 212, 314-315
African Tours and Hotels, 4
African Trust Fund, 10
Agricultural Development Corporation (ADC), 89
Alliance Girls High School, 330
Alliance High School, 16
Aluor Catholic Mission School, 2, 4, 81
American Youth Service Corps, 10
Association for Strengthening Agricultural Research in Eastern and Central Africa (ASARECA), 152
Association of African Universities (AAU), 18, 19, 153, 179, 217, 297, 314

Association of Chartered Certified Accountants (ACCA), 15
Association of Commonwealth Universities (ACU), 159, 242, 154
Association of Medical Councils of Africa (AMCOA), xvi, 154, 252-253, 259, 273, 286-287, 289, 293, 312-313
Attorney General's chambers, 19, 86
Australian Health Practitioners Regulation Agency (AHPRA), 313

B
Bank of India Advisory Committee, 92
Barclays Bank (of Kenya), 7, 208
Bata Shoe Company, 91
Bayer E. A Limited, 161
Bonn-Rhein-Sieg University of Applied Sciences, 201
Boy Scout Club, 7, 11, 13
British Association of Urological Surgeons, 287

British Government, 10
British National Health Service (BNHS), 299-300

C

Canadian Foundation for Innovation (CFI), 65, 160
Capital Markets Authority, 91-92
Central Bank of Kenya, 18
Centre for African Research on Enterprise and Economic Development, University of West Scotland, 219
Centre for Biotechnology and Bioinformatics (CEBIB), 158
Centre for Disease Control (CDC) Atlanta, 151, 162, 241
Centre for Disease Control and Prevention, 160
Centre for Global Public Health, 162
Centre for International Programs and Links (CIPL), 149, 166
Centre for Research Evaluation, Science and Technology (CREST), 242
Chandaria Foundation, xv, 92, 166
Chinese Confucius Institute, 166, 212, 221
Citibank, 91
Citizen Television Station (Royal Media Services), 89-90
Clinical Officers Council, 253, 255
Colorado State University, 150, 152, 202
Comcraft Group of Companies, 92
Commercial Bank of Africa, 74, 90
Commission for the Implementation of the Constitution (CIC), 136
Commission for University Education (CUE), 168, 315-318
Commission on Revenue Allocation (Kenya), 18
Commonwealth Africa Venture Capital Fund, 94
Conference of Rectors, Vice Chancellors, and Presidents of African Universities (COREVIP), 179, 217, 220, 314
Conference of Vice Chancellors, Provosts, Deans of Science, Engineering and Technology (COVIDSET), 218, 315
Confucius Institute Council, 150, 196-197, 205-206, 212, 313
Cornell University, 162
Court of Appeal, 1
Curtin University, 150

D

Danish Government, 10
Department for International Development (DFID), 242
Deposit Protection Fund, 91
Development of Research Uptake in Sub-Saharan Africa (DRUSSA), 242-243
Directorate of Criminal Investigation (DCI), 15, 321
Dr. David Livingstone Primary School, 7, 294-295

E

East African Breweries, 4
East African Business Council, 92
East African Community (EAC), 154, 159, 252-253, 256, 258, 260, 277
East African Industries, 93-94
East African Reinsurance Company Limited, 92
Egerton University, 78, 183
Electronic Information for Libraries (EIFL), 159

Equity Bank, 14
Erectile Dysfunction Advisory Council (EDAC), 58, 268, 303-305
Esso Limited, 93

F

Ethics and Anti-Corruption Commission (EACC), 136, 133
Fairmont Norfolk Hotel, 10
Federal of State Medical Boards (US), 293
Federation of Kenya Employers (FKE), 86, 101, 103, 120
Fellow Royal College of Surgeons (FRCS), 31-32, 36, 254
First Capital Bank of Zambia, 91
Ford Foundation, 10, 165, 209, 225

G

G4S Security Company Limited, 87
Gandhi Memorial Academy Society, 66, 92
Gandhi Smarak Nidhi Fund, 93
Gazi University, 211
General Medical Council of United Kingdom, 34, 259, 287
General Service Unit (GSU), 321-322
George Washington University, 203
Gertrude's Garden Children's Hospital, 91
Ghana Medical Council, 293
GlaxoSmithKline Limited, 161
Global Confucius Institute Council, 313

H

Hammersmith Hospital, 34-35, 49, 299, 303; Royal Postgraduate Medical School, 35
Hankuk University of Foreign Languages, 150
Health Professions Council of South Africa, 291, 293
Health Professions Council of Zambia, 289
Hillpark Hotel, 94
Housing and Building Research Institute (HABRI), 72

I

ICDC Investment Company (Centum), 94
Industrial Commercial Development Corporation (ICDC), 86, 89, 94
Information and Communication Technology Centre (ICTC), 157
Institute of Human Virology at the University of Maryland Baltimore, School of Medicine, 274
Insurance Advisory Board, 92
Intas Pharmaceuticals, 161
Inter-African Universities Program 1967 (INTERAF), 19, 297
International AIDS Vaccine Initiative (IAVI), 151, 161
International Association of Medical Regulatory Authorities (IAMRA), 252-253, 259, 287, 290, 291, 313
International Development Research Centre (IDRC), 165
International Federation of Library Associations and Institutions (INFLA), 159
International Finance Corporation (IFC), 89; business advisory council, 94
International Labour Organization (ILO), 120
International Livestock Research Institute (ILRI), 152
International Network for the Availability of Scientific Publications (INASP), 159

International Organization for Standardization (ISO), xv, 101, 103-104, 131-134, 168, 174
Investment Promotion Centre, 92

J

Jilin University, 200
Jina Primary School, 3, 5, 84, 294
John Hopkins School of Public Health Baltimore, 162
Joint Industrial and Commercial Consultative Committee, 92
Jomo Kenyatta University of Agriculture and Technology, 276-277

K

Kabaa Mission School (Machakos), 4, 40-41
Kabarak University, 315, 317, 344-345
Kagilo School, 3
Kakuzi Limited, 87
Kanazawa University, 150
Kansas University, 161
Karen Hospital, 75, 88-89
Kariokor market, 10
Katholieke Universiteit Leuven, 161
KCA University, 219
Keimyung University, 197
Kenindia Assurance Company Limited, 92
Kenol-Kobil Company Limited, 91
Kenya AIDS Vaccine Initiative (KAVI), 160-161, 164, 270
Kenya Association of Manufacturers, 92
Kenya Bankers Association, 91
Kenya Bureau of Standards (KEBS), 102-104, 131, 168, 174
Kenya College of Communications, 101

Kenya Colony, 11
Kenya Commercial Bank, 75, 91
Kenya Defence Forces, 14, 43
Kenya Ear Foundation, 92
Kenya Education Network (KENET), 158
Kenya High School, 16, 330
Kenya Hospital Association (Nairobi Hospital), 91
Kenya Industrial Estates (KIE), 89, 94
Kenya Institute of Curriculum Development (KICD), 324, 327
Kenya Institute of Management, 94
Kenya Library and Information Services Consortium (KLISC), 159
Kenya Medical Laboratory Technologists and Technicians Board, 255
Kenya Medical Practitioners and Dentists Board (KMPDB), xvi, xviii, 57, 252, 254, 258, 260, 272-280, 282-284, 292-293, 312-313
Kenya Medical Research Institute (KEMRI), 160
Kenya Methodist University, 249
Kenya National Examinations Council (KNEC), xvi, xix, 307-331, 340-342, 347
Kenya National Trading Corporation (KNTC), 94
Kenya Private Sector Alliance, 92
Kenya Revenue Authority (KRA), 78-79, 130
Kenya Seed Company, 163
Kenya Shell Limited, 10
Kenya Union of Domestic, Hostels, Educational Institutions, Hospitals and Allied workers (KUDHEIHA), 120, 227

Kenya Universities and Colleges Central Placement Service (KUCCPS), 219, 318
Kenya Universities Staff Union (KUSU), 188, 227
Kenya University Librarians Committee (KULC), 159
Kenya Wildlife Service (KWS), 14
Kenyatta National Hospital (KNH), 6, 12, 56-57, 160, 189, 192, 235, 260, 266, 270, 281, 304
Kenyatta University 74, 222, 309; School of Medicine, 18
King George VI Hospital see Kenyatta National Hospital (KNH)
Kisii University, 315-317; Eldama Ravine Campus, 316-317; Eldoret Campus, 316; Isebania Campus, 316-317; Kabarnet Campus, 316-317; Kapenguria Campus, 316-317; Kehancha Campus, 316-317; Keroka Campus, 316-317; Main Campus, 317; Migori Campus, 316-317; Nyamira Campus, 316-317; Ogembo Campus, 316-317
Kisumu County, 3, 6, 45, 76, 342
Kisumu Provincial Hospital, 11
Kitale Primary School, 11
KK Security Group, 91
Korean Foundation, 199

L

'L'Orchestre Lunna Success de la Capital', 8, 295
Lagos Island Maternity Hospital, 28
Laikipia University, 315-316; Nyahururu Campus, 317
Lenana School, 16
Linkoping University (Sweden), 150
Loreto School, Limuru, 2

M

MacArthur Foundation, 163
Maharishi Markandeshwar University (India), 150
Mahatma Gandhi Memorial Academy Society see Gandhi Memorial Academy Society
Makerere University, 18, 84, 87, 151-152, 154, 187, 204, 254; Mulago Hospital, 18
Malawi Medical Council, 293
Mang'u High School, 16
Manyani Camp, 10, 11
Manyuanda School, 3
Marenyo Dispensary, 6
Marlborough College, 10
Maseno University, 183, 215
Masinde Muliro University, 65
Mau Mau, 11
Medical Board of Australia, 313
Medical Council of Burundi, 260
Medical Council of South Sudan, 260
Medical Council of Tanganyika, 260
Medical Council of Zanzibar, 260
Medical Education Partnership Programme Initiative (MEPI), 240
Medical Practitioners and Dentists Board of Kenya (MPDBK) see KMPDB
Medox Pharmaceuticals, 185
Mekelle University, Ethiopia, 241
Melodica Studios, 8
Mercer University, 161
Meteorological department; Kololo Hill, 4, 41; Nanyuki, 4
Middle Tennessee State University (MTSU), 202
Mill Hill Catholic Mission, Yala, 2-3, 5

Ministry of Education, 19-20, 66-67, 71, 79, 108, 121-122, 323, 326-327, 329, 340-341
Ministry of Health, 108, 254, 275
Moi High School Kabarak, 344-345
Mombasa County, 292, 344, 346
Morrison Primary School (Bahati), 7
Mount Kenya University, 219, 220
MTT Agrifood Research Finland, 152
Muhanda School, 3

N

Nairobi Round Table No. 10, 152
Nairobi School, 11
Namliango, Makerere (Uganda), 2
Nation Media Group, 14, 75
National Aeronautics and Space Administration (NASA), 152-153
National AIDS and STIs Control Programme (NASCOP), 241
National Association of Resident Doctors of Nigeria, 33; Nigerian Resident Doctors Association, 121
National Council of Science and Technology, 92
National Economic and Social Council, 92
National Health Service (NHS), British, 299-300
National Health Insurance Fund (NHIF), 292
National Institutes of Health (NIH), 240
National Intelligence Service (NIS), Kenya, 228, 321
National Postgraduate Medical College of Nigeria,
National Research and Education Network (NREN), 158

National Youth Service (NYS), 10-11, 14, 325
New Partnership for African Development (NEPAD), 92
Nigeria Medical Council, 31, 32
Nigerian Resident Doctors Association, 33, 121
Norwegian Agency for International Development (NORAS), 165
Norwegian Research Council, 165
Nuffield Foundation, 10
Nursing Council of Kenya, 253, 255
Nyanza Province, 4

O

Obafemi Awolowo University, 19, 151
Office of the High Commission for Human Rights (OHCHR), 151
Office of the President (Kenya), 5
Open University of Tanzania, 222

P

Pan African Urological Surgeons Association (PAUSA), 269
Panpaper, 94
Partnership for Advanced Clinical Education (PACE), 241
Partnership for Innovative Medical Education for Kenya (PRIME-K), 240
Peking University, 150
Pfizer Laboratories (South Africa), 160-161, 269
Pfizer Limited, 57
Pharmacy and Poisons Board, 253, 255
Police Service (Kenya), 4, 10, 23, 227-228, 230, 322-323
Postal Corporation of Kenya (Posta), 17

Preliminary Inquiry Committee (PIC), 256
President's Emergency Plan Fund for AIDS Relief (PEPFAR), 241
PricewaterhouseCoopers (PwC), 66-68, 74, 87-88
Prime Bank (Kenya), 91
Prince of Wales School in Nairobi see Nairobi School
Professional Conduct Committee (PCC), 253, 256, 260
Public Service Integrity Programme (PSIP), 136

R

Radiation Protection Board, 255
Reckitt Benckiser Limited, 161
Reru School, 3
Rhino Ark Trust, 91
Rwanda Medical and Dental Council, 258, 260, 273, 286, 293

S

Safaricom Limited, 74, 87
Save the Children UK, 10
Seattle Pacific University, 89
Seed Enterprise Management Institute (SEMI), 162-163
Shanghai Finance University, 150, 203
Shiga University of Medical Science, 150, 204
Siaya County, 1-3, 234, 294
Simon Fraser University, 162
Soka University, 150
Sokoine University of Agriculture, 152
South and Eastern Africa Research Centre on Women's Law, 165
South and Eastern Africa Research Centre on Women's Law, 165
Special Universities Advisory Committee, 315

St. Helen's Kindergarten see Westlands Primary School,
St. Mary's School, 2, 16
St. Peter Clavers Catholic Church, Yala, 2, 5, 8
Standard Chartered Bank, 92
Stanford University, 109-113; Executive Program 2009 (SEP 2009), 94, 109-110, 223, 301; Graduate School of Business, 93, 110
Starehe Boys Centre, xx, 5, 9-10, 12-13, 15-16, 31, 33, 43-44, 82-83, 107-108, 121, 180, 245, 295-296
State University of New York (SUNY), 5, 160
Stellenbosch University, South Africa, 151, 153, 179, 241
Sterling Winthrop Company Limited, 7
Strathmore; College, 15-18, 44, 61, 82-83, 226-227, 296; School, 15, 51, 121, 297; Students Association, 16, 297; University, 18
Students Association for Legal Aid and Research (SALAR), 236
Students Organization of Nairobi University (SONU), 65-66, 103, 119, 228-232, 234-237, 250
Survey of Kenya, 11

T

Tanganyika Medical and Dental Council, 258, 260, 277
The Opus Dei, 17
The Oxford Committee for Famine Relief (OXFAM), 10
Tianjin University of Traditional Chinese Medicine, 161
Tianjin Normal University, 150
Tongji University, Shanghai, 150, 194

Total Kenya, 4
Training for Resource Efficiency and Climate Change Adaptation in Africa (TRECC Africa), 241
Tufts University, 162

U

Uchumi Limited, 14
Uganda Medical and Dental Practitioners Council, 258, 260, 285, 286, 293
Unilever, 93
Union Carbide, 94
University of West Scotland, 219
United Nations Development Programme (UNDP), 314
United Nations Educational Scientific and Cultural Organization (UNESCO), 153, 240, 314
United Nations University-Institute for Sustainability and Peace, 152
United States Agency for International Development (USAID), 162; Division of nutrition, 162
Universities Non-Teaching Staff Union (UNTESU), 120
University Academic Staff Union (UASU), 120, 140, 183, 227
University of Addis Ababa, 151, 154
University of Adelaide, 150
University of Alberta, 150
University of Botswana, 151, 154
University of Cape Coast, Ghana, 151, 154, 201
University of Cape Town, 151, 153, 161, 184, 187
University of Colorado State, 150, 152, 202
University of Copenhagen, 52, 160; DBL-Centre for Health Research and Development, 160
University of Coventry, 150
University of Dar es Salaam, 22, 86, 151, 154, 204, 241
University of Ghana, 19, 36, 151, 154, 201, 222, 241; Medical School, Legon, Accra, 19, 32
University of Ghent, 151, 210
University of Helsinki (Finland), 150-151, 198
University of Ibadan, 19-20, 22, 32-33, 35, 151; Faculty of Medicine, 20; Medical School, 22, 32, 35; Teaching Hospital, 32-33, 226
University of Ife see Obafemi Awolowo University
University of Illinois, 302
University of Ilorin, 31, 151
University of Imperial College London, 151
University of Johannesburg, 151
University of Jos, Nigeria, 5, 151
University of Juba, 151, 211
University of Khartoum, 151
University of Kumasi School of Pharmacy, 19
University of Kwa-Zulu Natal, 151, 153
University of Lagos, Nigeria, 5, 19-24, 31, 33, 35-36, 38, 49, 56, 61, 83-84, 121, 151, 227, 263-265, 297-298; College of Medicine, 24, 29, 38; Faculty of Medicine, 21; Teaching Hospital, 21-22, 25-28, 30-33, 35-36, 38, 46, 48-49, 51, 84, 121, 226, 264, 298, 300
University of Mac Master, 152
University of Manitoba, Canada, 150-151, 160, 162, 195, 271, 302

INDEX

University of Maryland Baltimore, 151, 196, 240-241; Global Programs, 151

University of Minnesota, 152, 162

University of Nagpur in India, 5

University of Nairobi; Alumni Association (UONAA), 72-73, 88, 113, 125, 131, 136, 141, 206, 237, 310; Alumni Centre, 113; Central Catering Unit (CCU), 164; Chandaria Arts Theatre and Auditorium, xv, 166; Chiromo Campus, xv, 138, 161, 234, 311; Chiromo Funeral Parlour, 161, 164; College of Biological and Physical Sciences, 70, 72, 156-158, 234, 171-172; College of Education and External Studies (CEES), 70, 72, 103, 155-156, 171-172; College of Health Science (CHS), 31, 55-56, 59, 60-62, 65, 70, 72-73, 83-85, 122, 132, 154, 159-162, 192, 207, 234, 240-241, 245, 260, 266, 270-272, 300, 304, 210-311; College of Humanities and Social Sciences, 70, 72, 79, 164-166, 250; Computing for Development Laboratory (C4D), 157; Confucius Institute of, 150, 166, 313; Enterprises and Services (UNES), 62, 67-69, 71, 79, 85-56, 92, 100, 172-173, 224; Fab Lab, 152-153; Faculty of Medicine, 18, 35, 55, 59, 61, 73, 82-83, 122, 245, 266, 300, 304; Institute of Tropical and Infectious Diseases (UNITID), 65, 160, 271, 272, 304; Jomo Kenyatta Memorial Library (JKML), x, 64, 134, 136, 155, 158-159, 164, 167, 336; Kakamega Campus, 158; Kenya Science Campus, 156, 164; Kenyatta National Hospital Campus, 160, 260; Kikuyu Campus, 72, 155, 158, 164; Kisii Campus, 158; Kisumu Campus, 156, 158; Lower Kabete Campus, 164; Meru Campus, 158; Mombasa Campus, 86, 165; Nairobi Law School, 165; Nakuru Campus, 158; Nyeri Campus, 158; Parklands Campus, 158; Pension Scheme, 86-87, 91, 174, 311; School of Medicine, 160-162, 266, 277; Seed Company (UNISEED), 163; Senate, 58-59, 62, 66, 71-72, 74-76, 90, 97, 100, 102-105, 108, 116, 118-120, 122, 166, 168, 210, 227, 229, 231-232, 249-250, 310, 316-317; Students Welfare Authority (SWA), 69-70, 76, 100, 104, 122, 133, ; Towers, xv, 86, 88, 93, 113, 165-168, 250, 305, 332-339; University Council, xiv, 30, 62, 66-67, 69, 71, 85, 87-89, 91, 94, 99, 106, 108, 133, 138, 249, 316-317; University Management Board (UMB), 62, 66, 69, 71, 75, 94, 100-105, 116, 118, 122, 171-173, 224, 231, 249; Upper Kabete Campus, 158, 163-164; Wangari Maathai Institute (WMI), 152, 163; Women Students Welfare Association (WOSWA), 85, 236, 237

University of Namibia, 151

University of Nigeria, Nsukka, 241

University of Oxford, 151

University of Pretoria, 151, 153

University of Prince Edward Island, 150

University of Rwanda, 218, 220, 151, 154
University of Santo Tomas, 197
University of Somalia, 151, 200
University of Sydney, 150
University of Toronto (Canada), 150, 151
University of Turkish Aeronautical Association, 150
University of Vancouver (Canada), 162
University of Washington Seattle, 89, 151, 160, 240-241, 302, 310
University of Western Ontario, 150
University of Witwatersrand, 151, 153
University of Yaoundé, Cameroon, 151
University of Zambia, 19, 151, 154, 222, 297; Medical School 297
University of Zimbabwe, 151, 154, 165

W
Watoto Kwanza Trust, 92

Wells Fargo Bank in San Francisco, 110
Western Province, 295
Westlands Primary School, 11
Westpac Banking Cooperation, 110
Widener University Law School (US), 165
Wilson Airport, 9
World Bank Group, 89, 94, 162, 187; Regional AIDS Training Network, 187
World Health Organization (WHO), 55, 252
Wyoming University, 152

X
Xiamen University, 150, 201

Y
Yokohama University, 150, 194
Yonsei University, 150

Z
Zhejiang Normal University, 150

Index of names of people

A
Achola, Prof. Ndinya, 267
Adam, Adam Mohammed, 18
Ade-Ajayi, Prof. Jacob Festus, 20-21, 27, 61, 83, 227
Ademiluyi, 23
Adeniran, Boniface Oye, 21
Adesola, Prof., 31
Aduol, Prof. Francis, 70-71
Agina, Dr. Okello, 18
Agunga, Charles Arnold, 2
Agyeman, Prof. Naana Jane Opoku, 178
Akama, Dr. M., 284
Akinkugbe, Prof. O., 28, 227

Akinnyanju, Prof., 26
Akongo, Veronica, 2, 40
Akumu, Dennis, 27
Akumu, Maria, 2, 81
Albright, Madeleine, 150
Aloo, Joan Sarah, vii, 1-7, 20, 37, 40, 43, 81
Aloysius, Ricky, 14
Amaku, Prof. Erete Offiong, 30-33, 50, 227
Angawa, Dr. James, xx, 6, 82, 295
Annan, Dr. Kofi, 179
Anthony, Joseph, 14
Anumonye, Prof., 27

INDEX

Anyango, Pauline, 2, 40
Anzala, Prof. O., 270
Arrumm, Dr. Brigadier General Christopher, 15, 43
Aryeetey, Prof. Ernest, 222
Asamoa, 22
Asilla, Mr. Wycliffe, 70
Athman, Aziza, vi
Atikpui, Mr. Elly, 293
Atwoli, Prof. L., 284
Awori, Mr. Jeremy, 208
Awori, Prof. Nelson, 55
Awuondo, Mr. Isaac Odundo, 74, 90, 127
Ayieye, Dickson, 19

B

Barasa, Jackson, 14
Barasa, Mr. Henry, 70
Baraza, Dr. Richard, 254
Barnard, Prof. David, 195
Barnett, Prof. William, 111
Bichage, Chrisanthus, 16, 18
Bilal, Dr. Mohamed Gharib, 182
Binaguaiho, Dr., 17
Bloomgart, Prof. L.H., 33,
Borusso, Mr. Silvano, 15, 17
Bosire, Dr. N., 284
Boyo, Prof., 26
Bulinda, Dr. D., 224
Burgleman, Prof. Robert, 111
Bwayo, Prof. J.; 270
Bwibo, Prof. Nimrod, 31, 55

C

Chandaria, Dr. Manu, viv-xvi, 66, 75, 92-93, 193, 216, 333
Chandaria, Mrs. Manu, 333
Cheruiyot, Mrs Elisheba, 345
Cheserem, Micah, 18
Christine, Agatha, 6-7, 294
Clement, Tony, 160
Clinton, Hillary, 150, 176

Cochran, Prof. Peter Blaze, 152

D

Danso, Dr. Alex, 267, 286
Davidson, Terry, 74-75, 91, 127
Dena, Mr. Hamisi, 127
Diagne, Prof. Baye Assane, 269
Dickson, Nial, 287
Divers, Boaz, 8
Dola, Pauline Anyango Magoha, 3, 5, 47
Dosekun, Prof., 22

E

Elebute, Prof. Ade, 30, 33
Elebute, Prof. Emmanuel Adeyemo, 84
Elebute, Prof. Oyinade, 24, 227
Elegbeleye, Prof. O., 28
Engman, Prof. Née Lomote, 32, 36
Erondu, Ngozi, 25
Esho, Prof. J. O., 30, 32
Essien, Dr. Odudu Augustus John, 36-37
Essien, Evelyn, 37

F

Falaiye, Prof. Olufemi, 26, 28
Farah, Dr. Idle, 224, 307-309, 333
Flynn, Prof. Francis, 111
Foster, Prof. George, 111
Frank, Tony, 150, 202, 272
Fraser, Simon, 162

G

Galgalo, Phillip, 14
Gallo, Prof. Robert, 241, 274
Gatama, David, 14
Gates, Bill Senior, 270
Gendia, Ertiman, 15
Gichaga, Prof. Francis John, 58, 60-62, 70, 78, 84-85, 108, 193, 266-267

Gicharu, Prof. Simon, 219-220
Gikonyo, Dr. Betty, 66, 73, 75, 88, 113, 125, 224, 275
Gikubu, Mr. Joseph K., 10-11
Gitobu, Prof. Julia, 66-67
Gitura, Kembi, 210
Gituro, Mr. Geoffrey, 10-11
Godec, Ambassador Robert, 185
Griffin, Dr. Geoffrey William, xx, 9-11, 15, 27, 31, 61, 82-83, 108, 226, 296

H
Hamisi, Mohammed, 16
Harvey, Mr., 12
Hassan (Congolese), 8
Hellwig-Boette, Ambassador Margit, 185
Hodge, Mr., 17
Hwang-Sik, Prime Minister Kim, 150, 178

I
Igiria, Mr. Peter, 70, 77, 126-127
Ilhi, Prof. Synn, 197
Imbuga, Prof. Mabel, 276-277, 219
Irungu, Prof. Lucy, 70, 147, 171-173, 188, 224-225, 234, 274, 307

J
Jeon, Mr. Nam Jin, 199
Jintao, President Hu, 150
Johnson, Prof. O., 28
Joss, Prof. Robert, 110

K
Kabasselleh, Ochieng, 8, 295-296
Kabira, Ambassador Isaya, 186
Kaggia, Bildad, 7
Kaggia, Dr. S., 277
Kagiko, 147
Kaimenyi, Prof. Jacob, 67, 70, 171-173, 191, 222, 274
Kairithia, Dr. F., 284
Kamau, Mr. Joseph, 15
Kamau, Mr. Michael, 181
Kameri-Mbote, Prof. Patricia, 165, 172, 191, 232, 315
Kanja, Waruru, 7
Karani, Prof. Florida, 215, 271
Kariuki, J. M., 7
Karogo, Mercy, 327, 340-342, 347
Karue, Mr. Michael, 70, 76-77, 126
Kataka, Mr. Awori wa, 70
Keidar, Ambassador Jacob, 207
Kemo, Alois Otieno, 52
Kenneth, Peter, 14
Kenyatta, First Lady Margaret, 275-276, 280-282, 284
Kenyatta, President Uhuru Muigai, 121, 154, 181, 318, 331, 334, 340-341, 347
Kerr, Mrs. W., 10
Khamis, Mohamed, 44
Khumalo, 291
Kiamba, Prof. Crispus Makau, 62-63, 66-67, 70, 78, 85, 121, 140, 176, 178, 183, 215, 271, 315
Kibaki, President Mwai, 65, 121, 180-181, 190, 288
Kibwage, Prof. Isaac, 224
Kigatiira, Prof. K., 277
Kiima, Dr. D., 284
Kimani, Prof. James Kirumbi, 62, 67, 79, 85, 172
Kinisu, Mr. Phillip, 67-69, 74, 87-88
Kinyua, Mr. Joseph, 66-67, 79
Kipng'etich, Julius, 14
Kipsang, Dr. Belio, 323, 340-341, 347
Kitonyi, Prof. Joseph, 70
Knapp, Prof. Stephen, 203
Kobonyo, Prof. Peter, 70
Kramer, Prof. Roderick, 111
Kreps, Prof. David, 111

Kuwong, Patrick, 27
Kwamin, Francis, 22
Kyambi, Prof. Julius Muasya 55, 67, 108, 254, 275, 311

L

Lasi, Prof. Mohammed, 25
Leazar, Prof. Edward, 111
Lema, Leonard Kileo, 22
Letlape, Dr Kgosi, 29, 293
Lin, Dr. Xu, 212
Lisiyampe, Richard, 189
Lugogo, Prof. Juma, 66
Lugwe, Mr. Robert, 70
Lumumba, Prof. P. L. O., xvii-xix
Lwakabamba, Prof. Silas, 217-218, 220

M

Maalim, Mahboub, 199
Maara, George J., 14
Maathai, Prof. Wangari Muta, 163, 183, 189
Mabadeje, Prof. Olu, 26
Mabayoje, Prof. Olu, 24, 28, 227
Macharia, Dr. Samuel Kamau, 74-77, 89-90, 128, 275, 287, 340
Macharia, James, 275, 287
Macharia, Ms. Nancy, 340-341, 347
Machayo, Ambassador Alfred, 37, 265
Magoha, Bernard Boniface, vii, 1-7, 37, 41-43, 81, 140
Magoha, Captain Charles Arnold Agunga, 2, 4, 20, 47
Magoha, Dr. Michael Augustus Achianja, vii, 38, 51-54, 108, 297
Magoha, Dr. Odudu Barbara Essien, vii, 31, 36-38, 51, 53-54, 225, 297
Magoha, Joseph Vincent Oyile, 3, 46
Magoha, Mary Consolata, 2
Magoha, Michael Achianja, 2, 42
Magoha, Richard Alex Nyabera, 3, 42, 48
Mailu, Dr. Cleopa, 284
Makasembo, Senator, 7
Martim, Prof. Ezra, 183
Masawa, Clinton Nyamuriyekunge, 22-24
Masime, Justice Raymond Otieno, 2, 18
Mathangani, Ms. Salome, 70
Mathenge, Dr. Robert, 14
Matiang'i, Dr. Fred, 315, 323, 340-341
Mbalu, Mr. S., 70
Mbalu, Prof. Michael, 58-59
Mbathi, Mr. Kitili, 127
Mbeche, Prof. Isaac Meroka, 70, 79, 147, 171, 172-173, 188, 222, 224-225, 307
Mbithi, Prof. Peter, 69-70, 79, 171-173, 190-191, 202, 222-225, 307, 309-310
Mbure, Jeff, 22
Mburi, Peter, 152
Mbwette, Prof. Tolly, 222
McDermott, Mr. Peter, 15, 296
Mcfie, Jim, 18
McOdawa, George, 18
McOloo, Morris, 225
McPhee, Prof. Sidney A., 202
McWha, Professor James, 218, 220
Merkel, Chancellor Angela, 150, 177-178
Mghanga, Mwandawiro, 14
Midamba, Prof. Noah, 219
Midika, Onyango, 7
Minwei, Prof. Chu, 203
Misore, Dr. Ambrose Ooko, 14-15, 19-20, 43
Mohammed, Maalim, 345
Mohammed, Yusuf, Prof., 200
Moi, President Daniel arap, 61, 180

Mothebe, Thabo, 22
Mozart, Wolfgang Amadeus, 108
Mshindi, Tom, 75
Mucheru, Joseph, 190, 341
Mugenda, Prof. Olive, 222, 309
Muhiddin, Prof. Mohammed, 25
Muhoro, Njeri, xx
Muigai, Attorney General Prof. Githu, 273
Mukwaya, Charles, 188
Mungai, Prof. Joseph Maina, xx, 18, 82, 108, 227
Muraguri, Dr. Nicholas, 275
Muriuki, Prof. Godfrey, 74, 88, 108, 232, 237
Murkomen, Senator Kipchumba, 334
Musekiwa, Norbert, 184
Mutahi, Dr. Loice, 280
Mutahi, Prof. Karega, 66-67, 79-80, 108, 121, 281
Mutoro, Prof. Henry, 70, 171-172, 188, 211, 224, 307
Mutunga, Chief Justice Dr. Willy, 191
Mutungi, Prof. A., 284
Muturi, Justin, 210
Muyodi, Dr. C., 284
Mwai, Duncan, vi
Mwang'ombe, Prof. Agnes, 70, 171-172, 225
Mwangi, Prof. Richard, 67
Mwea, Sixtus, 18
Mwinzi, Dr. Dinah, 323

N

Ndaguatha, Prof. Peter, 281
Ndegwa, Dr. David, 18-19
Ndetei, Prof. David, 219
Ndirangu, Dr. Kagiri, 56-57
Neale, Margaret, 111
Ng'ang'a, Nicholas, 74, 87-88
Ngassapa, Prof. David, 258, 277, 285
Ngilu, Charity, 160, 272
Ngoga, Dr. Eugene, 273
Ngondo, Ms. Rebecca, 70, 202, 232
Ngugi, Mr., 79
Ngugi, Ms. Sarah, 70
Ngumi, Prof. Zipporah, 59
Nhlapo, Prof Thandabantu, 184, 187
Nielsen, Mr., 12
Njau, Simon, 66-67
Njenga, Dr. E., 284
Njeru, Prof. E., 224
Njoroge, Patrick, 18
Njoroge, Prof. B., 224
Nkaissery, Joseph, 341
Nkposong, Prof. E. O., 32, 35
Noe, Christine, 184
Nwaefuna, Prof. Abua, 28
Nyaim, Dr. E., 284
Nyongo, Prof. Peter Anyang', 273-274
Nyutu, Jane, 220

O

O'Reilly, Prof. Charles, 111
Obado-Adera, Joseph Anthony, 14
Obama, President Barack, 150, 175
Obare, Agatha Christine, xx, 6
Obare, John Francis, xx, 2, 6, 20, 45, 294
Obuoforibo, Prof., 25
Ochiel, Dr. Stephen, 70
Ochola, Dr. T., 284
Odera, Simeon, vi
Odero, Mr. Leo, 19, 297
Odhiambo, Prof. Peter, 311
Odindo, Joseph, 14
Odinga, Raila Amolo, 182, 190
Odunjo, Prof. E.O., 26, 265
Ogengo, Prof. J., 224

Ogola, Julius, 43
Ogola, Lucas, 2
Ogola, William Edward, 2, 20, 24, 45
Ogonji, Dr. George, 14, 43
Okoth, Dr. Patrick Akuku, 18-19
Okullo, Prof. Joel, 258, 285, 293
Okuwobi, Prof. O., 28
Olaitan, Rev. Prof. Sammy Ade, 24
Oliech, Prof. Joseph, 56, 108, 267, 311
Oluchiri, Sila, 5
Omar, Binti, 292
Omodare, Prof. Paul, 26
Omore, Elizabeth, 2, 40
Omore, Romulus, 2
Ongeri, Prof. S., 270
Ongwachi, Chuchu, 22
Onyango, Prof. Fredrick, 183
Opot, Dr. Elly Nyaim, 273
Oreke, Dr. Bernard Oburu, 304
Osegbe, Prof. Dominic Nwankwo, 30, 32-33, 286
Ositelu, 22
Osterwalder, Prof. Konrad, 222
Otchere, 22
Otieno, Dr. Ibrahim, vi
Otoya, Boaz Juma, 43
Ouko, Josephine, 345
Owuor, Mary Magdalene, 2
Oyewole, Prof. Olusola, 217

P

Patel, Prof. James, 111
Paulino, Prof. Louis Antonio, 197
Pearse, Dr. Femi, 28
Perman, Dr. Jay A., 196
Perry, Prof. William, 111
Peter, 8
Peter, Prof. Lawrence J., 115
Pfeffer, Prof. Jeffrey, 111
Presley, Elvis, 8

Q

Quartey, Prof. J. M. K, 286

R

Ransome-Kuti, Prof. Olikoye, 27, 29, 84, 227
Rao, Prof. Hayagriva, 111
Rattansi, Dr. Vijoo, 213, 225, 309-310, 333
Rice, Prof. Condoleza, 111
Richards, Cliff, 8
Rinaldi, Niccolò, 150, 176
Ringera, Charles, 219
Rudakemwa, Dr. Emmanuel, 258, 273, 293
Ruto, Deputy President William, 334
Rwekaza, Prof. Mukanadla, 204

S

Sabwa, John, 295
Saloner, Prof. David, 111
Samnakay, Dr. Said, 267
Sanghi, Apurva, 187
Schuyler, Rev. Prof. D., 38
Sestero, Rev. Sister Christiana, 12
Sharma, Dr. S., 284
Shaw, Mr. Patrick, 9, 12, 14, 20, 82-83, 226
Shaw, Prof. Kathryn, 111
Shikely, Dr. Khadija, 292
Shultz, Prof. George, 111
Shunguo, Mr. Zhao, 184
Sihanya, Prof. Bernard, 232
Simba, Dr. John Nyangeri, 74, 77, 86-87, 94, 106, 172-173, 176, 190, 193, 216
Simukanga, Prof. Steven, 222
Siwisa, Vanga, 22
Smith, Folarin, 23
Smith, Modupe, 23
Snethen, Ms. Pamela, 12
Sperling, Dr. David, 16-17, 61, 83, 226

Ssentamu, Prof. John Ddumba, 187
Strauss-Kahn, Dominique, 182
Struthers, John, 219
Suda, Prof. Colette, 323
Szathmáry, Dr. Emòke, 271

T
Taylor, Prof. Selwyn, 32, 36
Temmerman, Prof. Marleen, 210
Thuo, Dr. R., 277
Tibatemwa-Ekirikubinza, Prof. Lillian, 204
Tuju, Raphael, 14

U
Ubiñas, Luis, 209
United Nations University (UNU), 222

V
Varma, Ambassador Yogenshwar, 186
Vatter, Prof. Jaime, 197
Vincent, Joseph, 3

W
Wachira, Mr. Jackson, 20
Wafukho, Ms. Rose, vi, 274
Waithaka, Solomon, 14
Wamugunda, Dr. Fr. Dominic, 70, 232
Wanjala, Dr. S., 284
Wanjohi, Mr., 13, 296
Wanjui, Dr. Joseph Barrage, 66, 68-69, 74, 77, 86, 93, 100, 109, 160, 166, 171, 176, 179, 188, 193, 215, 225, 308, 333

Warambo, Dr. Malaki Wilson, 254
Wario, Hassan, 181
Warner, Nan, 184
Wasawo, Prof. David Peter Simon, 62, 66-69, 74, 84-86, 267, 308
Wasuna, Prof. Ambrose, 55
Waudo, Prof. Stanley, 219, 277
Waudo, Francis, 280
Webuye, Humphrey, 187
Weisz, Mrs., 43
Were, Dr. F., 284
Were, Ms. Sarah, vi, 279
Were, Prof. Miriam, 66-67, 279, 284
West, Prof Martin, 184
Wilhelmsson, Rector Prof. Thomas, 198
Williams, Gordon, 34-35, 287
Wilson, Bella Ochola, 66, 75, 284
Witte, Reverend Father Michael John, 4
Wusu, Prof. O. O. Humponu, 27

Y
Yandong, Madam Liu, 205-206, 313
Yohana, Rafiki, 184
Yoo, Prof. Vak Yong, 266, 267
Yuanyuan, Prof. Li, 200
Yumbya, Mr. Daniel, vi, 273, 275-276, 278, 284, 292-293
Yussufu, Ahmed, 66

Z
Zulu, Dr. Mary, 289

www.ingramcontent.com/pod-product-compliance
Lightning Source LLC
Chambersburg PA
CBHW050301010526
44108CB00040B/1923